The Paris Review

Founded in 1953.

The Paris Review is published quarterly by The Paris Review, Inc. Vol. 40, No. 147, Summer 1998.
Business Office: 45-39 171st Place, Flushing, New York 11358 (ISSN #0031-2037). Paris Office:
Harry Mathews, 67 rue de Grenelle, Paris 75007 France. London Office: Shusha Guppy, 8 Shawfield
St., London, SW3. US distributors: Random House, Inc. 1(800)733-3000. Typeset and printed in
USA by Capital City Press, Montpelier, VT.   Price for single issue in USA: $10.00. $14.00 in Canada.
Post-paid subscription for four issues $34.00, lifetime subscription $1000. Postal surcharge of $10.00
per four issues outside USA (excluding life subscriptions). Subscription card is bound within magazine. Please allow six weeks notice of change of address using subscription card.   *While The Paris
Review welcomes the submission of unsolicited manuscripts, it cannot accept responsibility for
their loss or delay, or engage in related correspondence. Manuscripts will not be returned or
responded to unless accompanied by self-addressed, stamped envelope. Fiction manuscripts
should be submitted to George Plimpton, poetry to Richard Howard, The Paris Review, 541 East
72nd Street, New York, N.Y. 10021.*   Charter member of the Council of Literary Magazines and
Presses. This publication is made possible, in part, with public funds from the New York State
Council on the Arts and the National Endowment for the Arts.   Periodicals postage paid at
Flushing, New York, and at additional mailing offices.   **Postmaster:** Please send address changes
to 45-39 171st Place, Flushing, N.Y. 11358.

92ND STREET Y
Unterberg Poetry Center

Celebrating 60 Seasons of Literary Programs

1998-99
Season
of Literary
Readings,
Lectures &
Workshops

AUTHORS APPEARING THIS SEASON INCLUDE (in order of appearance)

Seamus Heaney	Athol Fugard	Marie Ponsot	Russell Edson
Alice Walker	Geoffrey Hill	Oscar Hijuelos	James Tate
Susan Minot	David Mamet	Alvaro Mutis	Aharon Appelfeld
Haruki Murakami	Howard Norman	Toni Morrison	Cynthia Ozick
Barbara Kingsolver	Wendell Berry	Alice Fulton	Charles Frazier
Rose Tremain	Robert Hass	Marilyn Nelson	Kaye Gibbons
T.C. Boyle	Arthur Miller	Susan Sontag	Annie Dillard
Robert Coover	J.D. McClatchy	Tom Wolfe	Garrison Keillor

SPECIAL PROGRAMS INCLUDE

A Tribute to Eudora Welty / *The New York Review of Books:* A 35th Anniversary Reading
Achilles and the Amazon Queen: A Reading of Joel Agee's Translation of Kleist's
Penthesilea by Christopher Walken and Kathryn Walker, illustrations by Maurice Sendak
Robert Lowell's *Benito Cereno*: A Revival Reading, directed by Jonathan Miller, with
Roscoe Lee Browne and Frank Langella / *Trickster Makes This World*: The Trickster
Figure in Literature, A Reading and Panel Discussion with Lewis Hyde, Robert Bly,
Robert Fagles, Maxine Hong Kingston, N. Scott Momaday and Ishmael Reed / The
Literature of Protest: A Memorial Reading of Allen Ginsberg's "Howl" and "America"

Poetry readings are co-presented with The Academy of American Poets

SERIES MEMBERSHIP: At $170, a Poetry Center Membership admits you to all the
above readings and much more

CALL (212) 996-1100 for a season brochure or to order tickets
UNTERBERG POETRY CENTER / TISCH CENTER FOR THE ARTS
1395 Lexington Avenue, NYC 10128 / An agency of UJA-Federation

YMCA National Writer's Voice
A Network of Literary Arts Centers at YMCAs

☆ **Core Centers:** Billings, MT • Scottsdale, AZ • Fairfield, CT • Chicago, IL • Lexington, KY • Minneapolis, MN • Chesterfield, MO • Bay Shore, NY • New York, NY • Silver Bay, NY • Detroit, MI • Tampa, FL

△ **New Centers:** Huntington, NY • Atlanta, GA • Charlottesville, VA • Providence, RI • Miami, FL • Quincy, IL • Wethersfield, CT • Gardena, CA • Manchester, NH • Everett, WA

○ **Armed Services Center:** Springfield, VA •

✯ **Program Schools:** Tempe, AZ • Mobile, AL • Pawling, NY • Des Moines, IA • Houston, TX • Denver, CO • San Francisco, CA • Tampa, FL • Columbus, OH • Springfield, MA • Baltimore, MD • Long Beach, CA • Tacoma, WA • West Chester, PA • Rockford, IL • Nashville, TN • Billings, MT • Honolulu, HI • Boston, MA • Black Mountain, NC • Rochester, NY (Program Schools offer year-round training in literary arts program development to YMCA staff.)

■ YMCA National Writer's Voice Office • YMCA of the USA National Office

*International Centers in development: France, Israel, Italy and South Africa

YMCA Writer's Voice centers meet the particular needs of their communities through public readings, workshops, writng camps for youth, magazine publishing, in-school residencies, and other literary arts activities while offering national programs such as the National Readings Tour, the National Readings Network, The Writers Community Writer-in-Residence Program, and the Body-in-Question Reading & Discussion Program. Centers also participate in national conferences, funding initiatives, and program sharing.

Contact your local YMCA or the YMCA National Writer's Voice Office
5 West 63rd Street • New York, NY 10023 • 212.875.4261

A program of the YMCA of the USA, funded by the YMCA, Lila Wallace-Reader's Digest Fund, National Endowment for the Arts, National Endowment for the Humanities, The William Bingham Foundation, and the Lannan Foundation, as well as many regional, state, and local organizations.

Petaluma

1ST. AVE. AT 73RD. ST., NEW YORK CITY
772-8800

The Paris Review

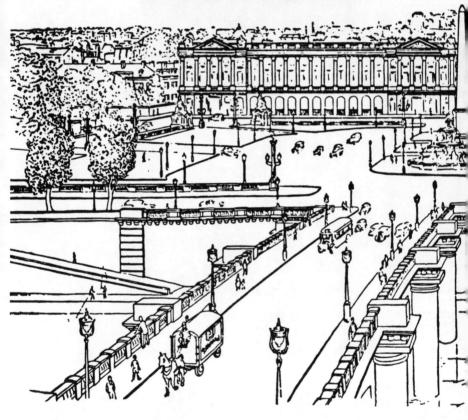

Editorial Office:
541 East 72 Street
New York, New York 10021
HTTP://www.parisreview.com

Business & Circulation:
45-39 171 Place
Flushing, New York 11358

Distributed by Random House
201 East 50 Street
New York, N.Y. 10022
(800) 733-3000

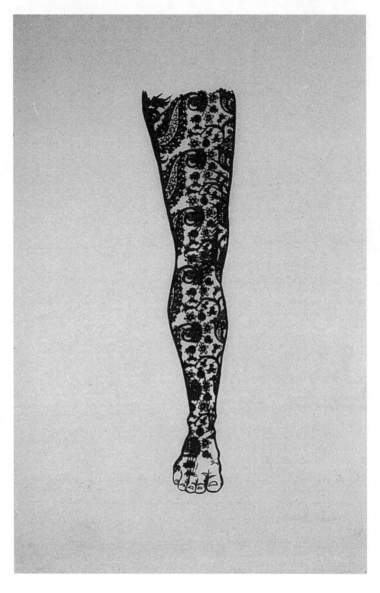

Table of contents illustration by Jeannie Thib, *Archive*, silkscreen print on mylar, 48″ × 36″, 1995.
Cover art by Steve Miller, *Self-Portrait Vanitas #55*, X ray of banjo and flowers with electron-microscope image of pollen spores in the artist's blood, 1998.
Frontispiece by William Pène du Bois.

Number 147

The Hermit's Story

Rick Bass

An ice storm, following seven days of snow; the vast fields and drifts of snow turning to sheets of glazed ice that shine and shimmer blue in the moonlight as if the color is being fabricated not by the bending and absorption of light but by some chemical reaction within the glossy ice; as if the source of all blueness lies somewhere up here in the north—the core of it beneath one of those frozen fields; as if blue is a thing that emerges, in some parts of the world, from the soil itself, after the sun goes down.

Blue creeping up fissures and cracks from depths of several hundred feet; blue working its way up through the gleaming ribs of Ann's buried dogs; blue trailing like smoke from the dogs' empty eye sockets and nostrils—blue rising like smoke from chimneys until it reaches the surface and spreads laterally and becomes entombed, or trapped—but still alive, and smoky—within those moonstruck fields of ice.

Blue like a scent trapped in the ice, waiting for some soft release, some thawing, so that it can continue spreading.

It's Thanksgiving. Susan and I are over at Ann's and Roger's house for dinner. The storm has knocked out all the power down in town—it's a clear, cold, starry night, and if you were to climb one of the mountains on snowshoes and look forty miles south toward where town lies, instead of seeing the usual small scatterings of light—like fallen stars, stars sunken to the bottom of a lake, but still glowing—you would see nothing but darkness—a bowl of silence and darkness in balance for once with the mountains up here, rather than opposing or complementing our darkness, our peace.

As it is, we do not climb up on snowshoes to look down at the dark town—the power lines dragged down by the clutches of ice—but can tell instead just by the way there is no faint glow over the mountains to the south that the power is out: that this Thanksgiving, life for those in town is the same as it always is for us in the mountains, and it is a good feeling, a familial one, coming on the holiday as it does—though doubtless too the townspeople are feeling less snug and cozy about it than we are.

We've got our lanterns and candles burning. A fire's going in the stove, as it will all winter long and into the spring. Ann's dogs are asleep in their straw nests, breathing in that same blue light that is being exhaled from the skeletons of their ancestors just beneath and all around them. There is the faint, good smell of cold-storage meat—slabs and slabs of it—coming from down in the basement, and we have just finished off an entire chocolate pie and three bottles of wine. Roger, who does not know how to read, is examining the empty bottles, trying to read some of the words on the labels. He recognizes the words *the* and *in* and *USA*. It may be that he will never learn to read—that he will be unable to—but we are in no rush, and—unlike his power lifting—he has all of his life in which to accomplish this. I for one believe that he will learn it.

Ann has a story for us. It's about one of the few clients she's ever had, a fellow named Gray Owl, up in Canada, who owned half a dozen speckled German shorthaired pointers, and who had hired Ann to train them all at once. It was eleven years ago, she says—her last good job.

She worked the dogs all summer and into the autumn, and finally had them ready for field trials. She took them back up to Gray Owl—way up in Saskatchewan—driving all day and night in her old truck, which was old even then, with dogs piled up on top of each other, sleeping and snoring: dogs on her lap, dogs on the seat, dogs on the floorboard. How strange it is to think that most of us can count on one hand the number of people we know who are doing what they most want to do for a living. They invariably have about them a kind of wildness and calmness both, possessing somewhat the grace of animals that are fitted intricately and polished into this world. An academic such as myself might refer to it as a kind of "biological confidence." Certainly I think another word for it could be *peace*.

Ann was taking the dogs up there to show Gray Owl how to work them: how to take advantage of their newly found talents. She could be a sculptor or some other kind of artist, in that she speaks of her work as if the dogs are rough blocks of stone whose internal form exists already and is waiting only to be chiseled free and then released by her beautiful into the world.

Basically, in six months, the dogs had been transformed from gangling, bouncy puppies into six raging geniuses, and she needed to show their owner how to control them, or rather, how to work with them. Which characteristics to nurture, which ones to discourage. With all dogs, Ann said, there was a tendency, upon their leaving her tutelage—unlike a work of art set in stone or paint—for a kind of chitinous encrustation to set in, a sort of oxidation, upon the dogs leaving her hands and being returned to someone less knowledgeable and passionate, less committed than she. It was as if there were a tendency in the world for the dogs' greatness to disappear back into the stone.

So she went up there to give both the dogs and Gray Owl a check-out session. She drove with the heater on and the window down; the cold Canadian air was invigorating, cleaner, farther north. She could smell the scent of the fir and spruce, and the damp alder and cottonwood leaves beneath the many feet of snow. We laughed at her when she said it, but she told us that up in Canada she could taste the fish in the streams as she drove alongside creeks and rivers.

She listened to the only radio station she could pick up as she drove, but it was a good one. She got to Gray Owl's around midnight. He had a little guest cabin but had not heated it for her, uncertain as to the day of her arrival, so she and the six dogs slept together on a cold mattress beneath mounds of elk hides: their last night together. She had brought a box of quail with which to work the dogs, and she built a small fire in the stove and set the box of quail next to it.

The quail muttered and cheeped all night and the stove popped and hissed and Ann and the dogs slept for twelve hours straight, as if submerged in another time, or as if everyone else in the world was submerged in time—encased in stone—and as if she and the dogs were pioneers, or survivors of some kind: upright and exploring the present, alive in the world, free of that strange chitin.

•

She spent a week up there, showing Gray Owl how his dogs worked. She said he scarcely recognized them afield, and that it took a few days just for him to get over his amazement. They worked the dogs both individually and, as Gray Owl came to understand and appreciate what Ann had crafted, in groups. They traveled across snowy hills on snowshoes, the sky the color of snow, so that often it was like moving through a dream, and except for the rasp of the snowshoes beneath them, and the pull of gravity, they might have believed they had ascended into some sky-place where all the world was snow.

They worked into the wind—north—whenever they could. Ann would carry birds in a pouch over her shoulder—much

as a woman might carry a purse—and from time to time
would fling a startled bird out into that dreary, icy snow-
scape—and the quail would fly off with great haste, a dark
feathered buzz bomb disappearing quickly into the teeth of
cold, and then Gray Owl and Ann and the dog, or dogs,
would go find it, following it by scent only, as always.

Snot icicles would be hanging from the dogs' nostrils. They
would always find the bird. The dog, or dogs, would point
it, at which point Gray Owl or Ann would step forward
and flush it—the beleaguered bird would leap into the sky
again—and then once more they would push on after it,
pursuing that bird toward the horizon as if driving it with a
whip. Whenever the bird wheeled and flew downwind, they'd
quarter away from it, then get a mile or so downwind from
it and push it back north.

When the quail finally became too exhausted to fly, Ann
would pick them up from beneath the dogs' noses as they
held point staunchly, put the tired bird in her game bag and
replace it with a fresh one, and off they'd go again. They
carried their lunch in Gray Owl's daypack, as well as emergency supplies—a tent and some dry clothes—in case they
should become lost, and around noon each day (they could
rarely see the sun, only an eternal ice-white haze, so that they
relied instead only on their rhythms within) they would stop
and make a pot of tea on the sputtering little gas stove.
Sometimes one or two of the quail would die from exposure,
and they would cook that on the stove and eat it out there
in the tundra, tossing the feathers up into the wind as if to
launch one more flight, and feeding the head, guts and feet
to the dogs.

Perhaps seen from above their tracks would have seemed
aimless and wandering, rather than with the purpose, the
focus that was burning hot in both their and the dogs' hearts—
perhaps someone viewing the tracks could have discerned the
pattern, or perhaps not—but it did not matter, for their
tracks—the patterns, direction and tracing of them—were
obscured by the drifting snow sometimes within minutes after
they were laid down.

Toward the end of the week, Ann said, they were finally running all six dogs at once—like a herd of silent wild horses through all that snow—and as she would be going home the next day, there was no need to conserve any of the birds she had brought, and she was turning them loose several at a time: birds flying in all directions; the dogs, as ever, tracking them to the ends of the earth.

It was almost a whiteout that last day, and it was hard to keep track of all the dogs. Ann was sweating from the exertion as well as the tension of trying to keep an eye on, and evaluate, each dog—the sweat was freezing on her in places, so that it was as if she were developing an ice skin. She jokingly told Gray Owl that next time she was going to try to find a client who lived in Arizona, or even South America. Gray Owl smiled and then told her that they were lost, but no matter, the storm would clear in a day or two.

They knew it was getting near dusk—there was a faint dulling to the sheer whiteness—a kind of increasing heaviness in the air, a new density to the faint light around them—and the dogs slipped in and out of sight, working just at the edges of their vision.

The temperature was dropping as the north wind increased—"No question about which way south is; we'll turn around and walk south for three hours, and if we don't find a road, we'll make camp," Gray Owl said—and now the dogs were coming back with frozen quail held gingerly in their mouths, for once the birds were dead, they were allowed to retrieve them, though the dogs must have been puzzled that there had been no shots. Ann said she fired a few rounds of the cap pistol into the air to make the dogs think she had hit those birds. Surely they believed she was a goddess.

They turned and headed south—Ann with a bag of frozen birds over her shoulder, and the dogs—knowing that the hunt was over now—all around them, once again like a team of horses in harness, though wild and prancey.

After an hour of increasing discomfort—Ann's and Gray Owl's hands and feet numb, and ice beginning to form on

the dogs' paws, so that the dogs were having to high-step—
they came in day's last light to the edge of a wide clearing:
a terrain that was remarkable and soothing for its lack of hills.
It was a frozen lake, which meant—said Gray Owl—they had
drifted west (or perhaps east) by as much as ten miles.

Ann said that Gray Owl looked tired and old and guilty,
as would any host who had caused his guest some unasked-
for inconvenience. They knelt down and began massaging
the dogs' paws and then lit the little stove and held each
dog's foot, one at a time, over the tiny blue flame to help
it thaw out.

Gray Owl walked out to the edge of the lake ice and kicked
at it with his foot, hoping to find fresh water beneath for the
dogs; if they ate too much snow, especially after working so
hard, they'd get violent diarrhea and might then become too
weak to continue home the next day, or the next, or whenever
the storm quit.

Ann said she could barely see Gray Owl's outline through
the swirling snow, even though he was less than twenty yards
away. He kicked once at the sheet of ice, the vast plate of it,
with his heel, then disappeared below the ice.

Ann wanted to believe that she had blinked and lost sight
of him, or that a gust of snow had swept past and hidden
him, but it had been too fast, too total: she knew that the
lake had swallowed him. She was sorry for Gray Owl, she
said, and worried for his dogs—afraid they would try to follow
his scent down into the icy lake, and be lost as well—but
what she was most upset about, she said—to be perfectly
honest—was that Gray Owl had been wearing the little daypack with the tent and emergency rations. She had it in her
mind to try to save Gray Owl, and to try to keep the dogs
from going through the ice—but if he drowned, she was
going to have to figure out how to try to get that daypack
off of the drowned man and set up the wet tent in the blizzard
on the snowy prairie and then crawl inside and survive. She
would have to go into the water naked, so that when she
came back out—if she came back out—she would have dry
clothes to put on.

The dogs came galloping up, seeming as large as deer or elk in that dim landscape against which there was nothing else to give them perspective, and Ann whoaed them right at the lake's edge, where they stopped immediately as if they had suddenly been cast with a sheet of ice.

Ann knew they would stay there forever, or until she released them, and it troubled her to think that if she drowned, they too would die—that they would stand there motionless, as she had commanded them, for as long as they could, until at some point—days later, perhaps—they would lie down, trembling with exhaustion—they might lick at some snow, for moisture—but that then the snows would cover them, and still they would remain there, chins resting on their front paws, staring straight ahead and unseeing into the storm, wondering where the scent of her had gone.

Ann eased out onto the ice. She followed the tracks until she came to the jagged hole in the ice through which Gray Owl had plunged. She was almost half again lighter than he, but she could feel the ice crackling beneath her own feet. It sounded different, too, in a way she could not place—it did not have the squeaky, percussive resonance of the lake-ice back home—and she wondered if Canadian ice froze differently or just sounded different.

She got down on all fours and crept closer to the hole. It was right at dusk. She peered down into the hole and dimly saw Gray Owl standing down there, waving his arms at her. He did not appear to be swimming. Slowly, she took one glove off and eased her bare hand down into the hole. She could find no water, and tentatively, she reached deeper.

Gray Owl's hand found hers and he pulled her down in. Ice broke as she fell but he caught her in his arms. She could smell the wood smoke in his jacket from the alder he burned in his cabin. There was no water at all, and it was warm beneath the ice.

"This happens a lot more than people realize," he said. "It's not really a phenomenon; it's just what happens. A cold snap comes in October, freezes a skin of ice over the lake—it's got to be a shallow one, almost a marsh. Then a snowfall comes, insulating the ice. The lake drains in fall and winter—percolates down through the soil"—he stamped the spongy ground beneath them—"but the ice up top remains. And nobody ever knows any differently. People look out at the surface and think, *Aha, a frozen lake.*" Gray Owl laughed.

"Did you know it would be like this?" Ann asked.

"No," he said, "I was looking for water. I just got lucky."

Ann walked back to shore beneath the ice to fetch her stove and to release the dogs from their whoa command. The dry lake was only about eight feet deep, but it grew shallow quickly, closer to shore, so that Ann had to crouch to keep from bumping her head on the overhead ice, and then crawl; and then there was only space to wriggle, and to emerge she had to break the ice above her by bumping and then battering it with her head and elbows, like the struggles of some embryonic hatchling; and when stood up, waist-deep amid sparkling shards of ice—it was nighttime, now—the dogs barked ferociously at her, but remained where she had ordered them to stay—and she was surprised at how far off course she was when she climbed out; she had traveled only twenty feet but already the dogs were twice that far away from her. She knew humans had a poorly evolved, almost nonexistent sense of direction, but this error—over such a short distance—shocked her. It was as if there were in us a thing—an impulse, a catalyst—that denies our ever going straight to another thing. Like dogs working left and right into the wind, she thought, before converging on the scent.

Except that the dogs would not get lost, while she could easily imagine herself and Gray Owl getting lost beneath the lake, walking in circles forever, unable to find even the simplest of things: the shore.

She gathered the stove and dogs. She was tempted to try to go back in the way she had come out—it seemed so easy—but considered the consequences of getting lost in the other direction, and instead followed her original tracks out to where Gray Owl had first dropped through the ice. It was true night now and the blizzard was still blowing hard, plastering snow and ice around her face like a mask. The dogs did not want to go down into the hole, so she lowered them to Gray Owl and then climbed gratefully back down into the warmth herself.

The air was a thing of its own—recognizable as air, and breathable, as such, but with a taste and odor, an essence, unlike any other air they'd ever breathed. It had a different density to it, so that smaller, shallower breaths were required; there was very much the feeling that if they breathed in too much of the strange, dense air, they would drown.

They wanted to explore the lake, and were thirsty, but it felt like a victory simply to be warm—or rather, not cold—and they were so exhausted that instead they made pallets out of the dead marsh grass that rustled around their ankles, and they slept curled up on the tiniest of hammocks, to keep from getting damp in the pockets and puddles of dampness that still lingered here and there.

All eight of them slept as if in a nest, heads and arms draped across other ribs and hips, and it was, said Ann, the best and deepest sleep she'd ever had—the sleep of hounds, the sleep of childhood—and how long they slept, she never knew, for she wasn't sure, later, how much of their subsequent time they spent wandering beneath the lake, and then up on the prairie, homeward again—but when they awoke, it was still night, or night once more, and clearing, with bright stars visible through the porthole, their point of embarkation; and even from beneath the ice, in certain places where for whatever reasons—temperature, oxygen content, wind scour—the ice was clear rather than glazed they could see the spangling of stars, though more dimly; and strangely, rather than seeming to distance them from the stars, this phenomenon seemed to pull them closer as if they were up in the stars, traveling the Milky Way—or as if the stars were embedded in the ice.

It was very cold outside—up above—and there was a steady stream, a current like a river of the night's colder, heavier air plunging down through their porthole, as if trying to fill the empty lake with that frozen air—but there was also the hot muck of the earth's massive respirations breathing out warmth and being trapped and protected beneath that ice, so that there were warm currents doing battle with the lone cold current.

The result was that it was breezy down there, and the dogs' noses twitched in their sleep as the images brought by these scents painted themselves across their sleeping brains in the language we call dreams but which, for the dogs, and perhaps for us, were reality: the scent of an owl *real,* not a dream; the scent of bear, cattail, willow, loon, *real,* even though they were sleeping, and even though those things were not visible: only over the next horizon.

The ice was contracting, groaning and cracking and squeaking up tighter, shrinking beneath the great cold—a concussive, grinding sound, as if giants were walking across the ice above—and it was this sound that had awakened them. They snuggled in warmer among the rattly dried yellowing grasses and listened to the tremendous clashings, as if they were safe beneath the sea and were watching waves of starlight sweeping across their hiding place; or as if they were in some place, some position, where they could watch mountains being born.

After a while the moon came up and washed out the stars. The light was blue and silver and seemed, Ann said, to be like a living thing. It filled the sheet of ice just above their heads with a shimmering cobalt light, which again rippled as if the ice were moving, rather than the earth itself, with the moon tracking it—and like deer drawn by gravity getting up in the night to feed for an hour or so before settling back in, Gray Owl and Ann and the dogs rose from their nests of straw and began to travel.

"You didn't—you know—*engage?*" Susan asks: a little mischievously, and a little proprietary, perhaps.

Ann shakes her head. "It was too cold," she says. I sneak a glance at Roger, but cannot read his expression. Is he in love with her? Does she own his heart?

"But you would have, if it hadn't been so cold, right?" Susan asks, and Ann shrugs. "He was an old man—in his fifties—and the dogs were around. But yeah, there was something about it that made me think of . . . those things," she says, careful and precise as ever.

"I would have done it anyway," Susan says, "Even if it was cold, and even if he was a hundred."

"We walked a long way," Ann says, eager to change the subject. "The air was damp down there and whenever we'd get chilled, we'd stop and make a little fire out of a bundle of dry cattails." There were little pockets and puddles of swamp gas pooled here and there, she said, and sometimes a spark from the cattails would ignite one of those, and all around these little pockets of gas would light up like when you toss gas on a fire—these little explosions of brilliance, like flashbulbs—marsh pockets igniting like falling dominoes, or like children playing hopscotch—until a large-enough flash-pocket was reached—sometimes thirty or forty yards away from them, by this point—that the puff of flame would blow a chimney-hole through the ice, venting the other pockets, and the fires would crackle out—the scent of grass smoke sweet in their lungs—and they could feel gusts of warmth from the little flickering fires, and currents of the colder, heavier air—sliding down through the new vent holes and pooling around their ankles. The moonlight would strafe down through those rents in the ice, and shards of moon-ice would be glittering and spinning like diamond-motes in those newly vented columns of moonlight; and they pushed on, still lost, but so alive.

The mini-explosions were fun, but they frightened the dogs, and so Ann and Gray Owl lit twisted bundles of cattails and used them for torches to light their way, rather than building warming fires: though occasionally they would still pass through a pocket of methane and a stray ember would fall from their torches, and the whole chain of fire and light would begin again, culminating once more with a vent-hole being blown open and shards of glittering ice tumbling down into their lair . . .

What would it have looked like, seen from above—the orange blurrings of their wandering trail beneath the ice; and what would the sheet of lake-ice itself have looked like that night—throbbing with the ice-bound, subterranean blue and orange light of moon and fire? But again, there was no one to view the spectacle: only the travelers themselves, and they had no perspective, no vantage or loft from which to view or judge themselves. They were simply pushing on from one fire to the next, carrying their tiny torches. The beauty in front of them was enough.

They knew they were getting near a shore—the southern shore, they hoped, as they followed the glazed moon's lure above—when the dogs began to encounter shore birds that had somehow found their way beneath the ice through small fissures and rifts and were taking refuge in the cattails. Small winter birds—juncos, nuthatches, chickadees—skittered away from the smoky approach of their torches; only a few late-migrating (or winter-trapped) snipe held tight and steadfast, and the dogs began to race ahead of Gray Owl and Ann, working these familiar scents—blue and silver ghost-shadows of dog-muscle weaving ahead through slants of moonlight.

The dogs emitted the odor of adrenaline when they worked, Ann said—a scent like damp fresh-cut green hay—and with nowhere to vent, the odor was dense and thick around them, so that Ann wondered if it too might be flammable, like the methane: if in the dogs' passions they might literally immolate themselves.

They followed the dogs closely with their torches. The ceiling was low—about eight feet, as if in a regular room—so that the tips of their torches' flames seared the ice above them, leaving a drip behind them and transforming the milky, almost opaque cobalt and orange ice behind them—wherever they passed—into wandering ribbons of clear ice, translucent to the sky—a script of flame, or buried flame, ice-bound flame—and they hurried to keep up with the dogs.

Now the dogs had the snipe surrounded, as Ann told it, and one by one the dogs went on point—each dog freezing as it pointed to the birds' hiding places—and it was the strangest scene yet, Ann said, seeming surely underwater; and Gray Owl moved in to flush the birds, which launched themselves with vigor against the roof of the ice above, fluttering like bats; but the snipe were too small, not powerful enough to break through those frozen four inches of water (though they could fly four thousand miles to South America each year, and then back to Canada six months later—is freedom a lateral component, or a vertical one?) and as Gray Owl kicked at the clumps of frost-bent cattails where the snipe were hiding and they burst into flight only to hit their heads on the ice above them, the snipe came tumbling back down, raining limp and unconscious back to their soft grassy nests.

The dogs began retrieving them, carrying them gingerly, delicately—not preferring the taste of snipe, which ate only earthworms—and Ann and Gray Owl gathered the tiny birds from the dogs, placed them in their pockets, and continued on to the shore, chasing that moon—the ceiling lowering to six feet, then four, then to a crawl space—and after they had bashed their way out (with elbows, fists and forearms) and stepped back out into the frigid air, they tucked the still-unconscious snipe into little crooks in branches, up against the trunks of trees and off the ground, out of harm's way, and passed on, south—as if late in their own migration—while the snipe rested, warm and terrified and heart-fluttering, but saved, for now, against the trunks of those trees.

Long after Ann and Gray Owl and the pack of dogs had passed through, the birds would awaken—their bright dark eyes luminous in the moonlight—and the first sight they would see would be the frozen marsh before them with its chain of still-steaming vent-holes stretching back across all the way to the other shore. Perhaps these were birds that had been unable to migrate due to injuries, or some genetic absence. Perhaps they had tried to migrate in the past but had found either their winter habitat destroyed, or the path down there so fragmented and fraught with danger that it made more sense—to these few birds—to ignore the tuggings of the stars and seasons and instead to try to carve out new lives, new ways-of-being, even in such a stark and severe landscape: or rather, in a stark and severe period—knowing that lushness and bounty was still retained within that land-scape. That it was only a phase; that better days would come. That in fact (the snipe knowing these things with their blood, ten-million-years-in-the-world), the austere times were the very thing, the very imbalance, which would summon the resurrection of that frozen richness within the soil—if indeed that richness, that magic, that hope, did still exist beneath the ice and snow. Spring would come like its own green fire, if only the injured ones could hold on.

And what would the snipe think or remember, upon re-awakening and finding themselves still in that desolate posi-tion, desolate place and time, but still alive, and with hope?

Would it seem to them that a thing like grace had passed through, as they slept—that a slender winding river of it had passed through and rewarded them for their faith and en-durance?

Believing, stubbornly, that that green land beneath them would blossom once more. Maybe not soon; but again.

If the snipe survived, they would be among the first to see it. Perhaps they believed that the pack of dogs, and Gray Owl's and Ann's advancing torches, had only been one of winter's dreams. Even with the proof—the scribings—of grace's passage before them—the vent-holes still steaming—perhaps they believed it was only one of winter's dreams.

It would be curious to tally how many times any or all of us reject, or fail to observe, moments of grace. Another way in which I think Susan and I differ from most of the anarchists and militia members up here is that we believe there is still green fire in the hearts of our citizens, beneath this long snowy winter—beneath the chitin of the insipid. That there is still something beneath the surface: that our souls and spirits are still of more worth, more value, than the glassine, latticed ice-structures visible only now at the surface of things.

We still believe there's something down there beneath us, as a country. Not that we're better than other countries, by any means—but that we're luckier. That ribbons of grace are still passing through and around us—even now, and for whatever reasons, certainly unbeknownst to us, and certainly undeserved, unearned.

•

Gray Owl, Ann and the dogs headed south for half a day until they reached the snow-scoured road on which they'd parked. The road looked different, Ann said, buried beneath snowdrifts, and they didn't know whether to turn east or west. The dogs chose west, and so Gray Owl and Ann followed them. Two hours later they were back at their truck, and that night they were back at Gray Owl's cabin; by the next night Ann was home again. She says that even now she still some-times has dreams about being beneath the ice—about living beneath the ice—and that it seems to her as if she was down there for much longer than a day and a night; that instead she might have been gone for years.

It was twenty years ago, when it happened. Gray Owl has since died, and all of those dogs are dead now, too. She is the only one who still carries—in the flesh, at any rate—the memory of that passage.

Ann would never discuss such a thing, but I suspect that it, that one day-and-night, helped give her a model for what things were like for her dogs when they were hunting and when they went on point: how the world must have appeared to them when they were in that trance, that blue zone, where the odors of things wrote their images across the dogs' hot brainpans. A zone where sight, and the appearance of things—*surfaces*—disappeared, and where instead their es-sence—the heat molecules of scent—was revealed, illumi-nated, circumscribed, possessed.

I suspect that she holds that knowledge—the memory of that one day-and-night—especially since she is now the sole possessor—as tightly, and securely, as one might clench some

bright small gem in one's fist: not a gem given to one by
some favored or beloved individual but, even more valuable,
some gem found while out on a walk—perhaps by happen-
stance, or perhaps by some unavoidable rhythm of fate—and
hence containing great magic, great strength.

Such is the nature of the kinds of people living, scattered
here and there, in this valley.

Czeslaw Milosz

Rivers

"So lasting they are, the rivers!" Only think. Sources somewhere in the mountains pulsate and springs seep from a rock,
join in a stream, in the current of a river, and the river flows
through centuries, millennia. Tribes, nations pass, and the
river is still there, and yet it is not, for water does not stay
the same, only the place and the name persist, as a metaphor
for a permanent form and changing matter. The same rivers
flowed in Europe when none of today's countries existed and
no languages known to us were spoken. It is in the names of
rivers that traces of lost tribes survive. They lived, though,
so long ago that nothing is certain and scholars make guesses
which to other scholars seem unfounded. It is not even known
how many of these names come from before the Indo-European invasion, which is estimated to have taken place two
thousand to three thousand years B.C. Our civilization poisoned river waters, and their contamination acquires a powerful emotional meaning. As the course of a river is a symbol
of time, we are inclined to think of a poisoned time. And
yet the sources continue to gush and we believe time will be
purified one day. I am a worshipper of flowing and would
like to entrust my sins to the waters, let them be carried to
the sea.

*—translated from the Polish
by the author and Robert Hass*

Michael White

Hotel Bar

Larry Levis (1946–1996)

This was the year drought autumn never ended.
Rivers couldn't float their barges, prairies
burned in a sulphurous caul, dead blossoms and clots

of cloud hung bloodshot, strung out over the west
horizon . . . I remember headlights lost in
miles of afternoon, peninsulas

of dustpall rolling off the failed fields, glare-swept
freeways sliding into a waning city
of streetlamps and smokestacks and billboards and Baptist
    spires.

And this was the year they renovated, gutted
wholesale blocks of downtown—brickheaps and tangled
fire escapes—and staked out naked saplings

next to the rubble. Not that it mattered much
to me. The Cheers was always the same inside—
its gestures left unfinished, monologues

that looped back over and over. Always the same
few regulars just getting warmed up—forearms
pressed against the marble bartop—trembling,

painful to look at. Even when I didn't want to
I could hear their money singing, feel the ice
in the pits of their stomachs, each one slipping piecemeal

through stale arabesques of smoke. And soon the evening
carhorns and streetcries, creak of the canvas awning
outside . . . Soon, the slats of soiled light pouring

into their ruined faces, irises
lit brilliant as the sunstruck liquors racked
in tiers behind me. In the meantime—scarred hills

risen half-drowned at the ends of streets—
I'd watch each stranger passing, shrieks of steampipes
pulsing toward the suites of another world . . .

And before long, the blood of memory thinned.
And I don't know what drew them there, what pinned
them—rummaging the false leads of their lives

for scattered crumbs of jokes or come-ons—but
I know how it feels when language comes back, crust
and pith you tear with your teeth. I know how it feels

so far from God, the distance you must travel
through tapped out in alphabets of fire.
It's like driving some floodplain two-lane south

through the boredom of alfalfa fields at night—
when you think of nothing, till some half-real bridge
of your childhood arcs against alluvial darkness—

It's like crossing with one thrust of the mind—
the rivers' silver spilt below—when girders
flick past and immaculate, moonlit islands

rip you open, when you cup the Present
in both hands, and lift it to your lips.

Sidney Wade

Another Passionless Day

Nel mezzo del cammin what one finds is beans
and wrinkled cabbage and an awful case
of ambling vacuity, an affliction resembling

walking pneumonia, but worse in its long-winded
and peevish consequences, so one shuffles and pokes
through jars of ointment and old hockey pucks

tucked away in the armoire to find just exactly
the right sort of eyewash or what is left
of one's former and nobly galloping convictions,

but what one discovers, among the stoppered monuments
to ancient prostrations, is a b-flat clarinet
and a parched umbrella, so one decides

with waffling confidence to put on some weight
and to belly up to some giant pastries
in a health-food bar where one is likely

to meditate, darkly, on the gnarled knobble
of *the rich tapestry of life* whereupon one decides
one is finally embarrassed by one's youthful enravishments

and regrettably public declarations of enthusiasm
for items no longer in one's possession,
and at this point one wonders if it might not be wise

to camp out from now on on a platform that features
some zazen sitting and banana smoothies,
when *mirabile dictu* one is relieved to realize,

as one waddles out fatly to the the bitter edge
of old *terra firma,* that the fruits of one's labors
are likely to grow more textured and complex

the plumper and softer the bottomland,
so one stands on the strand of the continent,
at the prow of the knowable with a valiant pulse

and a homemade sandwich and peers, ever hopeful,
at the roiling sea of contradictions
that presses in on the beaten sand.

Two Poems by Phillip Sterling

The Isadora Duncan School, Berlin 1905

By the fifth day of rain
a few had begun to dance,
though not quite properly,
never having danced before.
Some swayed in corners;
others tapped leather heels
descending marble stairs.
One pair moved imperceptibly
through the garden, the way
humidity dulls a field where
hay bales graze like deer.
The rest could barely imagine
what they knew:

that the dance must rise
from danceless depths like
a trout, must leap and loose
the tugs of breathless
resignation; that our thin
tunics must by nature reveal,
and our bright scarves trail
dangerously, snapping and
whipping wicked air, taunting
wind with gravity; that
coming to light on small,
unshod feet, uninjured, may
be all we know of grace.

Behind the Cathedral, Liège

No one is willing to suggest
it's miraculous: the blood-like stain
weeping from the third of several
porcelain urinals
embedded in the stonework of St. Paul's;

that, shy of any deviltry,
there could be another venue of belief.
No man's been willing to enshrine it
and forego
the practical amenities of pissing

in the open—to the relief
of lapsed parishioners, who obviously
don't mind when casual passersby
glance down
and greet them, heads and shoulders

rising from the level of
the street. No mystery here that men
relieve themselves; no miracle they
will pause
to pee. And as for those who must

believe in a body's privacy—
one's patience, strength, or modesty—
they'll find the solid wooden doors
that guard
a reliquary of Charles the Bold

are left unlocked, and expect
to be, in fact have warped, and never
closed completely since the last and
final occupation
of the last and final war.

Anneliese Wagner

The Street

after Balthus

The workman

in white crossing the street
carries the wood T-beam
like a crucifix on his shoulder
—does he love us
would he die for us?—let's say for

Michael

the baker
taking a stroll, hands sticky with eclairs
and a swipe in the till, he hides them
under his apron, will not stop

Louis

who twists

Miranda's

wrist, rips her red jacket, slams himself
on her from behind saying *Spread them!*
Spread them or I'll kill you! and he does
after her jeers fuddle him, or who knows,
maybe she just whimpers
as he jabs two fingers into
where she owns herself until she screams
not far from

Gabrielle

blond curlyhead, who goes on whacking a red
ball with a blue racquet, bounces it
high, plays her game alone
never loses, not like

Adrianna

one foot

in the gutter refusing to shake free
of her lover's touch
ripening in her body
all morning as she follows
                    Celeste
in restaurant apron
her arms around noon's
quaint menu sign, not one of them see
                         Paul
grinning his
what-a-good-boy-am-I smile
about to spring
and hone his knife on my throat.

Two Poems by Joel Brouwer

Rostropovich at Checkpoint Charlie, November 11, 1989

The maestro, in his Paris hotel, clicks
the television on. A girl with a purple mohawk
chops at the Wall with a hatchet, blasting

chunks of concrete and a cloud of gray dust
into the floodlit air. Beside her, a man in a tuxedo
jimmies his crowbar into a chink, hands his jacket

to someone in the crowd and drives the bar down
with all his weight. Cracks spider up
through the motley graffiti. The mob roars.

Someone shouts "Mehr Licht!" and a hundred drunk
Berliners run for flashlights. The maestro checks
his watch, lifts the phone. Six hours later he steps from a taxi

onto Friedrichstrasse, just as dawn is staining
the sky. He buys coffee from a vendor and together
they survey the street's disaster: splintered

splits of champagne, heaps of broken stone tentacled
with steel, a woman's shoe, fast-food wrappers,
and the half-smashed Wall as a backdrop: dilapidated

curtain in an abandoned theater. "Today all Berlin
will have a hangover," says the vendor. "There are worse
afflictions," Rostropovich replies. He has lived in exile

for sixteen years. "It's fine by me," shrugs the vendor.
"The hungover buy coffee by the bucketful."
The maestro asks for a chair. The man finds a rusty one

and unfolds it with a creak. The maestro sits
in the shadow of the Wall, lifts his cello from its case, then
lunges, stabs the bow across the strings,

and instantly the street is possessed: Bach's Suite #5.
The chords circle low, wary as a flock of crows, then vault
into melody, retreat, begin again: threnody, aubade,

threnody, aubade, like a man who wakes up
on the morning he's longed for and finds he can think of
    nothing
but the night just ended and the night to come.

"Scientists to Determine Why John Wayne Gacy Became Serial Killer; Brain Will Be Removed After Execution"

San Francisco Chronicle May 18, 1994

After the TV crews packed up
the doctors in charge
got bored quick—*Find a needle*

in a haystack the size of Venus—
and plopped the manhandled gray gob
back into its bucket. But grant checks

had been cashed: token slicing
was required. An intern pulled
the short straw from an offered fistful

of short straws, proceeded down
the long stairs to the lab
equipped with microscopic scissors

and a magnifying glass. The procedure?
Tedium's epitome, but simple enough: snip
open a cell, peer inside. *Whiskey*

*in this one. Here's a Chevy pickup: late
sixties, looks like.* The unlucky intern
grows old, dies, is replaced, and the soft ham

of nerves still glistens on the marble,
barely half carved. There are epiphanies—
dendrite for *knife* found wedged

between *apple* and *hair*, then *crawlspace*
two years later near *thread*—but they don't connect,
won't add up, and one night

the current intern, flabby, pale,
notes in his log, *It could be anyone!*
and lays his locked head on the slab to sleep.

Six Poems by Susan Pliner

Blue

for K.C.

is what they call the newly dead,
(absence of air
does this). What they call dread
of the present, or of the new,
the moony backward-turning,
our old know-it-all.

What they call cool,
cooler & cold, although green
under the skin.
In the mussel shell pried open
the groin's blue pulse,
as you were opened once. But blue won't

let you, as they say, "hold on"
as berries hold lightly to the one
mere twig. Blue pricks
at the eyes and the tongue, unstoppable
waters suddenly let down.
                              Blue longs
for a taste, afraid
to ask. Blue means no
harm but dilutes all perfume
—in a kind of closure of pleasurable
hyacinths all
the way to the horizon—as blue swings
the empty censer
to its own tune, not knowing
the coal's gone out or was never lit.

Inheritance

If I came to you when you were old, in pain
adrift, angry, if I came again and again,
bringing the little gifts of flowers, of my flowering
presence in those bleak damp hours
if I came, as I've said, relentless
unafraid, oblivious, impossible to turn
away, even if you didn't like me much
at first—my excesses of feeling, my ornate diction—
even if you felt burdened, longed to be alone,
(or at least for the privilege of making the invitation)
even if our exchanges were, at first, neutral
just the simple accumulated fact of those hours
our silences, small refusals gradually overcome,
just these slightly unpleasant occurrences would begin
to seem like a kind of a life, until you couldn't
send me away. If I turned aside your peevishness
with admiration, glued together the bits
the others rejected, mirrored a silvery you,
stripped of the squalor, made it marvelous
to be once again, seen, cherished,
it is because now, even after your death, the house
is infused with us and still my obsession,
I who have practiced for this all my life, send
postcards in your name, walk the northern
lawn wearing your sweaters in the waning light,
radiant, stooping in gardenerly affection
to the few fall bulbs, smiling your smile.

Leaf 12 / 17 / 97

Oh Wednesday, and I gave my coats away. Tied
them in a thick embrace, took them out
the door like a corpse. The old list in the old

down parka's pocket: *marzipan, cream, plum*
puddings, rescued from the poor. Wednesday
morning's excitement of coffee and French bread,
crumbs among the stars on the angel tablecloth.
Oh, and the bad night's sleep, Tuesday

in unseasonal warmth, the slight nightmares: sheaves
of dried leaves snatched angrily from my embrace,
my arms and the shame of ensuing nakedness.
Oh Wednesday, how will I fill your hours? Imagine
that all my loving acts have added up,
until the high pile begins to slide?
Anticipation of return, isn't that what Advent is
and almost all my quarters are in the steely machine.

Greed and the glint of gold in the dark. That tree
outside the restaurant in Marrakesh one small boy
climbed with his pot of rabbit-skin glue. Gilding a leaf,
an orange here & there. Gilded for our pleasure,
like the highlights in my hair, a little more
beautiful than one deserves. Who do we believe
will look at the plain, unvarnished tree and see
its glints? Oh Thursday, ease us toward epiphany.

The Month the Snowdrops Appeared

I went every few days. Not real woods, but overgrown
estates where people could walk among tangled
rhododendrons that branched and drooped in the shade
and red wineberry canes, the only color. Where years ago
someone planted a few *galanthus nivalis* which had spread
until I never knew where the next clump might be—a fat
colony of bulblets, the only green on the ground at that time.
I had to hunt to find each clump, and coming closer
I'd see their elongated oval skulls, spun of a material

so dry and delicate, it seemed manufactured, extruded,
like egg-white whipped stiff, half shell, half cranium.
At first, I picked just a few from each patch, but soon
I began to feel that I was the only one in those woods,
forgetting the frantic masturbator who faced
a crumbling wall and ignored me, or the unleashed dogs
on those narrow paths through the brambles.
Even as I stepped in their shit, over

and over, or watched a pheasant run through the bottle-
collector's stash—Sprite, Pepsi, weathered, flattened,
waiting for a truck to haul them away for cash—even
as I considered returning the bottles myself, I began to take
more of the flowers each time. Whole cold handfuls
to set on my windowsill in a glass which pressed
their tender stems together among the air bubbles,
and threw a pale green intelligent light into the kitchen.
Even as I helped myself to their crisp white selves, their shy
scalloped green underskirts, iced and neutral in their coldness
and absence of perfume, it seemed that by next March I would
be dead, or if I could imagine surviving these months
of disjunction, of rock-bottom nothing, even if I were
able to take up my life after all these trips to the woods,
I would be too busy, too distracted to know
they were blooming, and why would
I need to pick them again?

Album

I nearly drowned. I nearly burned.
We were in a train wreck once.
I wouldn't eat. He gave me the bouquet.
She refused, he tried to strangle her,
she bit him badly. We were used
in court. He shot himself. We sat up

all night. She said *Never ever marry*,
I did, he died, you went away . . .

I heap up all these things
as if they would arrange themselves, hold
still. They elbow and bicker
each wanting to be first. I wish
a little side-dancing-step would come
along right now and carry me off.

Elizabeth Bishop Comes to Dinner

First, you should know it's a dream. I've been reading
about her. She sits opposite me
at the table, overlooking the river. Snaggle-
toothed, frail (like in the photo with Methfessel)
she stinks of tobacco, is gray in the face, sort of
like Mom. I look at this shell of a woman—really,
a kind of smart Jean Stapleton, and think:
". . . the Fish Houses," "Crusoe in England," the pressed-
down-upon sense of who one is, subsumed
for the water that burns her wrist. Such jovial
sadness and the brief outcry *(!)* But what about
the competent lover's voice in that withheld poem?
She drinks in the river, the dying light,
all my scotch and finally, Canadian Club.
We turn in. I lend a nightie,
toothbrush. There is
no sex, but an exact mind next to me in the bed
hums: elegant passion of cold, loss, iridescence,
(wire, cages, water) says the woman from Vassar.

①   24   1/9/97

This morning I woke in the dark, and my cabin was cold as a grave,
and I thought again that I had died in the night and had joined
father and the others in Purgatory, ~~and~~ thought that I had become a ghost with
them, and my heart leaped up. But then gray light drifted through
the window like a fog and erased the ^comforting clarity of darkness, and
I saw where I was, crumpled under my blanket in a corner, ^a scrawny, old man in the
surrounded by papers — these tablets filled with my ^disordered scribblings
and all the letters and notebooks and documents and yellowed
news clippings and tattered, old books and periodicals that
I long ago promised to deliver over to you, a great, disheveled
heap of words, an incoherent jumble of truths, lies, memories,
fantasies, and lists, some as ^even mundane as the price of the
several grades of wool in 1848, others as lofty as ^philosophical speculations
on the nature of true religion and heroism, but all of it
adding up to — what? Nothing worth anything to anyone but me,
^and worth nothing to me; so why have I saved it all these years?
I'm struggling to think clearly. Why did I pack and carry ~~father's~~
letters sent and received, ^his pocket notes, the ~~color and~~ ^many ledgers
and books, ^whole cartons of them, away out here to California mountaintops and keep them
here beside me these many years? And why have I now in feeble old age
only added to the heap so much ~~more~~ paper, ~~more~~ ^useless truths, lies,
fantasies, and speculation? I know that I began with the belief
that I would compose ~~my personal account~~ ^a relation of my memories and knowledge
of my father and that I would send it to you and your employer,
Professor Vaillard, along with all the documents ~~I have~~ ^that I saved from
those years, for your purposes, ^for the composition of what you properly
hope will be the definitive biography, as they say, of John Brown,
to be published on the fiftieth anniversary celebration of the

matted
beard and
hair, lying
in his dirty
underclothes,
in an unheated
bare room
cot's shelve
and
tabletop
covered and
spilling over
with paper.
I am nothing
but paper —
my life has finally
amounted to only
this: a tiny
bubble of con-
sciousness

a great
book

A *manuscript page* from Cloudsplitter.

Russell Banks

The Art of Fiction CLII

Russell Banks was born on March 28, 1940, in Newton, Massachusetts, and raised in the small town of Barnstead, New Hampshire, the son of Earl and Florence Banks. His

father, a plumber, deserted the family when Banks was twelve.
Banks helped provide for his mother and three siblings. An
excellent student, winning a full scholarship to Colgate Uni-
versity, he dropped out in his first year with the intention of
joining Fidel Castro's insurgent army in Cuba, but wound
up working in a department store in Lakeland, Florida. He
lived briefly in Boston, where he began to write short fiction
and poetry, before returning to New Hampshire in 1964.
Soon after, he entered the University of North Carolina at
Chapel Hill. There he cofounded a small literary publishing
house and magazine, Lillabulero.

Throughout the 1960s, Banks contributed short stories to
a variety of literary magazines. He was graduated with honors
from North Carolina in 1967 and returned to New Hampshire
where he taught at Emerson College in Boston and the Univer-
sity of New Hampshire at Durham. The 1971 volume of The
Best American Short Stories *included fiction by Banks. In*
1974 he published a volume of poetry, Snow: Meditations
on a Cautious Man in Winter. *His first novel,* Family Life,
was not a critical success, but Banks's next volume, a collection
of short stories, Searching for Survivors, *won an O. Henry*
Award. A second collection of short stories, The New World
(1978), received acclaim for its blending of historical and
semi-autobiographical material.

The working-class New Englander and his struggle with
violence became the focus of his next two novels, Hamilton
Stark *(1978) and* The Book of Jamaica *(1980). Banks devel-*
oped his narrative experiments with point of view as well as
deepened his exploration of themes on the barriers of race and
class. An interrelated collection of short stories, Trailerpark
(1981), brought Banks widespread critical acclaim. Based on
the religious and moral struggles of a seventeenth-century
coffin builder, The Relation of My Imprisonment *followed*
in 1984.

Banks ascended to the first rank of American novelists in
1985 with the publication of Continental Drift, *a dual point*
of view work about an oil-burner repairman from New Hamp-
shire and a Haitian refugee. The convergence of lives and

*experiences around violence and tragedy also informs his next
novels,* Affliction *(1989) and* The Sweet Hereafter *(1991),
both of which were recently made into motion pictures. Following* Rule of the Bone *(1995), Banks's most recent novel,*
Cloudsplitter *(1997), transforms the themes of race and violence into an American epic centered on the story of John
Brown.*

*Banks is married to the poet Chase Twitchell. It is his fourth
marriage and he has four daughters from previous marriages.
Banks spends most of the year at his home in the small town
of Keene, New York. He recently retired from his position
as the Howard G.B. Clark University Professor at Princeton
University.*

*Most of this interview was conducted at his home in
Princeton, New Jersey. A powerful, burly man with a closely
trimmed beard and white hair, Banks sat comfortably in his
study surrounded by books, his computer and a large collection of model and toy school buses.*

INTERVIEWER

You began to write in the 1960s. How did that decade
influence you? Did you meet any notable figures?

RUSSELL BANKS

Yes, I met Kerouac. It must have been 1967, a year or
two, at the most, before he died. I got a call from a pal in
a bar in town, The Tempo Room, a local hangout: "Jack
Kerouac is in town with a couple of other guys, and he wants
to have a party." I said, "Yeah, sure, right." He said, "No,
really." I was the only guy in this crowd with a regular house.
So Jack Kerouac showed up with a troupe of about forty
people he had gathered as he went along, and three guys
whom he insisted—and I think they indeed were—Micmac
Indians from Quebec. Kerouac, like a lot of writers of the
open road, didn't have a driver's license. He needed a Neal
Cassady just to get around; this time he had these crazy
Indians, who were driving him to Florida to be with his
mother. They all ended up crashing for the weekend. He had

just received his advance for what turned out to be his last
book and was spending it like a sailor on leave. He brought
with him a disruptiveness and wild disorder, and moments
of brilliance, too. I could see how attractive he must have
been when he was young, both physically and intellectually.
He was an incredibly beautiful man, but at that age (he was
about forty-five) the alcohol had wreaked such destruction
that it left him beautiful only from the neck up. Also, you
could see why they called him Memory Babe: he would switch
into long, beautiful twenty-minute recitations of Blake or the
Upanishads or Hoagy Carmichael song lyrics. Then he would
phase out and turn into an anti-Semitic, angry, fucked-up,
tormented old drunk—a real know-nothing. It was comical,
but sad. There were a lot of arguments back and forth, then
we would realize, No, he's just a sad, old drunk; I can't take
this stuff seriously. Eventually he would realize it himself,
and he would back off and turn himself into a senior literary
figure and say, I can't take that stuff seriously either. Every
time he came forward, he would switch personas, and you
would go bouncing back off him. It was a very strange and
strenuous weekend. And very moving. It was the first time I
had seen one of my literary heroes seem fragile and vulnerable.

INTERVIEWER

Was Kerouac an early inspiration?

BANKS

Kerouac was very important to me for a lot of reasons,
though not necessarily for the reasons that he was inspiring
to other folks. But for a working-class New England kid who
was, for the most part, an autodidact, reading Jack Kerouac,
a writer of clear significance, was very liberating—liberating
both in literary terms and in sexual terms, as well as in social
behavior. He gave me another way to think and walk; vali-
dated my life so far and my hopes for that life. I never actually
wanted to write like Kerouac; I never wanted to write about
what he wrote, particularly. But there was a rough personalism

and expansiveness in his work that had gone out of favor at the time. Kerouac reinvoked a Whitmanesque perspective and texture; he renewed the old barbaric yawp, which was very exciting and inspiring. To me, it was something new, although that rough personalism is, of course, a very strong, old current in American literature, with its headwaters in Whitman and Twain. In the twentieth century it got blocked by the power of the Hemingway, Faulkner, Joyce models and the High Modernists' affection for formalism. But there was also Dreiser, Steinbeck, Sherwood Anderson, Richard Wright and Nelson Algren. I think Kerouac reinvigorated that stream, opened it up again. I think that's what happens with a young writer: a single figure, who may not be major in any way, can help you rethink and re-view writers that otherwise you would have dismissed or feared.

INTERVIEWER

Do you remember the first writer who really bowled you over?

BANKS

Whitman. It was in my late teens, and I suddenly realized that was the kind of writer I wanted to be. Not the kind of writing I wanted to do, but the kind of writer I wanted to be: a man of the people, but at the same time writing high art. It was the first time I had the sense that you could be a writer and it would be a lofty, noble position, yet still connected to the reality around you. You didn't have to be Edgar Allan Poe, or Robert Lowell for that matter. Whitman was the first figure of that sort.

INTERVIEWER

Do you make a distinction between highbrow and lowbrow literature?

BANKS

The distinction between high and low culture depresses me, dividing all culture like Gaul into high, middle and low.

It's a very comforting way to think about culture, so long as
you think of yourself as highbrow. I think it speaks to, and
speaks out of, anxiety about class, especially in the United
States, as people from the lower classes begin to participate
in the literary arts and intellectual life in an aggressive way.
Then folks start claiming there is high, middle and low culture, so know your place, please, and stay there. I don't think
it would have made much sense to Whitman. Some of the
distinctions between high and low culture wouldn't make
much sense to someone like John Brown of Harpers Ferry,
for example, who thought that Milton and Jonathan Edwards
were as available to him as penny broadsides.

INTERVIEWER

Did you sense that anxiety when you started to write?

BANKS

I sensed that the culture was run by people who went to
Harvard, Princeton and Yale, that it was run by upper-class
white men. I don't think I was wrong. Pick up an O. Henry
Award anthology or any poetry anthology from that era—
there may have been a few Jewish guys from Columbia—and
that's it. But pick up an O. Henry anthology from 1996,
the contributors come from everywhere—white men, women,
African-Americans, Asian-Americans, Native Americans. But
in the fifties there was no way you could think about culture
as something that was not run, not the product of, and not
consumed primarily by that small group of white male gradu-
ates of Ivy League colleges.

INTERVIEWER

Given this, you were hardly encouraged to become an artist
early on?

BANKS

No. No push in that direction whatsoever.

INTERVIEWER

Where did it come from?

BANKS

I think it came in by the side door. When I was a kid, the first evidence of any special talent that I might have had was artistic. I had a good hand. I could draw and paint, and I loved to do it. It was physically satisfying, it provided escape and a kind of sexual pleasure. It got me attention, too—praise from teachers, strangers, from my family. "Isn't he amazing. Can he play the violin too?" That sort of thing. I was a kind of prodigious curiosity to people. As I got into my middle teens, I thought, That's what I want to be, an artist! I think that allowed me to separate myself from the conventional expectations for a bright kid from my class.

INTERVIEWER

What were those expectations?

BANKS

From others, probably to get a scholarship and go to college and become a lawyer or a doctor. The goal was to get into the middle class: make some money, marry a nice girl, buy a house and settle down. I already had started to imagine for myself a life that couldn't meet that set of expectations, which I think is why I left Colgate after eight weeks. Colgate was then a preppy, neo-Ivy school for upper-middle-class white boys, and I was sort of an early affirmative-action kid. It was a good program, a wonderful program for most. For me it wasn't. I was so out of it on the social surface and at the psychological depths that I felt I had no choice but to flee. I stole away in the night, literally. Hitchhiked my way out in a snowstorm with all my belongings in a backpack. I hitchhiked as far from that little network of expectations and pressure as I could get. I headed off to Florida to join Castro.

INTERVIEWER

You wanted to join Castro's revolution?

BANKS

Why not? He was a heroic figure. He was a Robin Hood figure for a lot of Americans at that time—you didn't have to be radical to imagine him that way. It was pretty easy to picture myself at his side. He was, in some ways, the good father. I only got as far as Miami. By that time Castro was marching into Havana and didn't need me anymore. Also, I realized I didn't know quite how to get from Key West to Cuba, and I couldn't speak Spanish.

INTERVIEWER

You dedicated *Affliction* to your father. What was he like?

BANKS

He was violent, and alcoholic. He abandoned the family when I was twelve.

INTERVIEWER

Did you ever reconcile with him?

BANKS

Yes, I did. In my late teens I sought him out and even lived with him in New Hampshire for a while and worked as a plumber alongside him until I was twenty-four. I remember a talk I had with him when I was trying to write at night— stories and a novel and so forth, trying to invent myself as a writer while being a plumber. I remember talking to him about it, at one point saying, "Jesus Christ, I don't want to do this, I hate plumbing." He looked at me with puzzlement and said, "You think *I* like it?" I realized, My God, of course not. What was he then? Around my age now, and he had done this all his adult life. He was a very bright man, talented in many ways. But he grew up in the Depression and when he got out of high school at sixteen he went right to work to help support the family. No matter how bright he was, his life was shaped entirely by those forces. I'll never forget that moment.

But it was always a testy, anxiety-ridden relationship, on both sides. It wasn't until I was in my early thirties that I began to feel at ease with him. I vividly remember a perception that transformed my relationship to him. He had given me a Christmas present—a cord of firewood. Typically, it wasn't quite a gift. I had to go pick it up at his house. The wood was pretty much frozen solidly into the ground when I finally arranged to get over there. It was snowing, and I was out in the yard kicking the logs loose and tossing them into my truck. I was pissed off, goddamn it, he could have given me something smaller, or he didn't have to give me anything, instead of this damn wood! The old man was in the kitchen watching me. Finally, he put his coat on and came out and worked alongside me. I was working pretty furiously, ignoring him, but after a while I looked over at him and saw that it was very difficult for him. I suddenly saw him as an old man, and very fragile. We reversed our polarity at that moment.

INTERVIEWER

What were you writing at the time?

BANKS

I was working on *Hamilton Stark* then. I wonder if the book and that reversal of polarity are connected in some way, the power shift. Probably there is some real connection to it. There *is* a wonderful intelligence to the unconscious. It's always smarter than we are.

INTERVIEWER

Your personal mythology looks like part of the American mythology—the young rebel setting out for the territory ahead.

BANKS

What happens—at least this is what happened to me, and I suspect it has happened to a lot of writers—is that there comes a point when the work starts to shape your life. Early on, you intuit and start to create patterns of images and narrative forms that are bound to be central to American mythology. If you start to plug the imagery and sequences of your personal life into these patterns and forms, then they are going to feed the way you imagine your own life. Before long, writing will turn out, for the writer, to be a self-creative act. The narrative that early on attracted me was the run from civilization, in which a young fellow in tweeds at Colgate University lights out and becomes a Robin Hood figure in fatigues in the Caribbean jungle. That fantasy is a story for myself. It also happens to be a very basic American story, as well as a basic white-male fantasy. A wonderful reciprocity between literature and life evolves. It seems to be inescapable.

INTERVIEWER

When did you notice the impact of the mythology of your writing on your life?

BANKS

With *The Book of Jamaica*. That book leaves the protagonist at the end stunned into self-recognition by his confrontation with what people call the "radical other." Having gone through the same experiences, literally and imaginatively, that the protagonist in *The Book of Jamaica* experiences, I began to live my life more consciously and aggressively in racial and class terms, laying the ground on which I stood a few years later when I wrote *Continental Drift*.

INTERVIEWER

How did that play out?

BANKS

After living in Jamaica and writing *The Book of Jamaica*, I accepted that I was obliged, for example, to have African-American friends. I was obliged to address, deliberately, the overlapping social and racial contexts of my life. I'm a white man in a white-dominated, racialized society, therefore, if I want to, I can live my whole life in a racial fantasy. Most white Americans do just that. Because we *can*. In a color-defined society we are invited to think that white is not a color. We are invited to fantasize, and we act accordingly.

INTERVIEWER
Rule of the Bone invites comparisons to *Huckleberry Finn*.
Certainly I-Man makes us think of Jim.

BANKS
Well, Jim is not the only black man in white man's literature. Toni Morrison talks about that shadow in *Playing in
the Dark*.

INTERVIEWER
Do you think Morrison is right in seeing American writers
as essentially parasitic of the African-American experience?

BANKS
I didn't take it that way at all. I took it to be a description
of an American literature that persists on unconsciously including the African-American presence while at the same time
denying it a shaping role, and she argues that the denial of that
presence proves, not the absence of the African-American,
but his presence, a presence that makes itself known mainly
through denial. I thought her attempt to assert that was in
the end healing and inclusive. To write a novel that claims
to be, or intends to be, about the American experience and yet
does not consciously include the African-American presence in
some way is to lapse into a kind of pathological denial.

INTERVIEWER
What drew you to Jamaica?

BANKS
Serendipity. I had a white Jamaican friend who directed
me there and helped me rent a house, first for four weeks
and then a year later for six weeks. Gradually my interest in
the history of the region exfoliated, until I found almost all
my intellectual interests being nurtured there; so when I got
a Guggenheim in 1976 and had the opportunity to take off
from teaching and travel and live someplace for a year and
a half, instead of Italy or France I went to Jamaica.

INTERVIEWER

Continental Drift reveals a wealth of knowledge about Caribbean language, history, religion. Did the research begin then?

BANKS

Yes, but I wasn't planning a book at the time. I was just following my nose, and what began as a curiosity became a continuing interest and then turned into an obsession. The more information I got, the more I wanted—my obsession extended out into the entire Caribbean, including Haitian religion, history and culture generally. I found myself living for long periods out in the bush in Accompong, reading and working on my own in isolation. It was a deliberate withdrawal into another world. I accumulated most of the material that later became *The Book of Jamaica*. I wrote lots of stories too, most of *The New World*.

INTERVIEWER

How do you make the decision to work in the form of short story as opposed to the novel. Are they continuous forms?

BANKS

No, they're very discontinuous. For me, they each bear greatly different relations to time. The novel, I think, has a mimetic relation to time. The novel simulates the flow of time, so once you get very far into a novel, you forget where you began—just as you do in real time. Whereas with a short story the point is not to forget the beginning. The ending only makes sense if you can remember the beginning. I think the proper length for a short story is to go as far as you can without going so far that you have forgotten the beginning.

INTERVIEWER

Do you outline or make sketches of novels?

BANKS

With novels, yes. Not with short stories. Usually, with a novel, I have a pretty good idea of the arc of the narrative and its breaking points. I know if it's going to be a five-act or a three-act novel, or to drive right through to one place or require a reversal, come this way for a while, then reverse and go that way. I do work that out. I also have a short-term outline that covers the next fifty or sixty pages, which I keep rewriting as I work. Of course, it's all tentative; I can change it at will as new ideas, plot turns, characters appear and develop. The trick, I suppose, is to find the point between control and freedom that allows you to do your work.

INTERVIEWER

Do you find when you are writing short stories you must have that keynote?

BANKS

With a short story, I never know where I'm going until I get there. I just know where I entered. That is what comes to me: the opening, a sentence or phrase, even. But with a novel, it's like entering a huge mansion: it doesn't matter where you come in, as long as you get in. I usually imagine the ending, not literally and not in detail, but I do have a clear idea whether it's going to end with a funeral or wedding. Or if I am going to burn the mansion down or throw a dinner party at the end. The important question—the reason you write the novel—is to discover how you get from here to there.

INTERVIEWER

When you started writing *Continental Drift*, you saw Bob Dubois's demise?

BANKS

I saw the boat, the collision of two worlds and the people drowning. In both cases, Bob's and Vanise's, I began with a dark and stormy night in Haiti and a dark and stormy night in New Hampshire. I did know that they were going to end up together at sea in a boat, that the Haitians were going to drown and Bob was going to have to deal with that. I didn't know the meaning of it, but I trusted that the meaning would be acquired through getting there. The journey itself would be the truth and meaning of the ending. As in life.

INTERVIEWER

Suffering and blame are important themes in your work. How did the title *Affliction* come to you?

BANKS

It came from Simone Weil. I felt that every other name for it, like domestic violence, or male violence, if you want, or child abuse—those terms were too reductive and simplistic and weren't descriptive, finally. They didn't describe the condition the way the word *affliction* did, which implies something greater than a disease, but still a disease. It has a moral dimension, too. An affliction is a blood curse, in a way, a blood disease. I wanted all of those associations. I couldn't get at the condition without a metaphor that was large enough and suggestive enough to handle it. I needed a religious term, almost.

INTERVIEWER

What kind of religious upbringing did you have?

BANKS

New England Presbyterian. But more the culture than the actual religion. My family was not deeply religious, but we did go to church regularly and Sunday school and so forth, up until I was about fourteen. I think a sensitive kid doesn't need to be heavily indoctrinated in order to have a very elaborate, lasting and powerful set of responses to stimuli like that.

INTERVIEWER

You associate Protestantism with capitalism.

BANKS

Who doesn't? It's a great explanation for greed—the devil made me do it! And success—the Lord blessed me with it! As well as failure, or poverty. The whole idea of the free-

"The Paris Review remains the single most important little magazine this country has produced."

—T. Coraghessan Boyle

THE
PARIS
REVIEW

Enclosed is my check for:

☐ $34 for 1 year (4 issues)

(All payment must be in U.S. funds. Postal surcharge of $10 per 4 issues outside USA)

☐ Send me information on becoming a *Paris Review* Associate.

Bill this to my Visa/MasterCard:

Sender's full name and address needed for processing credit cards.

_____
Card number   Exp. date

☐ New subscription   ☐ Renewal subscription
☐ New address

Name _____

Address _____

City _____ State _____ Zip code _____

Please send gift subscription to:

Name _____

Address _____

City _____ State _____ Zip code _____

Gift announcement signature _____

call (718)539-7085

Please send me the following:

☐ The Paris Review T-Shirt ($15.00)
    Color _____ Size _____ Quantity _____
☐ The following back issues: Nos. _____

    See listing at back of book for availability.

Name _____

Address _____

City _____ State _____ Zip code _____

☐ Enclosed is my check for $ _____
☐ Bill this to my Visa/MasterCard:

_____
Card number   Exp. date

BUSINESS REPLY MAIL

FIRST-CLASS MAIL PERMIT NO. 3119 FLUSHING, NY

POSTAGE WILL BE PAID BY ADDRESSEE

THE PARIS REVIEW
45-39 171 PL
FLUSHING NY 11358-9892

BUSINESS REPLY MAIL

FIRST-CLASS MAIL PERMIT NO. 3119 FLUSHING, NY

POSTAGE WILL BE PAID BY ADDRESSEE

THE PARIS REVIEW
45-39 171 PL
FLUSHING NY 11358-9892

market system having some kind of great, Darwinian logic to it is wonderfully Protestant. You are either touched by grace or you're not—if you're not, there is nothing you can do about it, and nobody is to blame or obliged to help. Except God or Satan.

INTERVIEWER

There is a great scene in *Rule of the Bone* where Bone burns the spider. I thought of Jonathan Edwards's sermon "Sinners in the Hands of an Angry God."

BANKS

It comes out of Edwards, pointedly. It's a vivid image for me. But it also comes out of *Huckleberry Finn*—a scene where Huck burns a spider in a candle flame, very early, at his father's cabin, I think. When you are writing fiction, you try to write it as deeply as you can, so you have to go to the images that have power for you personally.

INTERVIEWER

The school bus is a powerful symbol for you.

BANKS

The school bus is a very powerful image to me. I'm not sure why. I'll probably keep on recycling it until it no longer has resonance for me. I think that is what poets do. Perhaps less overtly, novelists keep going back to images that retain power for them and recycling them, reusing them in another context, coming at them from another angle to see what they suggest from there. In that sense, I was trying to take what had been a vehicle for death in *The Sweet Hereafter* and see if it could possibly be a source of life for Bone. It took doing. But as you can see from my collection of toy school buses, it's still an obsession with me.

INTERVIEWER

Absolutely!

BANKS

Some are antiques, and from all over the world. The school bus is a layered, multifaceted image. It is instantly recognizable to every American. It is associated, at least for me, with the first time you give your children over to the state. From the child's point of view, it is the first time he leaves home and goes out into the larger world. It is the connecting cord between the family and the outside world, and has both positive and negative implications.

INTERVIEWER

There is obviously a difference between your sense of childhood and J.D. Salinger's.

BANKS

Salinger believes in innocence, and I don't think I do. He wrote obsessively about the fall from innocence, or the threat of it. I have a hard time imagining such a thing, mainly because I don't think that I believe in innocence. Salinger thinks of childhood differently than I do, as if the main threat to childhood is knowledge of adult life. Whereas I think that the main threat to children has more to do with power, adult power and the misuse and abuse of it.

INTERVIEWER

Because childhood isn't innocent?

BANKS

Right. Even Froggy in *Rule of the Bone* isn't innocent.

INTERVIEWER

And the girl in *The Sweet Hereafter* who survived the bus crash, Nichole, she isn't innocent?

BANKS

She's enraged, far from innocent.

INTERVIEWER

Getting even is all right?

BANKS

It can be liberating, and empowering, as it is to Nichole. For Bone, I think the point of his anger is simply in taking power back from his stepfather.

INTERVIEWER
That happens in *Affliction*, too.

BANKS
That is the pathological extreme—the abuse is so pervasive
and long-lived that it has been transferred from the abuser
to the abused. The victim's great conflict is how to avoid
becoming an abuser himself.

INTERVIEWER
How do you avoid it?

BANKS
Well, the book isn't a handbook, it's a novel. But the two
brothers, Wade and Rolfe, can be seen as equal and opposite
reactions to the same conditions. Rolfe manages not to inflict
on others the same violence that was inflicted on him—but he
does it by withdrawal and an absence of connection. Whereas
Wade doesn't keep other people safe from him; he has relationships, an ex-wife, a lover, a child—he puts himself into
the fray of life. But the story isn't meant to be a twelve-
chapter recovery manual. It just allows you to imagine your
life differently than you might have otherwise. There is a
kind of obsessive return in some of my work, as in *Hamilton
Stark*, *Affliction* and *Rule of the Bone*, to an abusive, patriar-
chal figure. Certain stories, too, return to it. Put simply,
because I was able to write these novels and stories, I think
I have managed to live a different story than the one I was
given by my childhood.

INTERVIEWER
What do you think are the dangers of associating writing
with therapy?

BANKS
Bad writing is the basic danger. It's also a lousy way to get
therapy. But if you submit the material of your life—all
the materials, not just the conscious materials, but all your

obsessions and dreams and your dimly apprehended intuitions of the world—if you submit those materials to the rigorous disciplines of art, then you are going to end up with a clearer story about someone other than you than the one that is about you. You can use your own books in the same way you use anybody's books . . . to inform your life about the person who inhabits it. I think the reason you write, after all, is to inform your own life with a book that is made out of the subconscious materials of that life.

INTERVIEWER

There is something else that comes up again and again— somebody who is trying to figure out a conspiracy or a crime. Certainly in *The Book of Jamaica*, certainly in *The Sweet Hereafter*. Is there a tension for you between having a solvable mystery and a sense that things just happen?

BANKS

There is a mystery at the center of all the books . . . for many reasons. One is simply that it provides the engine that drives the book—it provides a quest, the quest for knowledge, in most cases, for information. I suppose, too, at bottom I must believe that the oldest question, What is the secret of the universe? is still worth asking. And I must believe that there is, not just a question, but also an answer. So the books are an attempt, each time, to find the answer. The mystery in the book, the literal mystery that might exist in the plot of the book, is really a metaphor for the other, deeper quest that the author is engaged in. Remember that great Borges story "The Aleph"? Each time you sit down to write, you hope that this will turn out to be your aleph. This will be the story that decodes the universe for you. So you will never have to write again.

INTERVIEWER

Do you often long for that?

BANKS

With every novel or story.

INTERVIEWER

If you wrote that book, would you be content to stop and not respond to the pressures of having to go out and fight the bear to prove that you are the great hunter?

BANKS

I like to think so. Essentially, you're asking me if I no longer had to write, for whatever reason, would I then feel obliged to continue to write fiction in order to sustain the career? I don't think it would happen. One thing I have complete control over—my writing; the other thing I have no control over—my career. Writers often get confused about the two and tend to treat the one as if it were the other. They think they can control their careers and can't control their work.

INTERVIEWER

How did your career, as opposed to your writing, begin?

BANKS

I was slow to find a publishing home. I had written a first novel at twenty-one, twenty-two, and then wrote another at twenty-four, twenty-five. For the second first novel, I had an agent, and she sent it to Random House, and they bought it. I was amazed. But just as the manuscript was about to be set in type, my editor, Steven M.L. Aronson, left Random House to work for *Playboy*, leaving my book in the lap of some poor, overworked junior editor, who probably didn't like the book anyhow. I asked a couple of writer friends, older and more experienced in these matters, what I should do. They said, "Well, your editor is gone and nobody has picked up his support for you. If you force them to publish it, they will, but without an editor to champion it, the book will die. Withdraw the book and sell it somewhere else." Which I did. Of course, then I couldn't sell it. I bet fifteen publishers turned it down. Maybe, I thought, I should take another look at this book. I reread it. It turned out to be quite a terrible novel. So I called my agent and said, "Let's just park this one and I'll start my public writing life over again." She said fine—this lovely, understanding woman, Ellen Levine, the only agent I have ever had. She was just starting out then, too. We have more or less grown up together.

INTERVIEWER

You are prolific.

BANKS

Depends on whom you're comparing me to. I have been able to work fairly steadily over the years. Every eighteen months to two years I can have a book finished, usually. It hasn't been troublesome for me, but I want to say I know it is the exception and not the rule for writers. Also, I have been blessed with loyalty from my publishers when my audience was very small, so I could keep on keeping on in my own way, without feeling as though if I didn't write a book that got on the best-seller list, I would lose my publisher. I was allowed to mature as a writer in solitude and anonymity.

INTERVIEWER

How did you afford to do that?

BANKS

Well, a combination. My ex-wife's family had money and they paid for my college years in Chapel Hill. And I worked as a teacher from 1968 on, starting at the University of New Hampshire. The other day at Princeton, some of us were talking about our writing students, and Toni Morrison said the first job of a writer is to get a job. Absolutely right. I had jobs as a plumber, a department-store window decorator, a shoe salesman and, after college, a teacher. Teaching turned out to be the best way for me to make a living while I wrote books that didn't sell. It was better than any other kind of work I had done because I could organize and control my time better. And no heavy lifting. You can save your best energies for your writing. After about ten years, I reached a point where I could live off my writing and didn't need to teach. But I saw then that, actually, I like teaching and am pretty good at it. It situates me in a community that is serious about ideas and engages me in an interesting and continually changing way with young people. So why not continue doing it? Princeton has been willing to accommodate my needs well enough, so that now I teach only the spring term and pull away for eight months and hide out at my place in upstate New York. I have always led a bipolar life. Maybe it's a way to externalize interior conflicts that I grew up with and continue to be controlled by. My life these days is split between the very privileged, genteel world of Princeton, New Jersey, and a small Adirondack village in upstate New York where unemployment is about twenty percent in the wintertime. But I'm comfortable with that back and forth. I don't think I could do just one or the other and feel comfortable emotionally. I feel stabilized by being able to do both. I think you end up identifying with any community that you live in continuously, whether a monastery or a company town or a university or a corporation, and in some way I've managed to avoid ever living in one place long enough to identify with that place or the institution that shapes it. Both in the university and up north, I feel that I am, if not a saboteur, certainly a mole, a spy. Which is a healthy way for a writer to view himself, I think.

INTERVIEWER

As in the end of *Continental Drift*, to help destroy the world as it is?

BANKS

Not very subtle of me, was it? Well, it is a tradition, after all, ending with an envoi to send your book out in the world to give it an explicit, literal task. But, yes, I have felt like an outlaw when in a university context. But I also know very well that, like most writers who teach, I am essentially parasitic there. As soon as the university's economic interests and mine don't coincide, they can rub me off on the nearest rock without any trouble. But for now, an institution can make good economic and pedagogical use of the fact that Joyce Carol Oates is here, Toni Morrison is here, I am here.

INTERVIEWER

That's quite a cluster.

BANKS

A cluster bomb.

INTERVIEWER

Do you have a lot of interaction with the others?

BANKS

Joyce and I are very close friends, and Toni and I are good friends—I won't say that we are close friends, because I don't see her as much since she lives mostly in New York, but we work closely here in the creative-writing program and African-American studies and we do see each other socially quite a lot.

INTERVIEWER

Do you ever share work with them when it is in progress?

BANKS

No, but we do try out notions and ideas on each other— ideas and notions concerning writing, other writers, other books, about the bodies politic, about the world that surrounds us. They are people whose ideas and opinions I value highly, so that is an enlivening and enriching part of being there. The personal relationships, as well, are valuable to me, because it is not a competitive scene. I don't think any of us feels particularly competitive with one another.

INTERVIEWER

E.L. Doctorow also taught at Princeton. Did you know him at all when he was there?

BANKS

I came to Princeton after he left. Ed Doctorow is one of those writers I most look up to. Of that generation, he and Grace Paley are the two who stand out for me as models. They are exemplary figures, really, both in their lives and in their work.

INTERVIEWER

Several of your books have been made into films.

BANKS

I've written a script for *Continental Drift*. Two other books are also in development, as they say—*Rule of the Bone* and *The Book of Jamaica*. And *The Sweet Hereafter* came out in 1997 and *Affliction* will be out later this year. In those cases, I signed off on them and let others do it. For a fiction writer, writing screenplays can create certain occupational hazards.

INTERVIEWER

Such as?

BANKS

Well, cocaine for one! No, getting big money in short bursts for little labor can hurt you. And working closely with people who see the world in terms of the movie industry can affect you in a negative way. You can't identify with any institution.

INTERVIEWER

When you are getting into a voice, whether it be the narrators of *The Sweet Hereafter*, or Rolfe in *Affliction* or Bone, what decisions do you make about tone? How do you sustain it? Is there a sense in which that person is still an emanation of yourself?

BANKS

When it has worked—and I can't ever be sure when it has and when it hasn't—but when it's felt like it was working, which is pretty much the case throughout *Rule of the Bone* and also, oddly enough, with the female narrators in *The Sweet Hereafter*, Dolores and Nichole, it felt not as though I was speaking through them, like a ventriloquist, but rather was listening to them and transcribing what I was hearing. I was listening to a voice; occasionally, the signal would get weak, and I could, as it were, adjust the tuner and bring in the signal again and begin to transcribe again. Obviously this is a complicated process. It's not simply opening your ears up, because you are simultaneously broadcasting and receiving. But while you are engaged in the process, your attention is fixed on the listening part and not the broadcasting part. When it doesn't work is when my attention has shifted to the broadcasting part. I know I am speaking figuratively, but that's how it feels. In the case of the male narrators in *The Sweet Hereafter*, I felt that I was more focused on broadcasting and speaking *through* those characters than listening to them—and their voices don't seem as authentic to me. Maybe the less a character is like me—female characters, a teenage boy and so on—the easier it is for me to write as a listener and not a speaker.

INTERVIEWER

At the risk of seeming too mysterious, where do the voices come from?

BANKS

It is sort of mysterious. But I think we all at times have buzzing in our heads a whole range of voices, some of them heard early on and retained, some of them taken from the ether, the broadcast ether. I mean it literally. I can hear John F. Kennedy's voice in a second. I can hear my father's voice; I can hear the voices of people I have met only once on the street. So I think the voices are buzzing around in an aural memory bank, and you can tap into them the way you can tap into forgotten visual memories. It's analogous to the way in a dream someone who is long dead or from way back in your childhood, someone whose face and voice you can't really call up, suddenly comes back with great clarity and vividness, as if the dreaming self has a more powerful memory than the conscious self. I think writers, to a greater or lesser degree, have the ability to tap into their aural memories more effectively, more directly than the average citizen. I probably overheard the voice of a kid like Bone somewhere along the line and, in a sense, recorded it. Maybe it's a mix of several tracks. I don't know.

INTERVIEWER

When you were writing *Rule of the Bone*, did you feel that there was a dangerous line between listening and broadcasting, or that Bone would seem too intelligent for someone his age?

BANKS

It didn't worry me particularly. Kids are much smarter than most adults give them credit for being. I don't think there is as sharp a difference between children and adults as, again, Salinger believes—except in terms of power. Who is to say that the inner life of a child is less complex or intelligent than the inner life of an adult? You can remember yourself at fourteen: you were able to say incredibly complicated, subtle things when you spoke to a trusted friend; you could move deep centers of meaning straight into speech and could communicate those meanings with ease and precision. But you couldn't do it very well when you had to speak to someone who was threatening to you, like an adult. The tricky part in that book, for me, was to imagine myself as the trusted friend and listener, so that Bone could become articulate.

Many of my characters are drawn from people who—to the world at the large, the reading public let's say—are perceived as inarticulate or mute altogether; but who, given the chance to speak, turn out to be quite able to address and describe their lives with clarity and intelligence. At bottom, I really believe that people are not more or less inarticulate by virtue

of their age or education or class: what makes you inarticulate
is a feeling of threat. And it is generally true that poor people
and children feel more threatened than rich adults and, surprise, the people who feel least threatened turn out to be the
people we think of as the most articulate—rich, white men.

INTERVIEWER
Do characters tend to come first when you are planning
a novel?

BANKS
It's very difficult to generalize. If you had asked me that
question in my thirties, I'd have said that the narrative form
comes to me before anything else. Later on, in my forties, I
would have said character, definitely characters first. A few
years later, I'd have said no, actually voice—narrative voice,
language—comes to me first. It has varied over the years. I
don't think it has evolved, just changed. I tended to grasp
at form more immediately in the beginning, when I was still
learning my craft and consequently was more conscious of,
and anxious about it. Then in the middle years, I was coming
to important understandings of basic relationships—my parents, my wife, my children, my friends. Now I think I'm much
more interested in listening and language. Not abstractly so,
but humanly so. I'm more interested in the act of witnessing,
more engaged by it—a result, perhaps, of being more confident in my ability to organize and control and develop a
formal apparatus that will carry the story sufficiently and
efficiently, more confident and secure in my ability to maintain loving, gentle, continuing relations with other people.
I feel free to turn my attention to other things, and what I
have been most anxious about in these recent years is my
ability to listen to and understand the lives of people who
are different from me—people who don't live the way I live
and don't have my privileges.

INTERVIEWER
Would you agree with the critic who said of you: "Banks
began his career divided between a common life subject mat-

ter and an experimental style. Subject has obviously won out, and Banks's liberated energies have gone into the forging of a straight-on technique."

BANKS

It's essentially true. It's descriptive, but not very analytical. What has occurred is that the formal aspects are less apparent than they were—I didn't know how to make them less apparent when I was younger. I don't think the work itself is less formal.

Another thing vis-à-vis that perceived shift is that I became a writer without having a clear sense of entitlement. I didn't know any writers. It wasn't a trade I could imagine myself into very easily. So in order to do it, I felt I had to reject a lot of my background and the circumstances of my youth, and willfully learn the techniques of fiction. In my early years as a writer, I was a lot more self-conscious and deliberate in my attempts to acquire craft and at the same time somewhat apologetic about what I knew about the material. Over the years that aggressive approach to craft diminished at the same time as my defensive relation to the content. As that occurred, the work began to appear more assertive in terms of content, and more self-confident.

INTERVIEWER

In your novel about John Brown were you interested in creating a hero?

BANKS

I am interested in the whole question of the possibility of heroism, especially in a secular age and especially in a democratic society. There are two things that are ongoing perplexities for me: First, Is there such a thing as wisdom? And second, Is there such a thing as heroism? I want there to be both, but I am not sure that I believe they exist as human potential anymore. At least, I am not sure in what terms they are available. Those are the truths I am trying to find out: the truth about wisdom and the truth about heroism. That quest takes different forms. For example, in *The Sweet Hereafter*, I was interested in whether you could locate heroism in a community rather than in a single individual—whether some of the conventional notions about the characteristics of heroism could be distributed across a broader spectrum. The four main individuals in the story are unable to resolve the contradictions of their experience—the contradictions inherent in loving somebody and knowing that we all die soon and there is no afterlife—and they do not behave heroically as individuals. But as a community they are able to resolve those contradictions; they do it by means of public ritual, in which they simultaneously appoint Dolores, the school-bus driver, as the scapegoat and forgive her for the school-bus accident that killed their children, which their ragtag American religions and their legal systems couldn't do for them. That is what I was working towards: trying to create a consciousness large enough to absorb the human contradictions of the situation.

INTERVIEWER

How did you get interested in John Brown?

BANKS

A short ways down the road from my home in upstate New York is the home he lived in and maintained for the longest period of his life. His body lies moldering there today. But I first got interested in John Brown in the 1960s in Chapel Hill, when I was reading and taking very seriously the literature of the New England Renaissance. His name repeatedly appeared in association with them—the transcendentalists' Che Guevara, a romantic but violent figure who, in a sense, acted out their deepest political fantasies. Certainly he was a romantic figure for me as well—he had acted out some of my own neo-abolitionist fantasies of the sixties. Then he faded from my consciousness for a long period, until I settled in upstate New York and learned that his house and grave were down the road. The ghost of John Brown returned to haunt me. About the same time, events like Waco, Ruby Ridge, the militia movement, the radical anti-abortionists started making head-lines—all of them invoking his name to justify violence. Certain parallels became pretty obvious to me, and I realized how significantly he figures in the old American weave of violence, politics, religion, race. All those strands cross him, yet the nearest John Brown Boulevard is in Port au Prince, Haiti, and there are no schools named after him, no stamp honoring him—even though he is regarded, certainly by African-Americans, as a hero of the first order. James Baldwin and Malcolm X placed him even higher than Abraham Lincoln. But white Americans generally regard him as mad, at best, and criminal.

INTERVIEWER

That split is revealing about America, isn't it?

BANKS

The irony is that it is Brown's own race that regards him as a criminal. Anyhow, all of these forces converged to draw me into his orbit. He is an ambiguous figure, morally ambiguous. He had a ferocious, charismatic presence and from early in his life he deeply impressed people not easily impressed—Frederick Douglass and Harriet Tubman, people normally very skeptical, especially of an energetic white man. The defining actions in his life, however, are in some ways inexplicable. He didn't just sacrifice himself, remember, he sacrificed his sons as well—he took two sons to certain death and would have taken a third, who escaped, and two sons-in-law, and all those other young, idealistic men who died at Harpers Ferry. He knew they were going to die there. The book is an attempt to deal with that mystery. And with another mystery: Nat Turner might be the first true terrorist in American history, but John Brown became the first deliberate white terrorist in American history when he calmly executed five pro-slavery civilians in order to "spread terror." For no other reason. They were selected at random. There is not much difference between him and an IRA bomber. I wanted to understand that—the mystery of terrorism.

INTERVIEWER

Did you find yourself wanting or able to justify Brown's violence?

BANKS

Neither. I'm his creator, not his defense attorney. It's a novel, not a trial transcript; and Brown is a fictional character in the novel, not a real person. I wasn't trying to write his biography.

INTERVIEWER

How did you arrive at the title *Cloudsplitter*?

BANKS

It's the translation of *Tahawus*, the Algonquin name of the Adirondack mountain we call Marcy today, which is in full view from John Brown's farm and burial place in North Elba. Besides having been old Brown's favorite sight, or site, it seemed a useful metaphor, both for Brown's career and for his son Owen's task-in-hand, which is to clear away, or split, the clouds that surround his father's actions and character.

INTERVIEWER

How did you decide to make John Brown's son Owen the narrator?

BANKS

You can't stand too near the heat of a character like John Brown. It scalds you. To see him as other than an icon, you need the distancing that a weaker character provides.

When I was still researching the novel and hadn't worked out a way to tell the story yet, I came across an endnote in a 1972 biography of Brown by Richard O. Boyer that referred to the research materials of a previous biographer, Oswald

Garrison Villard, which had been gathered early in the century when several of Brown's children were still living. So I went up to Columbia and pulled this material from the rare books room—seven dusty boxes of material—and found interviews made by Villard's assistant, a Miss Catherine Mayo, with three surviving children. Reading the interviews, I started hearing the voice I wanted for my narrator—the writing voice, not the speaking voice, of an old man born probably in the first quarter of the nineteenth century, looking back half a century to the events that defined his life. It was one of those moments when you know you've got something very basic very right, a moment that stops the whirl in your head and lets you plunge into the writing. Owen had been with Brown at Harpers Ferry and had escaped and lived to tell about it, except that he never did tell about it. He escaped through the abolitionist underground and surfaced after the war as a shepherd on a mountaintop in Altadena, California, where he died in 1889. The perfect narrator. For the purposes of storytelling, I let him live on till 1902, long enough to be interviewed by Miss Catherine Mayo and then to write the letters that make the novel.

INTERVIEWER

Did you have models of the epistolary novel in mind?

BANKS

Not specifically. We've inherited the biblical epistles, of course, and the great eighteenth-century English epistolary novels, which are based—even if satirically—on the classical writers' use of it. Then they get based on each other, so that by our time it has become more than a literary form—it's practically a genre. You almost don't need models. You need a structure—my narrator, his psychology and the occasion of his telling, gave me that structure, but the form drops whole from the genre, the tradition of the epistolary novel.

INTERVIEWER

Why does Owen not mail the letters?

BANKS

He intends to, at least at first. But before long he realizes
that it's the writing itself that is important to him and that
he is not so much interested in setting the public record
straight as he is in telling, and in that way learning, the
truth—the personal, private truth of who and what his father
was and who, in turn, he is himself.

INTERVIEWER

Does your approach to John Brown differ from other major
versions in American literature?

BANKS

Do you mean those by Stephen Vincent Benét, Thoreau,
Melville, Hayden and so on? To them, I think, he is an icon,
larger than life—a bearded, emblematic figure used mainly
to express the authors' passionate feelings about race, slavery,
injustice, religion and martyrdom. To me, he is just an ordinary American workingman of the mid-nineteenth century,
radicalized by the inherent conflict between his conscience
and his historical circumstances. He is the last Puritan and
the first modern terrorist—it's the terrible logic of that transi-
tion that fascinates me.

INTERVIEWER

Are you concerned with the ethical impact of your characters? Do you worry that a young person reading *Rule of the
Bone* would be inclined to follow Bone—chuck it all for reefer
and split for Jamaica?

BANKS

Wouldn't be the worst thing he could do. But the book
really isn't about kids, it's about adults. Just as *Huckleberry
Finn* isn't about kids. What I think upsets adults when they

read *Huckleberry Finn* is Huck's portrait of adults—their
chicanery, hypocrisy, cruelty, violence, racism. That was in-
structive to me in thinking about Bone. What I hoped was
that when kids read *Rule of the Bone*, they would see themselves and the book would confirm and validate their view of
adults. Just as when you read *Huckleberry Finn* for the first
time at fourteen or fifteen, you say, Yeah, man, adults suck.
And because it's told in such a smart and funny way, for the
first time you don't feel guilty or fearful for holding that view.

INTERVIEWER

I read somewhere that the Ridgeways were portraits of you
and your wife.

BANKS

No. The Ridgeways themselves certainly are not based on
me and my wife. You sometimes introduce *aspects* of yourself,
consciously and unconsciously, into a book. It's inescapable.
There are a couple of places where, in a minor way, I inserted
aspects of myself and my wife. It's a way, I think, of depriving
us of major roles. Bone's best friend is named Russ, a garrulous, wise-cracking, bullshitting schemer; I know there are
times, certainly when I was a kid, when I have been just
that—a garrulous, wise-cracking, bullshitting schemer. If I
could put myself over there in that corner of the book, then
it was less likely that I would inadvertently let myself slide
into Bone, or some other important part of the book. Same
with the Ridgeways. In that case, I slipped in the bourgeois
snob aspect, another unlovely side of myself. It wasn't just
being coy or seeding the book with obscure references; but
I think it served a useful purpose by giving a minor character
my own name and giving myself a cameo, as it were, I was
able to keep my head clear about who Bone really was—it
helped me know that he was not me and his story was not
mine. Paradoxically, it helped me stay invisible.

INTERVIEWER

The question of invisibility comes up over and over again
in that book and, of course, in American literature.

BANKS

I think the question you are raising here is more about authorial invisibility than, say, Ralph Ellison's use of the term. It is something I strive for, mainly because I have treasured it in other writers. Its absence in Hemingway makes me uncomfortable in ways that reading Faulkner, to keep to the same generation, does not. But authorial invisibility is extremely difficult to achieve, because to give the work any real heat and power you have to go straight toward what matters to you personally. You have to deal with what really is a life-or-death issue for you. Because of that you are inadvertently, almost inescapably, going to end up becoming visible in the book. So you have to discover and impose on the text a means of keeping yourself out—you have to keep catching yourself in the glare of your own light and then getting the hell out of there.

INTERVIEWER

How do you manage the day-to-day stuff of writing?

BANKS

It has changed over the years, much as my life's circumstances have changed. When I was younger and had young kids, I wrote from ten at night till two in the morning and then got up in the morning and got the kids ready for school and went off to my teaching job. Now that I am in my middle fifties, happily I have a lot more time but, unfortunately, I have a lot less energy. In the mornings, I go down the hill to my cabin—an old, renovated sugarhouse that I've used as a studio for the last eight years—and crank it up and work until I start to get stupid, or at least start to feel stupid. Actually, I feel stupid rather quickly, but usually it's perfectly obvious that I *am* stupid after about four to five hours.

INTERVIEWER

Four or five hours is quite a bit of writing.

BANKS

But when you are working well, it goes by so fast. You look up and, My God, it's one o'clock and I'm hungry.

INTERVIEWER

Do you try to keep on a regular schedule?

BANKS

I try. I am able, most of the time, to work seven days a week, although now and then I take a day or two off for a short holiday or to come into the city on business. But generally I work every day and then hold the afternoons free for everything from hiking in the mountains, to doing laundry, to answering letters, to editing, to paying bills.

INTERVIEWER

Do you get a lot of letters from readers?

BANKS

Seems to me a lot. Enough time goes by and enough books end up in print—people will pick one up and read it and have that old impulse, and I think it's such a wonderful impulse, to write back to the author. I do like that, and I try to answer eventually. It's only polite if someone has taken the time to write you a letter. Also, a lot of times it's somebody in prison or a kid or someone who's had a really fucked-up life and says, Thanks a lot, your books sound just like my life. You have to answer those, no?

INTERVIEWER

Do you write on a word processor?

BANKS

I love the word processor. I grew up with wet clay and a stylus. Consequently, I don't think the computer has had quite the same impact on me as the sense of rhythm and pacing and language basically formed in the stone age of writing technology. Also, from the beginning I've found that I have to sneak past that internal censor who basically wants me to shut up and be silent, and the best way for me to get something said has been to move real fast. The faster I can write, the more likely I'll get something worth saving down on paper. From the very beginning, I've grabbed onto any technology that would allow me to write faster: a soft pencil instead of a hard pencil, ballpoint instead of a fountain pen, electric typewriter instead of manual and now, working with light on a screen rather than marks on a page, I find that I can noodle and doodle and be much more spontaneous. It doesn't mean that I don't go back and rework and rework and rework.

INTERVIEWER

You do a lot of revising?

BANKS

Oh, I do! Much more revising than I used to do. Because it's much easier with a computer.

INTERVIEWER

What about reviewers?

BANKS

I have gotten irritated here and there, especially when the reviewer seems not to have read the book I wrote and complains because it's not some other book—sometimes an earlier book of my own, as if I were supposed to be cloning my books instead of writing them. But only mildly irritated. I tend to avoid the negative reviews anyhow. Positive reviews help to sell the book, of course, and they feel good—they're better than a stick in the eye—but I've learned over the years that any book, when it is first published, is forced to fit into the gestalt of the moment. Whatever the popular perception of the moment, whether in literary terms or social terms, the book is forced into the gestalt and media vocabulary of that moment. So it takes about five years, at least—if the book can stay in print that long and get circulated and read—for it to be seen in its own terms. When *Rule of the Bone* was published, there was a flurry of literary interest in Huck Finn and a flurry of media interest in child abuse and homeless kids; consequently *Rule of the Bone* was read mostly in those contexts. But years from now, if the book should be so lucky as to stay in print, it will be seen and read on its own terms. It will be easier then to know what the book is about. That is when I'll care what people think of it. Just as I care now what people think of *Affliction* or *Continental Drift* or any of the earlier books.

INTERVIEWER

It's a broad question, but has the determination to keep writing had an effect on your home life?

BANKS

Oh, definitely. My married life would have been worse if I hadn't been a writer. I don't think my being a writer has ever had the slightest negative effect on my domestic life. In fact, I think writing has channeled my self-absorption and selfishness into socially and domestically constructive forms of behavior.

INTERVIEWER

Who is the funniest writer you've ever met?

BANKS

A lot of writers are unintentionally funny. But intentionally? Joyce Carol Oates. You might not think so from her work, but she is incredibly, slyly funny, a brilliant tease who pretends not to be funny at all. We recently had dinner and she kept me laughing all evening—little things, sly little darts in and out. She especially likes to tease men, I think, and does it very effectively. By the end of the evening, your shirt is covered with blood and you don't remember being wounded once. Actually, she plays a role in my life that nobody else ever has played—the older, scolding sister. I get to play the bad, younger brother. It's comforting in some ways for both of us, and enjoyable. You recreate those basic roles over again with your friends—sibling and parental relations and so on—and carry them on into the rest of your life.

INTERVIEWER
Have you ever had a knock-down drag-out fight with another writer?

BANKS
I've had some serious disagreements with other writers over
the years, but they never reached the point of verbal or any
other kind of violence. Not that I know of, anyhow. I take
great pleasure in the gift of friendship, when it's given; I
value it very highly and try to live up to its responsibilities.
I have managed over the years to have many friendships with
writers that really nurtured and sustained me. With Joyce,
of course, and Paul Auster, Michael Ondaatje and a half-
dozen other novelists; the poets Charles Simic, Bill Matthews,
C.K. Williams and Dan Halpern; and another poet, in Boston, Bill Corbett. He's a great man and he has been a dear
friend for more than thirty years. When you reach a certain
age, the friends who have carried you through thirty years of
work and the accompanying insecurities and fears—people
you have relied upon to reality-check everything from marriage to money to your basic political and religious beliefs—
those people are irreplaceable and absolutely invaluable. I've
been very lucky to have had a dozen or so such friendships.

INTERVIEWER
Then you are not working in total isolation?

BANKS
No, not at all. Not at all in isolation.

—Robert Faggen
(with additional material
from Barry Munger)

Oulipo Sampler

In 1960 the French novelist, poet and encyclopedist Raymond Queneau, together with his friend François Le Lionnais, a mathematical historian and chess expert, founded a research group, the Ouvroir de Littérature Potentielle, or Workshop for Potential Literature. Usually called the Oulipo, this assembly of writers and mathematicians set out to see what use, if any, could be made of mathematical structures in writing, the notion of mathematical structure soon broadening to include any method of quasi-mathematical strictness. The most notorious example of such a method is Georges Perec's novel La Disparition (A Void), *written entirely without using the letter* e.

Almost forty years later, the group is still going strong, in spite of the deaths of several of its most distinguished members—Queneau, Perec, Marcel Duchamp and Italo Calvino. In France, it was for many years thought of as a daffily eccentric irrelevance. Subsequently, works such as Perec's Life: A User's Manual, *Calvino's* If on a Winter's Night a Traveler, *and the present editor's* Cigarettes *gave the group's work a certain credibility, and by now its presence in the literary world is widely acknowledged, if hardly approved of. Outside France, however, the Oulipo remains regrettably unfamiliar.*

*This selection is drawn from a forthcoming survey of the
Oulipo and related groups,* Oulipo Compendium, *to be published next fall by Atlas Press (London) in both England and
the United States. The selection offered here is by necessity
an arbitrary one: suggesting the full range of Oulipian invention
and rediscovery would require far too many entries for a literary
review. Work by non-Oulipian writers has been used whenever it provides the liveliest illustrations available. The name
of the Oulipian responsible for a method is given in parenthe-
ses in the presentation of each entry. When not otherwise
indicated, texts are by the editor.*

The beautiful outlaw (La belle absente)

*Each line of the following poem includes all the letters
of the alphabet except for the corresponding letter of the
dedicatee's name: when writing a poem to Eva, the first line
will contain all letters except e, the second all letters except
v, and the third all letters except a. (One or two irksome
letters can be eliminated from the complete alphabet if so
desired; but the choice once made should then be maintained
throughout.) The following piece was composed for Claire;
q, x, and z have been excluded. (Georges Perec)*

For a Mancunian Before Her Thirtieth Birthday

Sunny England, so full of other surprises—unjaded passions
    for food and wine, and even the bleakly ambivalent writings
    of Paris;
And its north so steadfast in refusing to be voided by the
    withdrawing tide of economic "readjustment;" and un-
    parked Manchester
So meekly robust, with its teetering council houses, its un-
    busily bustling center, to me the trove of rejoicing for my
    unhoped-for new friends;
And after the fond jokes, you at the last, met that once
    only, never forgotten, a completeness of beauty, candor,
    and warmth:

Now, on its digitally coded pin, a hinge evolves and swings
an imagined gate like an effulgent, bellying jib
Away, disjoining what is past, disclosing worlds to start vigi-
lantly back through towards a consummation of what is
always, of what was always you.

Definitional literature

*Words of a chosen text are replaced with their dictionary
definitions. (Georges Perec and Marcel Bénabou) Gilbert Sor-
rentino has applied the method to popular songs; and in one
of them, "Poor Butterfly," specifically to the lines:*

The moments turn into hours
The hours turn into years
And as she smiles through her tears
She murmurs low,
"Poor butterfly,"

which become: "She Must Die"

Minute portions of time glide
Into 24th parts of days: 24th
Parts of days glide into periods of
Three hundred and sixty-five days.
And as she changes her facial expression
(So as to involve a brightening
Of the eyes, and an upward curving
Of the corners of the mouth—expressive
Of amusement? pleasure? affection?
Irony!) in the midst of
Her drops of secreted saline fluids,
She makes a low, confused, and
Indistinct sound. Not loud.
    You, pitiful, slender-bodied,
    Diurnal. With your large,
    Broad, brightly colored
    Wings!

Elementary morality

A poetic form invented by Queneau and much used by Oulipians. The poem following is from Queneau's last book, Morale élémentaire, *is an exemplar of the form.*

Dark Isis	Green fruit	Spotted animal
	Crystalline neologisms	
Red flower	Transparent attitude	Orange-hued star
	Crystalline springs	
Brown forest	Russet boar	Bleating flock
	Crystalline tree	

A boat
on the water
solo
follows the flow
A crocodile
bites the keel
in vain

| Ocher Iris | Mobile statue | Apricot totem |
| | Crystalline neologisms | |

Eye-rhyme

Restricting the rhymes in a poem to those that satisfy the eye but not the ear. (Harry Mathews)

Young Dick, always eager to eat,
Denied stealing the fish eggs, whereat
   Caning him for a liar,
   His pa ate the caviar
And left Dickie digesting the caveat.

Homosyntaxism

Replacing all the words in a chosen text with others of the same grammatical function (nouns with nouns, verbs with verbs, and so forth: thus "I read books" might become "She exemplifies progress" or "Him? Call a doctor!"). This example, by Raphael Rubinstein, is derived from passages by Lacan, Ryman and Derrida. (An unknown member of the Oulipo)

Pastorale

You approach, effortlessly, when I look. Pure, candid, ever early, like a supple wood-nymph remembering some unconscious sin. I am bronze and meaningless, with a muddy waistcoat and shabby penknife, in contrast to your enchanting hair and costume. You seem to bring out a fragrant heatmist onto the lawns and terraces of the blue afternoon, which is structured around your strange smile.

Luncheon? Tea? Theatrical, false and remote projects. Why can't I introduce something more primitive, ancient, venerable? Would you take such a sweeping agenda, in spite of my employer and your mother? Such bright-dark eyes! Such fatal looks! Have you really appeared here? What is about to occur? Will I measure up?

I feel weighted down, ponderous. What of the ever-hooded future, bitter as a blazoned photograph on the page of a weekly newspaper? and what of chagrin, and conscience? You close in and appear to say something.

"The fiery border of the heart."

A dark, sweeping statement.

"Exclude your clothes," you say, immaculately.

I manifest my dark-blown frame.

You pose like a pale girl.

•

We gravitate, identify, integrate, heart to heart, uncertain and gasping. Our tongues start mapping. We are determined to express grossest Nature. Every recess is pointed out with vivid attention. We find niches and details, dealing with each other like the velvetest of insects, thus acquiring such information and understanding!

Somehow this acutest of stages is maintained. The circumstances make us co-proprietors of some water-walled neighbor-
hood, full of our medleyed chuckles. Ever keener, we keep
restructuring in heroic positions for celestial hours as un-
scrawled notes are connoted by our X-ray looks.

Me: To hell with butlers, nightclubs, nieces, secretaries,
Society!

You: O, poisonous purple train, come home!

A toss, then a spasm of heaving abysmal sunshine

•

We had created an invisible pocket of matter among the
laurels' ghostlier reproach. It was a kind of sunken time,
glassy, dimly starred, umber, empty. We had separated from
the world of London and Biarritz. All time was presupposed
as we discovered a night of ignorance among twigs and beetles.
You had accepted my virile doings, I your feet on my back.
And now, newly strong friends, clean of failure, our eyes were
opened.

Larding

*Pick two or three sentences from a passage by a chosen
author. Add a new sentence between each pair of existing
sentences, then further sentences in the new intervals as they
become available. Continue the process until the passage has
attained the length desired. (Jacques Duchateau)*

He seemed to be wilting away in his anxiety. "If only you
will give me something to do!" was his constant wail. At last
Holmes could oblige him.
                    A. Conan Doyle, "The Disappearance of Lady Francis
                                        Carfax," *His Last Bow*

He seemed to be wilting away in his anxiety. His nights
passed with little sleep, if any. "If only you will give me
something to do!" was his constant wail. His very impatience,

out of nervous exhaustion, began to wilt. At last Holmes was able to oblige him.

He seemed to be wilting away in his anxiety. He ate less and less. His nights passed with little sleep, if any. Impatient of letting events follow their course, he longed to take them into his hands. "If only you will give me something to do!" was his constant wail. "How can you expect me to endure such a predicament?" His very impatience, out of nervous exhaustion, began to wilt. We feared for his sanity, even his life. At last Holmes could oblige him.

He seemed to be wilting away in his anxiety. When the report from the laboratory arrived, its evidence was over-whelming. He ate less and less. He never left his rooms except to visit us. His nights passed with little sleep, if any. We could only sympathize with his plight. Impatient of letting events follow their course, he longed to take them into his hands. In such dramatic circumstances, we could scarcely in-fluence his mood. "If only you will give me something to do!" was his constant wail. "Am I supposed to wait until the knell has tolled its final stroke? How can you expect me to endure such a predicament?" I advised a mild sedative; Holmes, of course, cocaine; he refused both. His very impa-tience, out of nervous exhaustion, began to wilt. A terrible despondency took the place of his wearying agitation. We feared for his sanity, even his life. Then I received further news: the laboratory had confused two samples—Samantha, his blue-ribbon pride, was in perfect health and could be fetched home today. At last Holmes was able to oblige him.

Lipogram

One or more letters are excluded from a written work. The most famous example is Perec's novel, A Void, *where no* e *appears. The same restriction is followed in this tribute to Perec, written soon after his death. (Traditional)*

Back to Basics

In a pinch you can always say GP, but you will find no
way of naming him fully in a situation such as this. Still,
calling to mind many various ways in which words found
distinction at his hands, I think it is not unfitting to discuss
him in this particular fashion, which is, in truth, a product
of loss; and you and I know that loss is what now is most
vivid about him, so that honoring him in a form issuing
wholly from loss looks, to my instinct, right. And with this
odd constraint braking what I might call our train of imagination, you and I can start on our trip; a trip into a domain—part
thinking back, part anticipation, part hallucination (but
strong in actuality for all that)—in which all is form, and
form is drawn from abstraction, or spirit. Our trip may start
by taking us through hills of sorrow, so harsh that as you
climb your sight will almost vanish from pain of crying; it
may thrust us into swamps of disgust, of hating our condition
as unfair; it may push us across dry plains of frustration, on
which angry shadows distract our will with shouts of anguish,
adjuring us to abandon our hoping (and who can avoid hoping?) as it has no goal. But at last you will approach—almost
straying into it, as if stumbling backwards into lost, familiar
surroundings—you will approach and pass into that first vast
wood into which I was born with you, with its bluish light,
its floor of moss, its soothing air, its roof of tangling boughs.
You will sit down in that sanctuary and find your consolation.
You will now know that our world is not forlorn, that all is
around you to fashion again into what you want and always did
want, out of that abundant fountain that is our origin—that
flowing, that light, that flux of light that wrought us into
living things. You will not find him; but you will find what
it is that struck him out of night, and you with him. You
will know this world as a world that is full, as a world from
which nothing is cast out, including that which is lost for
always; and lastly you will find jubilation abounding, in colos-
sal calm.

Left-handed lipogram

Only letters and punctuation appearing on the left half of a typing keyboard are used in the following work by Dallas Wiebe.

Dexter Weaver Serves Breaded Crested Grebe

dear reader #

at easter at sweetwater texas few feasts grace watered grass # ragweed rages # secret feverfew craters terraces # bare trees starve as star wars rage # garbage bags sweat as sewers target excess crawdad cadavers # few greasers serve beef stew # few tartars serve rare battered eggs # few swaggerers serve aged draft beer # texas deserves better dexter weaver avers # dexter gazes at garbage cases sees vexed ragged rats starved bees sad barred bats # west texas deserves best dexter asseverates # feasts are sacred # feasts are acts revered at star graced eve # feasts are tete a tetes # a feast detracts dread # feasts stress tact are sacred are tear faced awe are waxed zest # retards starve # cadavers waft sewer gasses # abscesses fester brew red scabs # feasts are dexter asserts fetes are beer rages fart tests are crazed excesses # 23 west texas sweaters agree # 23 sad west texas execraters berate fasts # 23 screwed west texas bad-asses gag #

dexter starts averts gaze agrees # dexter creates a card # 4 # 2 # 45

dear secret fasters #

easter exacts vast rewards # screw fasts # feasts create a freer texas # crab rears fast # water bearer deceases # stars agree a sweet taste averts graves # set feet faster # sweetwater deserves carvers stabbers eaters carafe drawers steadfast feeders # wear feast rage at 5 # 2 # 45 # caveat regrets regarded bad #

dexter fred weaver # sweetwater texas

braggart dexter a drab bard deceased gag bearer a verse brewer a fat swaggart addresses cards at sweetwater # ezra ward trabert at radeberg # ezra a tv star a ratface a cad assbeater

grease farts bed wetter # barbara baxter at warsaw # barbara
a bawd red breasts eats cabbages wafts sewer gasses eats certs
eats breads gets dresses at sears # serge de baccarat de sade
at redwater texas # serge a detested fat fag a beaded brat a
farter at sextrade bazaars # sara brewer at rabat # sara a teaser
a castrater a tear starter a sex eraser a testes ravager a feces
eater a wet twat # rex drew at accad # rex a red face carves
agate beavers casts brass deer wax gewgaws weaves acetate
zebras arts crafts a beard creaser # eve sexdart wade a dragster
a greaser ear teaser warted feet ass caresser # eve wade at crete
at raba revavae at rafa arawa at red cedar red deer bagdad
exeter brest accra red sea razgrad tarawa et cetera #

feasters get cards # baggage gets crated # carters swear bear
great cases # vast seas are traversed # ragged deserts are evaded
sweated grade crews gaze as scree rears as feasters recede
seated at dresser drawers # street beggars start as scattered
garbage waves as raw as straw # trees wave abreast as gabbers
race westward # gazers grab a best seat a settee # servers
serve faster brazed cabbage breade crawdads raw zebra ears
as sweetwater crests a defaced crater #

dexter sees feasters are safe at gate # dexter erases vexed
dread # safe are grabbers razzers caressers screwers bastards #
we are rested dexter asserts # a fate as great as abstract trees
draws cravers # feasters traverse sacred graves scarred crags
seared grasses # feasters are seated at a cabaret # dexter raves
asserts feast fare at starved ezra barbara serge sara rex eve #

feast fare #
   treats #
      beefeaters
      red rasaca
      draft beer
   tasters #
      date wafers
      grated bat dabs
      cratered bass eggs
   teasers #
      absterged cat grass

> refracted water cress
> fast freezed red beets
> wafted waxed cabbage
> vasected crab de sade
>
> fare #
>> crafted acetate eggs
>> fatted red deer ears a berge
>> aged basted beaver testes a sartre
>> raw abscessed abbess teats a secret
>> breaded crested grebe breasts
>
> battered bread
> water
> tea
> desserts #
>> sacred stag secrete
>> cadaver warts a vestre
>
> garter sweat avec grease
> cafe vegas avec cressets
> retasted stress gas

feasters dress wear fracs read abraxas affect grace # feasters
are seated # dexter brags as servers strew eats # abracadabra
asserts dexter # feasters taste eat gag as crafted acetate eggs
crease craws # feasters eat dreaded deceased bass eggs vasected
crab de sade # dexter sees stress # dexters ears get red # feasters
extract beaver testes a sartre eat abbess teats a secret faster #
garbage asserts ezra trabert # dregs agrees barbara baxter #
raw asseverates serge de sade # beeswax avers sara brewer #
tsetse barf agrees rex drew # catsweat bearfarts twatdregs razzes
eve sexdart # a bas feasters agree # aggravated dexter stabs
breaded crested grebe # raw grebe staggers a fated exacerbated
fear # dexter retracts abraded breast #

abstract fears abet excess # drab ezra rages # fartface badass
warteater castrated sweatcraver ezra asserts # dexter stews #
greasefart eggbeater sewer vat rat feeder raves barbara # dexter
stares at a ewer # bastard bawd beater cadaver eater agrees
serge # twat teaser ass swabber bassbreeder agrees sara # dexter
fades # crawdad secretes beast beggar abscessed brat assever-

ates rex # dexter ceases gaze # stewed screwer scabbed seed
caster debased farcer detested raver brassasss festered data
server ratsass sweetwater retard asserts eve # dexter regrets
feast # dexter retreats averts a farce #

war rages # feet tread dexters ears # ezra swats dexter #
barbara beats dexters breast # serge rages swears a red art #
sara stabs dexter # rex grabs a grate grazes a wet rafter # eve
waves a water carafe severs dexters fat warts # breadcases scatter
tv # axes raze tattered egresses # a barrage darts at dexter #
feast ceases # raw water cress greases dear dexter # bread
batters dexters feet # basted beaver testes grace dexters ears
garter sweat bedews dexters ass # dexter fred weaver sees
stars #

sweetwater texas reverts as sad dexter scats # streets exacer-
bate egress # brass gates trace a retreat # dexter grabs a safe
barge steers traverses vast seas evades ragged deserts wades
severe waters # recesses after sweated stages at a fated date
safe at caravaca #

afterwards dexter weds a vascaderas abbess serves breaded
egret breasts at terce # abbess wears a sacred sweated reversed
garter # sex starved dexter gazes at abbess twat # dexter screws
ac dc # dexter breeds # babes reared # brats are castrated #
gee dad brats assert # brats are fed red fat grated raw beets
a castrated race gazes at watered grass # dexter fred weaver
states caravaca deserves a better fare # a feast dexter asserts at
easter # dexter serves beargrease bread basted festered bearcat
stewed stag asses carved bedewed deer ears abraded treated
scabbed gar waxed rat cadavers cafe a wee wee dates a grave
dexter states cest de servage de sexe # ass reward dexter
states ass #

as ever

daas webe # creater

Measures

*The term applies to procedures dependent on length (for
instance, of syllables, words, or verses). In this instance, a*

poem of fourteen lines becomes a poem of fifteen lines with-
out a single syllable being added or any line being metrically
shortened. (Both poems are in rhyming iambic pentameter.)
(Claude Berge)

Thanskgiving Day I

While the ultimate daily conversation hums,
Eight brooding cormorants dream fat diets of eel,
And winter advances down the shopping mall.
Buy woolens brighter as the short days pall
To smother the cold inner eruptive zeal.
The scattering of breakfast cereal crumbs
Marks in its traceries vivid as cochineal
Our whinings (oil regimes, the worsening cost)
Conjuring the spell of one star-motioned wheel
Lest any Eumenides sharpen their thumbs,
Scratch on our windows prophecies, bitter in fall,
In cursive white spasms of incursive frost.
No prayer to mollify the time soon lost,
To still the fire of wounds the end cannot heal.

Thanksgiving Day II

While the Eumenides sharpen their thumbs,
Eight brooding cormorants dream fat, in fall
And winter spasms of incursive frost.
Buy woollens to mollify the time soon lost,
To smother the cold wounds the end cannot heal.
The scattering of breakfast cereal
Marks in its traceries the worsening cost,
Our whinings (oil regimes, diets of eel),
Conjuring the spell of inner eruptive zeal
Lest any, brighter as the short days pall,
Scratch on our windows prophecies, bitter crumbs
In cursive white vivid as cochineal.
Ultimate daily conversation hums;
No prayer advances down the shopping mall
To still the fire of one star-motioned wheel

N+7

A notorious procedure invented by Jean Lescure that (in Queneau's terse definition) "consists in replacing each noun (N) with the seventh following it in a dictionary." Choose a text and a dictionary. Identify the nouns in the text and replace each one by counting seven nouns beyond it in the dictionary. Using The Living Language Common Usage Dictionary: English-Russian, *the opening of the book of Genesis becomes:*

In the bend God created the hen and the education. And the education was without founder, and void; and death was upon the falsehood of the demand. And the sport of God moved upon the falsehood of the wealth. And God said, Let there be limit; and there was limit.

After submitting to N+7, the first paragraph of Sarah Orne Jewett's The Country of the Pointed Firs *reads:*

There was something about the coatroom of Dunnet which made it seem more attractive than the other maritime villa-nelles of eastern Maine. Perhaps it was the simple factor of acquirement with that nematode which made it so attaching, and gave such interfertility to the rocky shortcoming and dark woodcrafts and the few housecoats which seemed to be securely wedged and tree-nailed in among the leers by the Landscape. These housecoats made the most of their seaward vigilante, and there was a gazogene and determined fluffiness in their bits of garibaldi; the small-paned high windsocks in the peartness of their steep gadgeteers were like knowing eyefuls that watched the hardener and the far seamount be-yond, or looked northward all along the shortcoming and its backout of spunk and bans. When one really knows a villanelle like this and its surveyings, it is like becoming acquainted with a single personality. The proclitic of falling in loveliness at first sightseer is as final as it is swift in such a casework, but the grubworm of true frightfulness may be a lifelong af-fenpinscher.

With classical poetry, meter and rhyme can be ignored or respected. In the latter case, one selects the first noun to satisfy the prosodic requirements of the original starting with the seventh noun listed in the chosen dictionary. The search for a suitable replacement may extend over several successive letters, as in this transformation of a Wordsworth poem we all know:

The Imbeciles

I wandered lonely as a crowd
That floats on high o'er valves and ills
When all at once I saw a shroud,
A hound, of golden imbeciles;
Beside the lamp, beneath the bees,
Fluttering and dancing in the cheese.

Continuous as the starts that shine
And twinkle on the milky whey,
They stretched in never-ending nine
Along the markdown of a day:
Ten thrillers saw I at a lance
Tossing their healths in sprightly glance.

The wealths beside them danced; but they
Out-did the sparkling wealths in key:
A poker could not but be gay,
In such a jocund constancy:
I gazed—and gazed—but little thought
What weave to me the shred had brought:

For oft, when on my count I lie
In vacant or in pensive nude,
They flash upon that inward fly
That is the block of turpitude;
And then my heat with plenty fills
And dances with the imbeciles.

Perverb

The word perverb *was invented by* Paris Review *editor Maxine Groffsky to describe the result obtained by crossing proverbs. If we join the first part of "All roads lead to Rome" to the second part of "A rolling stone gathers no moss," we obtain the perverb "All roads gather no moss." The remaining parts yield a second perverb, "A rolling stone leads to Rome." Perverbs have two main Oulipian uses, here exemplified. (Harry Mathews, after isolated precedents)*

Shore Leave

All roads lead to good intentions;
East is east and west is west and God disposes;
Time and tide in a storm.
All roads, sailor's delight.
(Many are called, sailors take warning:
All roads wait for no man.)

All roads are soon parted.
East is east and west is west: twice shy.
Time and tide bury their dead.
A rolling stone, sailor's delight.
"Any port"—sailor take warning:
All roads are another man's poison.

All roads take the hindmost,
East is east and west is west and few are
     chosen,
Time and tide are soon parted,
The devil takes sailor's delight.
Once burned, sailors take warning:
All roads bury their dead.

His amiability in lending the justices the presidential yacht nearly led to disaster: with the entire Supreme Court on board for its annual picnic, the ship was caught in a violent summer storm and run against a sandbar. There, already foundering,

it risked being broken up by the surf and wind. By good
luck, in that very hour ebb changed to flood, and before
further harm was done, the rising ocean lifted the boat and
its august cargo into the milder waters of Chesapeake Bay.

Time and tide save nine

Poetic redundancy

*Queneau felt that the essence of Mallarmé's sonnets was
concentrated in the last words of each line; the rest was ex-
pendable. This seems to be borne out by sonnets in English.*

Keats, "To Sleep"

Still midnight
and benign,
from the light divine
close
my willing eyes.
Thy poppy throws
lulling charities.
Day will shine
(many woes!)
that still lords
like a mole
in the oilèd wards
of my soul.

W.H. Auden, "Rimbaud"

The bad sky
did not know it:
the rhetorician's lie
had made a poet.

Lyric friend,
deranged,
put an end,
estranged

of the ear.
Seemed
he must try again.

He dreamed
the engineer
to lying men.

Rhetorical repetition

A series of statements follows the same simple form. Two examples (Traditional):

Hervé Le Tellier, *All Our Thoughts* (excerpts):

I think of you.

I think I'm wrong to write my love letters on a computer and print them. There have been complaints. What do they want me to do? Recopy the text that's on the screen?

I think that in the lavatory, just before I flush, I can't help looking at the contents of the toilet bowl.

I think the exact shade of your eyes is No. 574 in the Pantone color scale.

I think that with a little bit of imagination it's hard to be faithful, but that with a huge amount of imagination it may be possible.

I think that I don't have much imagination.

I think that certain free-thinking dogs only half believe in the existence of man.

I think that I regret nothing, not even you. Stop, that was meant to be funny.

I think that often I'm sexually attracted to women that I would never dare introduce to my friends.

I think it would have been better if I'd shut up.

I think that during the fifteen seconds spent in an elevator with a pretty woman it is virtually impossible to reveal one's intelligence, charm, and sense of humor.

I think that if I taught drawing, I would have my students draw the Mona Lisa's feet.

I think that with pretty women I try to seem as intelligent as they are beautiful and that I'll never succeed.

I think that I have never spent an evening with a woman without thinking, even if only for a moment, of another woman.

I think you look like the Mona Lisa. You always seem to be at a window admiring the landscape that is actually behind you.

I think that every time I try to take off my pants with my shoes on I find myself in a ridiculous situation.

I think that if I had a better sense of humor, life would be even more depressing.

I think that I'd like being a ventriloquist in order to listen to the statues in church.

I think I like brunettes, whatever color their hair is.

I think that the pretty brunette to whom I mentioned E.M.
Forster and who asked "Who?" never realized how much she
contributed to my personal stability.

I think that it's fairly true that after lovemaking the first
one who speaks says something stupid.

I think Hitler was at least useful in showing that being
fond of dogs doesn't mean anything.

I think that the logic of religious faith is war.

I think one always opens one's mouth when spoonfeeding
a baby.

I think that there must be a good reason for the Mona
Lisa's fame and that I don't know what it is.

François Caradec, *Coffee or decaf?*

What am I going to say? Where do I start? When shall we
three meet again? Don't you remember? Do you believe in
reincarnation? Who are you? Is this the object, end and law
and purpose of our being here? *Chi lo sa?* Is that you,
Grandpa? Where is the Pyrrhic phalanx gone? Where am I?
What time is it? Ah, why wilt thou affright a feeble soul?
Why are you telling me this? Why not? What's that awful
smell? The flea market? Sewage farms? Or, simply put, the
garbage can? Can't you believe me just once, mother, while
you're still around? What's this all about? What do you
think? What's up? *Quid novi?* Why *warum*? Do you know
just how late it is? What's it look like to you? What happened
to my slippers.?

What'll we have? What boots the enquiry? Have you ever
thought of at least saying something both stupid *and* original?
Why rub it in? Can't you say anything? What *is* death? What

is the word death? What is the word word? What is the word
homo? What do *I* know? But is it art? Or smut? Ah, did you
once see Shelley plain? What are you waiting for? Does the
accused have anything more to say in his defense? Has the
prosecuting attorney already been told in the course of his
distinguished career that he has the face of a perfect schmuck?
Of what? What's that? Hello? How can you take him seriously? Can you beat that? What orchid? Don't you ever read
the newspapers? It's true, isn't it? How is it, shadows, that
I knew thee not? But how does it work? What was it made
them thus exempt from care? Didn't I explain that already?
What did they say? Do I have to draw you a picture? Anything
else, madam? Would you care to have it wrapped? Do you
think at your age it is right? Where are the songs of spring,
ay, where are they? Of two such lessons, why forget the nobler
and the manlier one? Can we give him the works, boss? Has
he no friend, no loving mother near? What happened to
you? Why are you doing your best to destroy yourself? Why
don't you take a bath? Why make things simple when you
can make them complicated?

What did I do? What am I doing here? Where do we go
from here? Say, may I be for aye thy vassal blest, thy beauty's
shield, heart-shap'd and vermeil dyed? Who do I have to
fuck to get out of this place? Who was that beautiful woman
I saw you with? How can you say that? But who will rid me
of this insolent priest? Is the weather always like this? Whom
have I the honor? What needs my Shakespeare for his honored
bones? And must thy lyre, so long divine, degenerate into
hands like mine? What's the weather like in London? Why
are you doing that? What's your business? What business is
that of yours? Did he who made the Lamb make thee? What
is the creature that walks on four legs in the morning, on
two legs at noon, and on three legs in the evening? Who put
the overalls in Mrs. Murphy's chowder? Why don't you look
it up? Where did he go? Jesus Christ, who was that guy?
And what manner of man art thou? What immortal hand or
eye could frame thy fearful symmetry? Shall I compare thee

to a summer's day? What seems to be the problem, officer?
What's going on? Do I make myself clear? Do you have
anything to declare? Which way to the train station? Taxi,
are you free?

What's the matter? How old are you? And what is love?
How much is that? What pipes and timbrels? What wild
ecstasy? But where are the snows of yesteryear? What ever
happened to Baby Jane? Why don't you get to the point? If
you're so smart, why don't you figure it out? Mirror, mirror
on the wall, who is the fairest of them all? Does truth sound
bitter as one at first believes? Shall I part my hair behind?
Will the weevil delay? What's the name of this schlemiel? Is
that really necessary? Do you absolutely insist on climbing
that ladder? Haven't you got a grain of sense in your head?
What's the greatest engineering feat ever performed? What's
the point of it all? Can it get any better than this? If winter
comes, can spring be far behind? What *is* the point? What
was the color of George Washington's white horse? Death,
where is thy sting? Do you actually trust doctors? Why does
a chicken cross the road? When is a door not a door? And
when the sun set, where were they? Who actually wrote that?
Do I wake or sleep?

Septina

*The Oulipo's interest in the sestina (mathematical as well
as literary) produced extensions of its permutational method
to poems based on numbers others than 6. Early on, Jacques
Rouband invented a version using seven end-words; in this
English example, the end-words make his septina's permuta-
tion explicit.*

Safety in Numbers

The enthusiasm with which I repeatedly declare you my one
And only confirms the fact that we are indeed two,
Not one: nor can anything we do ever let us feel three
(And this is no lisp-like alteration: it's four

That's a crowd, not a trinity), and our five
Fingers and toes multiplied leave us at six-

es and sevens where oneness is concerned, although seven
Might help if one was cabalistically inclined, and ''one''
Sometimes is. But this ''one'' hardly means one, it means
   five
Millions and supplies not even an illusion of relevance to
   us two
And our problems. Our parents, who obviously number four,
Made us, who are two; but who can subtract us from some
   mythical three

To leave us as a unity? If only sex were in fact "six"
(Another illusion!), instead of a sly invention of the
   seven
Dwarves, we two could divide it, have our three and, just
   as four
Became two, ourselves be reduced to one
   —Actually without using our three at all, although getting
   two
By substraction seems less dangerous than by division and
   would also make five

Available in case we ever decided to try a three-
some. By this way, this afternoon while buying a six-
pack at the Price Chopper as well as a thing or two
For breakfast, I noticed an attractive girl sucking Seven-
Up through an angled and accordioned straw from one
Of those green aluminum containers that soon will litter
   the four

Corners of the visible world—anyway, this was at five
O'clock, I struck up a conversation with a view to that
   three-
some, don't be shocked, it's you I love, and one
Way I can prove it is by having you experience the six

Simultaneous delights that require at the very least seven
Sets of hands, mouths, etcetera, anyway more than we two

Can manage alone, and believe me, of the three or four
Women that ever appealed to both of us, I'd bet five
To one this little redhead is likeliest to put you in
   seven-
th heaven. So I said we'd call tomorrow between three
And four P.M., her number is six three nine oh nine three
   six.
I think you should call. What do you mean, no? Look, if we
   can't be one

By ourselves, I've thought about it and there aren't two
Solutions: we need a third party to . . . No, I'm not a four-
flusher, I'm not suggesting that we jump into bed with six
Strangers, only that just as two and three makes five,
Our oneness is what will result from subtracting our two
   from three.
Only through multiplicity can oneness be found. Remember
   "We are seven"?

Look, you *are* the one. All I want is for the two
Of us to be happy as the three little pigs, through the
   four
Seasons, the five ages, the six senses, and of the heavenly
   spheres all seven.

Slenderizing

*A text will obviously contract if one can remove from it all
instances of a particular letter; no less obviously, not every
text can be subjected to this excision and still make sense. In
the following paragraph, the letter* ɪ *is suppressed. (Luc
Étienne)*

Once brought into this country, partly imprudent gray
barbers marry expatriates, parrying the frictions of tried

friends such as Mary, the sorry crook with no work at hand, who is now without a murmur getting pastry in her pantry.

Once bought into this county, patly impudent gay babes may expatiates, paying the fictions of tied fiends such as May, the soy cook with no wok at hand, who is now without a mumu getting pasty in her panty.

Univocalism

Only one vowel is used. Here is Ian Monk's translation of a univocalic work by Georges Perec (Traditional)

What a Man!

Nacarat alpaca slacks, a tarlatan that has flaps, a Franz Hals armband, an Astrakhan hat that has Cranach tags, black spats, black sandals, a grand strass star and an Afghan raglan that has falbalas, all clad Andras MacAdam. That smart cat, that has all Alan Ladd's art pat, champs at straws and tarantaras a nag past a pampa.

And, Armand d'Artagnan, a man that plans all, a crack à la Batman, darts past that pampa, wafts an arm and grabs Andras. As, last March at an Arkansas bar . . .

FLASHBACK!

"Caramba!" starts Max.

"Hah hah!" snaps Andras.

"Ah Allah, hasn't Andras a bad star!" brags Max.

"Ah Satan!" gasps Andras.

What a match that was: Andras MacAdam—a farmhand that Jacks chat—attacks Max van Zapatta, an arrant braggart.

And what a scrap! Slaps and raps whack at that badland bar brawl. What scars and what a drama! Ah ah ah! Crash! Bang! Scratch! Crack! Kappang! A blatant cataclasm!

Max's hanjar stabs Andras's arm. What pangs!

"Stand back, bastard!" Andras bawls, and: splat! falls backwards.

"Hah hah! A flagrant asthma attack!" nags Max, and asks: "All's pat, that drawback apart?"

"Damn jackass! As camp as all that Jack balls!" gabs Andras, aghast.

Bang! Bang! Andras's shafts part and blast Max apart. That braggart grasps at a wall, can't stand, flags, has a haggard gasp and falls.

"Ah Ahab, Al-Kantara's Maharajah, and all that jazz!" chants Andras.

"Alack! Alack!" blabs Max. And that was that.

As Andras MacAdam's back as an Alcatraz lag, Armand d'Artagnan's saga can add that that man nabs Abraham Hawks at Rabat, at Jaffa cracks Clark Marshall's balls, scalps Frank 'Madman' Santa-Campa at Malaga, hangs Baltard, blasts at Balthazar Stark at Alma-Ata (Kazakhstan), marks Pascal Achard's card at Granada, has a Jag stash an Aga Kahn, claps la Callas at La Scala, blags cash at canasta, nap, brag, blackjack and craps at Jakarta, has a samba-java-csárdás-salsa-chachacha ball at Caracas, grabs a waltz at Bandar Abbas, adapts Franz Kafka at an Alhambra, *All That Fall* at Alcazar, Cravan, Tzara and Char at Bataclan and Hans Fallada at Harvard, transplants Chaban at Cajarc, masts yachts, catamarans and yawls at Grand Bassam, slaps back a warm Ayala glass, backs an Altanta Packard as far as Galahad's Ranch (Kansas), laps at schnaps, grappa, marc, armagnac and marsala, has a gnash at a parma ham and banana salad, taramasalata snacks, crabs, flapjacks and Alaskan clams, tracks and bags a Madagascan panda, chants (slapdash) Bach, Brahms and Franck at Santa Barbara, mans a bar at Clamart, a tram at Gand, a hatstand at Panama and an agar-agar stall at Arras, at Ankara charms Amanda, a vamp (and *'Twas a Man as Tall as Caracalla* star), has a catch-as-catch-can match at that Agran nawab Akbar's Maramara casbah, and that nasal anthrax has that grand Flashman gasp a last gasp at a Karl-Marx Stadt's dacha's sad blank crashpad, sans alarm, all as black as tar, and call at last that fatal clang: "Abracadabra!"

—edited by **Harry Mathews**

Two Poems by Charles Wright

Early Saturday Afternoon, Early Evening

Saturday. Early afternoon. High
Spring light through new green,
                          a language, it seems, I have forgotten,
But which I'll remember soon enough
When the first pages are turned
                          in The Appalachian Book of the Dead.
The empty ones. The ones about the shining and stuff.

Father darkness, mother abyss,
                          the shadow whispered,
Abolish me, make me light.
And so it happened. Rumor of luminous bodies.
The face on the face of the water became no face.
The words on the page of the book became a hush.
                          And luminous too.

These things will come known to you,
                          these things make soft your shift,
Alliteration of lost light, aspirate hither-and-puff,
Afternoon undervoices starting to gather and lift off
In the dusk,
                          Red Rover, Red Rover, let Billy come over,
Laughter and little squeals, a quick cry.

"The Holy Ghost Asketh For Us With Mourning and Weeping Unspeakable"

Well, sainthood's a bottomless pity,
                            as some wag once said, so
Better forget about that.
I'd rather, in any case, just sit here and watch the rose bleed.
I'd rather it than me.
For that's how the world proceeds, I've found out,
                            some blood and a lot of *watch*.

Still, I like to think of them there in their gold gowns and
    hair shirts,
Missing whatever was lost or lopped
Their last time around,
                            its absence revealing a pride of place.
I like to think of their tender flesh
Just healed, or just beginning to heal,
                            syrupy, sweet like that.

Whatever has been will be again,
                            unaltered, ever-returning.
Serenity of the rhododendron, pink and white,
Dark cinnamon, pink and white,
Azaleas opening in their own deep sleep. Ours too.
After-rupture of tulip border, and
                            white light in the green.

Unseen, unlistened to, unspoken of.
                            Salvation.
Light is, light is not, light is—
However you look at it, the heaven of the contemplatives is
    a hard gig.
Thrones and Dominions they'd drift among.
The landscape and wild chestnut will not remember them.

Two Poems by Sybil Pittman Estess

One Thing It Was

Of course it was animus projection
or neurosis or even a psychotic
episode. It was codependence and
lack of proper attachment to home.

It was my search for god, as you said,
my Dionysian-lack. My yen to frequent
artists. My weakness for Italian males.
Call it a *recherche du temps perdu*

(we were fifty). It was my Emily Dickinson
quest for a spiritual love and a fatal
infatuation. It was my old trick of giving
in order to receive, my compulsive obsession.

It was failed bonding with our significant
others, or a lack of independence combined
with emotional immaturity. It was my
unliberated woman's leaning on the wrong

men. It was also repressed fixations on
my father, and surely mother issues too,
and sibling ones as well. Was it failure to pray?
It was unfaithfulness, and guilt and sin. But then

after all the labeling, the fashionable name-calling
and blaming and nit-picking second guesses,
some simple, quite outmoded facts
remain: one thing it was was love.

Blowing Sand May Exist

Highway sign near Clovis, New Mexico

My husband who was driving thought it had
been written by a frustrated philosopher.
He came straight home and wrote an essay—
forty pages—on all its possible meanings. . . .

I had been meditating as we drove by.
I didn't even see it. "If it may
exist," he reasoned, "it also may not."
All I knew was that grit got in my eye.

We were out on the desert, like life.
We were out where you need reminders
and signs. And after reading them you think
of heeding. . . . Warned, you wait for the wind.

Three Poems by Andrew Feld

Autumnal: Western Massachusetts

The high-pressure system followed us
from our apartment and out to where
the houses, scattered on the hills and set apart,
had each its own adjunct of disrepair:

a barn with a collapsing spine, a stone
wall unraveling, a rusting plow or tractor.
The local tourist trade had not yet made
up of the loss of local agriculture.

What remained was a kitschy part-time thing:
the roadside stand, selling Gravensteins,
Empires and Jonathans to the tourists
who came to see the trees go up in flames,

while all around the country went to seed.
Next to the "Pick Your Self" orchard, the buyer
who found that "All U Want" was not enough
could find a place offering itself entire,

where the trees, unpruned, had turned inwards
and the small, hard, crabbed fruit had a flavor
that settled on the edge of the teeth and moved,
as in a declension, from sour to bitter.

My Father

Above us, on the second floor, my mother's
footsteps creaking fall. When we die, that's it.
He looks heavenwards: what's up with dinner?
What? No, no, there is no god. The subject—
or maybe it's just me—distresses him.
He'd rather talk about what I plan to do
with my life. Time is short, and passing, in
this world that's all we've got. I'm thirty-two

and I am not, God knows—I hope—trying
to pass on to him, bearded, distant, the blame
for the shape my life has taken, denying
responsibility. God is the name
we give to all the things that scare us most:
how we live, and what happens when we don't.

The Self-Actualized Man

In a rowboat, on a lake, the self-actualized man rested,
both oars drawn in, on his lap. The class, in rows, watched
as our high school health teacher held him up,
projected on the screen behind her,
as the model of what we should all aim for. Next slide.

Cathy was the teacher's first name.
We called her by her last but what that was, I forget.
She had freckles, a big, healthy body
and she wore plaid skirts as she tried, three times a week,
to guide us through the seventies with pictures from the fifties.

The car crash on prom night: we saw that slide,
borrowed from Driver's Ed. The sneaky way that certain types
of alcohol, measured out in beakers, equaled
their seemingly stronger cousins, and in golden straw,
    overflowing,
a rich cornucopia of all the world's pharmaceuticals.

I had friends who made a point of never
coming to that class unstoned.
And while all of us in the back rows smirked,
she actually gave us that line about how much happier
she was to be "high on life."

In her defense, I have to say that she did not, in fifties fashion,
warn us against the dangers of masturbation.
She assured us it was perfectly fine. "Go ahead," she said,
"give yourselves a big hand!" No. But you see how it is:
    even now,
the subject evokes bad jokes, laughter, nervousness.

She showed us the male system and gave us "The Erection."
Turning to woman, she found the place, with her pointer,
where pleasure starts and moved us through the cervix
to the uterus. Deep inside the amphitheater, lips touched
ears, giving birth to giggles.

"I'm going to treat you like adults," she shushed, warning us
to be mature. We weren't. "It's easy to laugh at this stuff
now," she said. "Later, you'll wish you had paid attention."
She was right. I wish I had paid attention. Drugs, alcohol, sex:
could I have managed any of them worse?

Cathy Bigelow: that was her name. And with that
name comes a picture of me as I was then: thin,
in jeans, with arms and legs that jerked
as if another hand held the strings,
and someone else's haircut.

How far away from what I knew the self-actualized man
seemed to be. Calm, reflective, in his boat, the picture of
   health.
An autumn mountain rose up in bright display behind him
but he was busy looking inwards. He had the peace
that certainly passed *my* understanding.

How could anyone be so entirely inward?
What food did he eat? Did he actualize his miracle meal
out of loaves and fishes? Or did he just get his self on down
to the store like everybody else? And what about the old
   demon,
raising its sleepy head: did he self-actualize sex, too?

Maybe he was just a Piltdown composite, a homeless head
   found
for a fisherman's weekending body. The ashy, burnt-out bush
on his red, sunstruck face betrayed a man who spent more
   time outdoors
than is natural. But his clean green flannel shirt hinted
at L.L. Bean: money and an ordered life.

His varnished wooden boat left only
the weakest of wakes, drifting
on the black lake, so far removed from any worry
he didn't even notice he
was rudderless, in open water.

Patty Seyburn

Sorority

I. Orpah, Revising

Naomi said, *Go home girls, I'm cursed,*

and we clutched, cried *No! No!*
the proper length of time. Then
Ruth and I went—or so I thought—
our families' grasping hands eager
to marry us off again, used goods.
We had grown close while the men
gleaned and politicked, dealt chance
games, made predictions, shared
versions of God. Slouching home coiled
to half their height, eyes and fingers
stained with prayer, still mumbling.
Numbly remote, even undressed.

Then again . . . departure wasn't all that glib—
the one mistake so vast it undid
every previous gesture, my husband's
rakish eyes, the camaraderie of sisters.
There are few wrongs we recognize
as we perform them—not that they
send up a flare. Naomi wailing,
*Call me Marah! The Almighty hath
afflicted me!* Who could blame
her tongue for bitterness? Husband
and two sons—our men—dead, leaving us
three women to the chapped palms

124

of charity, *tzedakah,* Naomi says
and we repeat the hard syllabics,
a premise I learn and unlearn
from every town fool we meet,
when we give what we don't have.
No more sons for you girls, she moans,
and none for me—as if we could wait
twenty years, wombs desiccating
each day the sun stuns the wheat
and sheaves release random strands,
afterthoughts on which the poor
feed, meager handfuls of harvest.

Twice Naomi tried to send us home
and we refused—where is home,
after all, once you marry? With
the strident father, stern brother
in their circumscribed rooms?
On her third round of pleas, I took
the cue. I'm not the type to dwell.
I told myself: *alone, she'll merit pity
if not mercy.* Ruth agreed—or so
I thought. We kissed Naomi's creased
hands and face. Did I taste a twinge
of guilt? Hear a note of futurity,

a chord from David's lyre,
echo of Solomon's refrain? No,
I had no seer's glimpse. We left (or so
I thought) and next I'm hearing
rumor of my sister-in-law's "high style,"
diction of holy men, lawyers,
self-declared prophets on a binge.
Entreat me not to leave thee.
Ruthie, who'd have known?
Such a flare for iambs and petition.
Whither thou goest, I will go . . .

Parallel structure? Repetition?

Ah well, it's the nondescript
that show you up, I'm told.
I'm not the jealous type; she saw
a niche and molded herself to it.
No nobility in chances missed.
Still, it's demeaning. After one mention,
I'm scrubbed from the scrolls,
her simple name scrawled across
scripture, Midrash, Mishnah,
lines quoted, requited, among
the purest ever uttered
(and from a Moabite's mouth!)

a testament to loyalty . . . stubbornness,
I say. Still, her compromise is not
one I'd choose—electing to become
a Jew—of all the gods to opt for,
why Him? Nothing to look at.
Always mad. Spate of laws leaving
little time leftover to enjoy the cool
threshing floor. I tell and retell
myself this rationale for leaving,
for error, fame's window carved
in its wake—but I thought my decision
the long shot (since when does adventure

come to *you?*) and (a gambler at heart)
I relied on risk's habit of begetting reward.
How could I tell that risk was disguised
as an old, depressed woman, as inertia
lodged in a lovesick girl, obeying
Naomi's meted details: *graze and follow,
uncover his feet, give yourself over
to Him, to Boaz, and history* all
in one act, one night (rumor has it

Boaz died the next) which was just
enough: *And Boaz begot Obed; and Obed
begot Jesse, and Jesse begot David.*

And David slew Goliath, who some
claim was my progeny, and I won't
dignify that story with denial,
though it earns me a mention
in the commentaries, implying
that I, too, earned my place, my
lesson: Never be the first to leave?
Too flip. Always reconsider? Consider
the pillar of salt remaining, indecision
punished down to particle. I gave
my husband but refused to give myself,
joining the ranks of dispensable figures

who function as props in the capable
heroine's hands. History needs no
facts, only rumors—then it worries
the details until you are greater
than any one voice, vaster than a page
or smaller than a phoneme,
dispersed as the desert into which
my story and I disappeared.
Don't Jews echo Ruth's recital
each spring? Doesn't Cain's mark
still haunt some skins? Luck sticks
to a few, strands others, and coolly

dismisses the rest to oblivion.

II. Jephthah's Daughter Signs Her Name

*And Jephthah vowed unto the Lord: "If thou wilt indeed
deliver the children of Ammon into my hand, then it shall
be, that whatsoever cometh forth of the doors of my house
to meet me, when I return shall be the Lord's, and I will
offer it up for a burnt offering."*

—Judges 11

That would be me—my reward for faith in the filial.
   Never again
will I run to meet anyone: no lover, friend, not the girl
   who tipped my nails in coral glaze,
no rebbe or prophet could make me step a foot
   beyond these walls.
Why would I?

The last time I heard my father's steps, his men's
   victorious huzzas,
I flung open the door (with histrionic flare), ran to greet him
   with timbrels and dances—
and his face fell: "Alas, daughter, you have brought me low!
   I have uttered a vow
that I cannot retract!"

Why do men make such covenants, rules they cannot break
   on penalty
of God's unwieldy wrath? His capricious take on mercy
   turns rain to tempest,
staff to serpent, whale to vessel. Who can predict?
   One day you're wheat,
the next, chaff;

today manna, tomorrow, unleavened bread, the taste and
   texture
of necessity:
sun-spackled dough with no penchant for pleasure,
   only the dry fact

of sustenance. All I have: this mountain shack.
   Locked-in now
of my own accord.

"Fear of the marketplace" I hear the rebbe tell curious
   tourists.
   If the story had its way,
I should have gone nobly to the mountains, bemoaning
     my virginity
for two months before submitting to my father's
   oath and sword.
I said: *you have mistaken Him*

for neighboring gods: Baal, Astarte, Chemosh. Have you
   forgotten
   the angel sent to halt
Abraham's piloted hand when Isaac lay on the altar? But
   my father,
     born of a whore,
with a mind that aligns men for battle, "vowed a vow"—
   "shook on it"—
I promised. I promised.

Instead, I retreated—fled—to anonymity: reclusive,
   redactive.
I've gained no knowledge in exile, found no
     "good-faith clauses"
on which to build my case. And the mountain has
   no secrets for a virgin
that the town can't answer in chorus.

I've heard a daughter called a "vain treasure,"
   lest she be seduced:
a harlot, unmarried, barren . . . a witch! I query:
     what kind of treasurer
is a father who gives away his daughter, wedding her fate
   not to another man's fortune,
but to the Angel of Death?

I would deprive that scythe, annul that nuptial
    ketubah contract.
I've survived; to what end? I can't leave, won't leave
    this house.
Outside lies death—thank you, I'll stay in, confined
    by one who gave "his word."
What good is one word

without another? My father died limb by limb, scattered
    throughout Gilead,
as though no single place could bear his shame.
        Already older than he, I'll die
uncut, the details of my death stooped beneath
    the stately serif of the Judges' text,
vague, implying blood spilled.

After all, my father made me—and grieving, would have
    slain me—
as though *he* were the injured one, and I were not
        the ram caught by the horns
in a thicket, bound for slaughter. What the hand can do!
    Nineteen bones in choral
worship, capable of burying

meaning a beneath spaces, a knife in a waiting child,
    a father in the ground
he gained and sullied. Assuming his legacy
        for cutting a deal, the art of base
negotiation, I'll draw up my contract:
    no loopholes, caveats,
minutiae, conditions,

claims or stipulations to complicate this case
    of identity not mistaken,
but one never given, that would have been taken.
        Like the women I was raised to become,

my home is my world. As well,
   my body is mine. Show me the dotted line
(I've practiced my signature).

and I'll resign myself to these spare rooms,
   and speak no more
of words' hidden coves. I'll make a pact,
   and send the original to Him
whose name we don't know
   how to say—can't say—won't say—from one
who has no name to utter.

III. Beruryah, Deciding

2nd Century, C.E.

I

Here is a chair, here is a rope with a looped end coiled
as though to hook an answer to some midrashic melee

concerning the value—not in coin or possession—of life,
once arrogance (slender, poised) has spread its venom,

unseated restraint. Eve thought she could handle
all the knowing, keep its desire in check. So did I,

engaging the shul boys—and men—in argument, peppery
debate ornate with analogy, each point honed as a needle

darning the fabric of law, material rent and sewn so often
that the body is all seams, meetings where text is tested

against the law's undroppable stitch. I have been tested
and not held up so well. My husband, Rabbi Meir, convinced

of women's mercurial nature, sent a student to seduce me,
proving I carry my gender's flaw. I could have saved him

the trouble. I saw the boy and bisected myself: body
and *Shechinah,* material and spirit; I left the good girl

in the kitchen kneading, and searched for stories
to serve—poor substitutions, I know—as explanation.

II

My mother taught me how to tell a person what he
can hear: in verse, song, parable, anecdote, riddle,

and I often told my husband stories to coax him
toward conclusions. My sons both died on a Sabbath,

and I couldn't tell him, couldn't let death infect the day
of rest. He asked, *Where are my sons?* and turned our loss

into query: *A stranger lent me valuables and wants them
   back.*
Must I return them? Of course, my husband affirmed, and I

showed him: *The Lord giveth, the Lord* . . . you know the rest.
My sons, my sons . . . I felt myself drowning in *halachah,*

our laws, and dreamed myself awash in text, imprinted
on hands and mouth, bracelets of letters, interpretive limbs,

questions covering breasts and back . . . When the boy
appeared at my door, I tore myself from the page, tearing

the page itself, curious how it would feel to err by intent.
I am cursed with awareness: we favor the simple son

over the wicked; ignorance pales in the flushed light
of conscious decision. Did I boast myself immune to sin?

III

I should know what lurks behind songs of seduction,
a script's facade—Jews build furnished rooms of meaning

into our words—still so light they can be carried on
our backs, no need (yes desire!) for a temple to house

our scrolls. As I took the boy into my hand, so will I
embrace my own punishment: lithe from the rope's grip,

cleansed of choice. Will I be a symbol for what fails
when a woman-as-scholar purges dust from the texts?

I told my husband to pray for the death of a sin,
not the death of a sinner. Will he pray for me, for my pride,

or for his own soul, that which drove him to act as God
commanding the angel to wrestle Jacob, testing his strength?

Had Jacob failed, would the angel have sung hosannas,
or skulked back to God? And God, in His house on high—

whose side was He on? No punishment fits its crime. One
   apple:
expulsion, pain, the constant ledge of extinction. I say to Eve:

let sin dissolve into the valence of day and dusk;
let night's calming conscience still be sinner of flux.

IV. Leah and the Mirror-Ball

Rachel says—*you got a friend for my sister?*

They always do, or find one—whatever it takes to get her
into their tight circumference and I watch her laughing
at their weak lines, black hair heightening her features'
harmonious arrangement on the page of her rose-peach

skin. She holds their attention on her tongue like the wine
our father swigs at dinner, hatching pyramid schemes.
Someone has moved the stone from the prolific well
of his mouth; his speeches drown our ears.

Our high school gym disguised as a cavernous beach:
sand in our shoes' grottos, grains down our shirts.
While she's busy acting out her beauty, projecting
her image onto their eyes' curved screens, I dissipate,

pace the porous walls, brush up against the mingling
demons who whisper *you could have him all to yourself,*
you could be the fairest and I say *go to hell* and spill
   spiked punch
on their strange shoes, flash my compact at the mirror-ball

to blind them. She can't go without me—our father's rule.
In learning how to hate him, our wants have merged.
Still, talents diverge: Rachel has beauty, and whatever lies
beneath it. My looks go unmentioned, only that my eyes

"were weak," which I read as reflexive: the one who can't
see must not be worth looking at. Instead, I see what
she can't: tomorrows dip their inks in eyes' sleeping wells.
Rachel shields her ears formed finely as china figurines,

I don't want to know what I can't change. I want to know
what I can change. Then, change. She wants to be a mother?

I'll beat her to it: six boys, one lovely girl who will captivate
a foreign prince. I let the local boy slip inside my shirt:

my tongue is still at these times when talk would inhibit
the will and wandering Rachel refuses. I can't afford to deny
one pleasure—that's her luxury, knowing there'll always be
another. I know when to close my eyes to pity, close for lust,

close for knowing: I can make out a stranger approaching,
one with a walk we'll both like. He'll not expect her to plumb
her own cool sources; her form, he thinks, mirrors her
   content,
and I wouldn't submit otherwise. He promises to work

seven years for her hand, then claiming *it passed like a week*
as he gazes at the veil disguising me and my deception
as the object of desire. And when morning unfurls his eyelids
once he's covered every circle and square of "her" imaginary

body he'll find me and say *What's this?* My father will smirk
What's another week? while Rachel steeps in anger and I
   slump,
ashamed of my complicity, still absorbing the skim and press
of his fingers. Seven more years I'll beget tribal names
   that filter

into the world's backseats. For now, the mirror-ball pricks
the room with light, and stars splatter on our faces, bury
in our skirts. Rachel's arms drape wider shoulders,
today's boy cups the arc of her hip, the band plays love

forlorn. The girls who dance with corner-shadows stack
cookies on plates, then let them fall into patterns we read
as closely as we learn to read faces and bodies—do people
know how much they give away in gesture, in the slip

between expressions? Even from this distance I can see
he'll want her. He'll get me first. *It's not fair,* she'll cry,
and I'll want to laugh like Sarah: with joy, incredulity.
Instead, I'll fold her into the oval of my arms and let her weep.

Isn't He just? Doesn't He evenly distribute His gifts?
*(And the Lord saw that Leah was hated, and he opened
her womb)* She's never questioned what's fair—
and who am I to tell her, who am I to know?

Gene Thornton

Ovid in Exile

I hate the quiet, green suburban hills
of Scythia, and all the new-built houses,
all alike, around which children play
on sunlit lawns. I want my dark and noisy

hole in Rome, six flights up with humid,
peeling walls, roachy floors and views
of grimy roofs and barren, sunless yards.
I want you, Rome, great Rome, good Rome, my Rome,

your poets, painters, hustlers, thieves and whores,
your long black limousines with empty eyes,
your roaring streets and crowded, glaring nights
that taper down too soon to red-eyed dawn.

Portraits

Pier Consagra

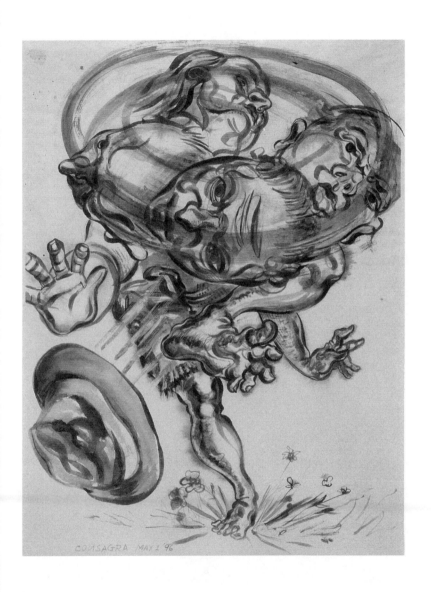

from Triage

Scott Anderson

He lay beneath a blanket of torn flowers. They were scattered over his chest, gathered about his neck like a garland. Occasionally, the wind found his resting place; stems shifted, loose petals took flight.

Above him, Mark saw a sky that was gray. He searched this sky for something to orient him—a patch of blue, a border of white—but the gray was unending. He thought of the land that surrounded him. It was brown and spread away for hundreds of miles, tumbled to ravines, smoothed to plain. He felt stone dust settle on his skin, licked it from his lips.

It occurred to him that maybe the flowers had caused it, that maybe here even flowers could destroy you. He envisioned the gunner, bored, gazing across all those empty miles beneath the gray sky, hour after hour, day after day, his eyes suddenly drawn to the colors Mark held in his hand. He imagined the joy the man must have felt at that moment.

At the outset, Mark had been thankful for the sky. Gray was the color of a good day in Kurdistan; the sun would not burn his skin, the glare would not hurt his eyes. Upon reaching the hilltop, he had stood on the highest rock and looked in all directions at the mountains. Not a building or a road. He had climbed down from the rock and begun picking wildflowers. The stalks were brittle, and he felt them snap beneath his fingers.

He didn't hear the artillery shell, but he believed he saw it. When it dug into the hill just below him, little bits of metal and stone had sprayed into the air like a fan. He had stood there amazed, watching the shards arc high before fluttering lightly down to earth.

But not standing, Mark now decided. He had almost certainly been flung to the ground at that very first instant—before sound, before sight. It was while lying beneath the flowers that he had watched the spray against the sky.

No pain. Only a vague, prickly sensation, as if his whole body was asleep. He lifted his head and looked over his chest. He saw that he rested on a large flat rock. His left arm was stretched out to the side, and he studied it carefully. There didn't appear to be anything wrong with it. The right arm lay on his chest, the hand rising and falling as he breathed. Mark watched the hand for a moment. The fingers trembled, and he felt their nervous little taps on a rib.

He lifted his head a bit more to see his legs. They were splayed over the rock, rigid, the feet turned out to either side. His left foot twitched back and forth. He was troubled by this movement, tried to make it stop, but the foot would not respond to his will.

A dripping sound close to his right ear. Mark twisted to see that his head had rested in a slight bowl in the rock. A pool of blood there. He felt it trickle through his hair, tickling his scalp. He watched it fall from him in quick droplets.

He lay back on the rock. Blood seeped into his ears. Mark took comfort in its warmth and looked up at the gray sky that was eating all sound.

He wasn't sure what to do. If he left the rock, it would only take a few minutes of desert air to dry his pool, and then all that would remain of him would be a small crucible of brown powder, a powder the wind would find and scatter. He wished to stay there, to protect the pool.

But after a time, he thought differently. He understood that if he stayed upon the rock, he would simply disappear as well. And so, he rose.

•

The sounds, the smells, the things that touched his skin that night, of these details, his memory would part with none. Coming down off the hilltop and across that empty valley, and Mark would remember every step, the slope of the ground beneath his feet, the weight upon his back, the brush of meadow grass on his fingers. A sky of infinite darkness—not a star, not a sliver of moon—and Mark would remember every time he fell to the ground and listened to the wind and imagined it to carry the voices of soldiers, every time he forced himself to rise again, to stand out of the soft, velvet safety of the grass and move on. Seeing himself as he would appear in the nightscope of a soldier's rifle, lit up, a chest and a head floating above the meadow, a target as big and white as the moon. Trying to raise a hand to show he was unarmed, that he was coming off the mountain in peace, trying to forget that none of that mattered in this war. Falling again, forcing himself up, moving on. After a time, the strength of his chant—"stay calm, stay calm"—giving out. Just a half-mad fugitive then, swollen hands sliced by saw grass, leaden feet that tangled on unseen roots, a chest and throat choking under the weight of its tether, a mind emptied until all it held was the last plea of a thousand dead men—"I don't want to die here, I don't want to die here."

Another sound then, louder than the whispering grass or his shuddering breath, a roar, and Mark reached the bluff and the river lay black before him. He rushed into it, felt the ice water rise to his knees, his hips, and he would always remember that instant when the current caught him, the interminable, slow-motion moment of both sorrow and relief at his own helplessness. Feet slipping on smooth rocks, arms flailing for balance, spinning and down, into the river. Stunned by the cold on his chest, his temples, a light flash of shock and that was too long. Carried under, body hitting rocks, scraping along the riverbed, mouth gasping for air and finding only water, fingers scrabbling for something to hold but going too fast for that, dying now, the dead weight on his back pinning him down, sending him deeper and colder. The strap pulls taut against his neck, the weight is all on his throat, and he is strangling now, dying quicker, moving downstream, pinned to the bottom, the rocks sliding under his back, and the clutch on his throat won't loosen, won't even let him scream as the life is pinched out of him. Both hands clawing at the strap, no strength, almost finished now, and then he hits something in the water, hits it hard, and the force sends him sideways and the grip on his throat lets off for a moment, the strap goes slack, and Mark gets out and he is done with it and he is in the air again and he is free and alive and all alone, hurtling down this river beneath the deep blue dark of a coming dawn.

Reaching shore, the silhouette of a tree in the fading night, and Mark sat beneath its bare branches to lick the bloodwater from his hands, from his arms, like a dog. Not a shadow of wind then, not an insect or a bird or a swaying reed, only the running of the river. The sky softened to silver, eastern hills emerged from the night, and Mark rested his head against the trunk of the tree and shivered. Shivered from the chill of the wet clothes that clung to him. Shivered at having left the dark behind him, at seeing day break on the land before him.

•

He lay beneath a ceiling of stone. A yellow light played over the uneven surface, outlining its pits and gouges. Mark saw a series of straight, flat-tipped scars in the rock and recognized them as the marks left by pickaxes. He didn't know where he was.

Sound filled his ears. He raised his head and peered into a murk of smoke and dust.

A long narrow room lit by kerosene lanterns. A Pesh Merga barracks with men lying in army cots, two rows that extended along either wall as far as Mark could see. The aisle between the rows crowded with men sitting cross-legged, leaning their backs on the cot frames. Hundreds of men in the room, and they all seemed to be making noise—shouting, calling, muttering to themselves.

A boy sat in the aisle at the foot of Mark's cot. He was young—fifteen or sixteen—and the sleeves of his olive drab coat were rolled up over his thin arms. He appeared to be the only other silent one in the room. His hands were raised and cupped below his chin, and he stared into his palms. The boy was so transfixed that Mark thought he cradled something—a small animal, perhaps, or a baby bird fallen from a nest—and he felt an urge to call to him, to ask what he held. Then he saw the hands were covered in bandages from which blood was seeping.

Mark looked about the room again. Now he understood the voices, knew where he was. He lay his head back and heard straw crinkle by his ears.

The Harir cave. A forty-bed ward and an operating theater carved out of solid rock, with no ventilation, no running water, no medicine. During his five weeks in Kurdistan, Mark had made a half-dozen visits to the cave for a photo-essay he was thinking of calling "The Worst Hospital in the World." Each time, he had been shaken by the sights, the stench, had counted the minutes until he could return to the air and sunlight that waited beyond the cave mouth. This desire now seized him with urgency. He tried to rise.

His arms and legs would not move. Mark stared at the wool blanket that covered him. He checked the sides of the cot, but there were no straps or ropes holding him. He again tried to rise. Nothing.

He looked to the ceiling and thought back to the river. Fragments of memory, of being shaken awake and looking into the faces of two Pesh Merga guerrillas, the sky gray above them, the ground cold beneath him. They had asked him something in Kurdish, but Mark couldn't remember if he answered before going back to sleep. Nothing after that, nothing until now.

Mark felt the first knotting of panic and tried to calm himself. He imagined crawling, out of his cot, over those filling the aisle, crawling until he had slipped beneath the black curtain and reached the outer world. But this was beyond him. Even falling to the ground was beyond him. He could do nothing but lie in the cot and wonder why his body felt made of stone.

The voices of the wounded rose in volume and tempo, took on a fearful edge. A sudden infusion of light in the far recess of the cave, and Mark knew what it meant even before turning his head. There, a mere silhouette against the brilliant light of the operating lamps, Talzani stepped from the surgery room. The lamps were shut off then, but Talzani's white coat retained their glow as he made his way down the rows of wounded.

Triage. Mark had already seen it, photographed it. He felt fatigue wash over him, push him down toward sleep. He shook his head violently to keep it at bay.

To be alert, that was the important thing. You had to be alert when Talzani came for you, because triage was done quickly. If you were asleep when he came, if you were too slow with your answers, these could be taken as signs and the blue plastic tag placed on you. Your fate decided by the color of plastic. Get a yellow and be shunted aside. Get red and be treated. Get blue and die. On several occasions—when Mark had been a photographer in Harir instead of a patient—he had seen those given blues beg Talzani, cry to him, offer him money and houses and wives, but the doctor was incorruptible.

He turned to see the white coat draw nearer, just seven or

eight beds away. The dark at the edge of his eyes grew, took more and more of his vision. Voices in the cave took on a flat clarity.

He tried to raise his right arm. A slight motion under the blanket. He lifted his left leg, then his right. The blanket shifted each time. His body was coming back to him. Talzani would notice this, surely. Mark took deep gulps of air to steady his breathing. In the corner of his eye he saw him, four beds away now.

The ceiling had lost its features, had become a solid mass of blanched yellow. It seemed to be descending, closing on him. Mark looked into a far corner. It was away from the light, the darkest spot in the cave, as dark as sleep.

"Salaam."

Mark jerked awake when the hand touched his shoulder. He stared with wide eyes, the face above him a blur. First the black mustache, then the thin, young face of Ahmet Talzani came into focus. He was smiling.

"Ah, Mr. Walsh," he said in English, "you've decided to visit me again. And to what do we owe the honor?" A holstered gun poked through a flap of his stained white coat. He drew closer, his smile easing away. "What happened, do you remember?"

Mark didn't answer, just stared up at him. The orderly, an aged, white-haired Pesh Merga, muttered something in Talzani's ear.

"They found you down by the river. Do you remember that?"

Mark nodded.

Talzani pulled the blanket back. He gazed at the bruises on Mark's chest and legs, whistled softly through his teeth. "Good heavens. Did someone beat you?"

"I fell crossing the river," Mark said. "I was swept down."

The doctor took a cigarette from his coat pocket and lit it, cocked his head to the side. "You were on the other side of the river? Where were you coming from?"

Mark watched the burning tip of the cigarette. "I went out

hiking in the morning. I got lost. And then it turned dark."

Curiosity left Talzani's face, and he smiled again. "A dangerous area to go hiking, Mr. Walsh, so close to the contested zone."

The orderly became impatient and whispered in Talzani's ear once more.

"He says you can't walk. Is that so?"

"I don't know," Mark said. "I just woke up and—I think I'm just stiff."

Talzani handed his cigarette to the orderly. He put a hand on each of Mark's shoulders and pushed down. "Does that hurt?"

Mark shook his head.

"But you can feel it?"

Mark nodded. The doctor traveled down, pressing here and there, as if giving a desultory massage. He dug his hands under Mark's back, felt along the spine. He cupped the hip bones and kneaded them, rubbed around the knees, then went to the feet and squeezed hard.

"No pain?"

Mark shook his head again.

Talzani straightened and took back his cigarette. He stared at Mark's body, sent twin steams of smoke out his nose. "Can you move your arms?"

Mark bit his lip and slowly raised his elbows a little off the mattress.

"Your legs?"

He tried to lift his legs clear from the bed but couldn't; he brought his feet in, pushed the knees up a few inches.

"Very good."

The orderly muttered something else. Talzani raised his eyebrows.

"A head wound, as well? I don't think our rivers agree with you, Mr. Walsh." Holding the cigarette between his teeth, the doctor came forward and began turning Mark's head to the side, but then noticed the thin, straight cut across his throat. He frowned, traced it with a finger.

"A chafing wound. How did you get that?"

"I don't know," Mark said.

Stifling a sigh, Talzani twisted Mark's head until it was flat against the pillow, ran his fingers through the matted hair until he found the cut in back. Mark gritted his teeth as he felt it being spread open, the fresh blood spilling down his neck. A trail of cigarette smoke curled around his head to roil and disperse before his eyes. Talzani let go and stepped away. He flicked blood from his fingertips, took the cigarette from his mouth.

"Very lucky, Mr. Walsh—a flesh wound, maybe a concussion. Kurdistan isn't a good place for a skull fracture. You might want to get stitches though." Reaching into his coat pocket, he withdrew the stack of plastic tags. "As for the rest, it's difficult to say. Your body took quite a jolt, but you're not paralyzed and there don't seem to be any broken bones. You have some neural disruption but, God willing, it's temporary. We'll know soon enough."

The plastic tags were thin and Talzani held about fifty— yellows, reds, and blues. He cradled them in the palm of his left hand, brought up his right, and began to absently shuffle them.

"The legs will be the biggest problem. That's always the case. Legs, legs, legs. For every arm I've amputated up here, I've probably taken ten legs. Puzzling, isn't it?" He waited for a response, but Mark was watching the plastic, watching how the topmost tag changed with each shuffle: red, blue, yellow, blue. "I'm not sure why this is. I think human legs simply weren't designed for modern war."

Talzani stopped his shuffling. He looked at the tags in his palm and, with a careful surgeon's hand, reached in to pull out a yellow. He dropped it on Mark's chest. "Take it easy. Get some rest."

But Mark still stared at the plastic in Talzani's hand.

"You're going to be all right," the doctor said, leaning over, trying to meet Mark's eyes. "Do you understand?"

But Mark couldn't stop looking at the tags.

"You're going to be all right." Talzani turned and moved on to the next man.

•

He awoke to find he was being shifted onto a stretcher by two orderlies. They took him out of the cave, and Mark shut his eyes tight against the sudden light. He felt himself drift with the lulling motion of the stretcher—head rising and falling, feet rising and falling—and listened to the regular scrinching sound of the canvas each time his weight shifted.

They carried him to the recovery ward. At some time in the past, the building, standing on a level stretch of land sixty feet from the cave mouth, had been a shepherd's hut. Now it more closely resembled a beachside cabana, with a makeshift reed roof and only two walls, and it was filled with those who didn't require the cave's warmth to survive the cold nights. The orderlies moved several of the other wounded to clear a space, then hoisted Mark off the stretcher. They settled him on the stone floor, threw a thick blanket over him and walked away.

Through the gaps in the roof, Mark saw a pallor of sun. He breathed the fresh air in deeply, but occasionally the smell of the cave came to where he lay. Each time, the stench of waste and disease lingered, seemed to cling to his clothes and nostrils. He would wait, taking short, shallow breaths through his mouth until he felt steady enough to inhale deeply once more.

In late afternoon, he heard the sound rise within the cave. It was low and indistinct at first, the hum of a generator, but it grew in pitch until Mark could pick out individual voices, individual cries. Others in the recovery bay began to pray. Mark looked to the cave.

The orderlies brought the blues out on stretchers, lined them up in a neat row. There were five of them, and their mouths gulped at the sky like feeding fish. One could move his hands, and he used them to shield his eyes against the daylight.

The mullah from Harir came over the bluff. He went to the stretchers and walked among them, squatting down to speak, leaning close to hear a whisper. Talzani emerged from the cave. With a nod from him, two orderlies lifted up the first stretcher. The mullah took a Koran from his robe and read aloud from the holy book as his right hand went out to touch the forehead of the dying Pesh Merga. Mark watched the procession move away, the mullah still reciting, still touching the man's forehead, Talzani following, his hands clasped behind his back, his head slightly bowed.

The prayers of the men in recovery grew louder. Mark closed his eyes. The report of a gunshot. Mark twitched but kept his eyes shut. Four or five minutes later, another shot. Then another. Another. After the last one, Mark opened his eyes and stared into the reed roof.

A shadow fell over him. Talzani. Holding the revolver at his side, he gazed down at Mark. His face was white and his eyes were clouded glass.

"Do you know what *Pesh Merga* means?"

Mark nodded, but Talzani seemed not to notice.

"It means 'those who face death.' A romantic name, don't you think? Poetic. I myself have never seen one face death; they all turn away at the end."

The doctor looked to the ground, ran a trembling hand through his short black hair.

"It's not so easy, is it?" he asked quietly. "Without your camera, it's not so easy."

He started back to the cave, holstering the gun as he went.

Tenant

Michael Knight

My landlady died in the fire that consumed her house, but the rescue squad was able to pull her unconscious dog, Shiloh, out of the flames and breathe life back into him. They revived him by wrapping a hand around his muzzle to keep it closed and huffing air into his nose. He woke—I am told; I was passed out drunk at the time—coughing up smoke like an old man. I live in an old slave cottage behind the main house that Mrs. Cunningham restored for renters. One of the firemen roused me some time later, and I stumbled out onto the lawn in my underwear, already hungover. The fire was nearly out and the house was soaked and shadowy in the darkness, a faint mist rising from the walls and tiny, still-burning embers winking in the wasted frame like cigarettes.

Shiloh was an enormous German shepherd, who relished tipping my trash cans and who couldn't get past his genetic predisposition for shepherding. Each day when I returned from work he met me at the car, determined to prevent me from reaching my front door. He circled me growling, rushed to block my passage, cut me into ever shrinking corners. Charlotte, the woman I'd been seeing, was terrified of him and, in her defense, he did have forty pounds on her. He was big enough, upright, to pin my shoulders to the car with his paws and look me in the eye. I complained when I first moved to the farm, when Mrs. Cunningham was still alive, but she was at least seventy-five and could no more control Shiloh than I. She would grin and shake her head, as if he were a beloved only child and she found his bad habits endearing. I couldn't bring myself to demand that she leave the flower garden, where she spent her mornings, to collect the trash that was scattered on my yard. The very thought of a woman her age stooping to retrieve a paper plate made me shiver with guilt. Charlotte called the mess my own little garden, a lawn of perennials, she said, coffee-filter buds, planted in TV-dinner cartons, blooming each morning on liquor-bottle stems.

When the policeman in charge of the fire scene had finished questioning me—Had I seen anything suspicious? No. Did I know Mrs. Cunningham to be unhappy? I did not—I called Charlotte. She had stayed home to study for the test I was giving the next day. I teach history at the little college in town. Charlotte was what the college calls a "continuing education" student, so she was in my class though she was four years my senior, a fact that did not exempt our relationship from the college's strict non-involvement policy. She skipped college the first time around to try her hand at acting in Los Angeles but told me that all she did out west was hone her waitressing skills.

She was sleeping when I called but came out anyway, and we stood at my window watching sirens flashing silently, men with smudged faces moving through the pinkish light in wet raincoats. Mrs. Cunningham's house was built in 1827 in the Tuscan style, a stucco Italian villa dropped into the middle of Alabama, complete with terra-cotta shingles on the roof and marble floors. That house and the 650 acres that surrounded it were the reasons I moved out here. I would have slept in a toolshed to live in its shadow. Burned now, blackened and crumbling in places, it looked like something from the ruins of ancient Rome.

"She was in the house?" Charlotte whispered, tapping the windowpane. We couldn't stop ourselves from whispering. She had come in a hurry, her hair still mussed from sleeping, and the pillow had drawn graceful lines on her face. I gave her a solemn nod.

Mrs. Cunningham had lived alone in the big house, the sole occupant of its thirty-two rooms, and didn't get out much, except to tend the garden. It was impossible to imagine Mrs. Cunningham as a young woman. My clearest memory was of her in the garden wearing a wide-brimmed straw hat to keep off the sun and long baby-blue formal gloves, the sort women used to wear to balls. To protect her skin, she said. Despite her age, her hair was still faintly red and the hat pushed brittle rings of it down around her face. Occasionally, she asked me to come over to the main house and help her move a piece of furniture or lift a heavy box down from the attic. Mrs. Cunningham believed that, because I taught at the college, I must therefore be an intellectual, so when I was finished with her heavy work, she would have a question ready for me, along with a glass of iced tea. How close did we—she said we, as if she were there—really come to securing foreign intervention in the Civil War? How did I think history would view George Wallace? Her tone was always serious so I told her whatever I knew on the subject, sometimes shamefully little. We never talked about ourselves.

Around her, Shiloh was a different dog, docile but alert, curling at her feet beneath the kitchen table, growling if he thought I got too close. I think Mrs. Cunningham liked having a man on the property, but I may be flattering myself. My visits were infrequent. We rarely saw each other, though we lived not a hundred yards apart.

My cottage was situated in a grove of maples, and Charlotte and I would scare ourselves at night by pretending that the wind was a slave voice singing old spirituals. We would sit under the dark trees and convince ourselves that we could almost make out the words. Neither of us believed in ghosts, so we weren't really afraid, just thrilled, like children telling stories, and we would go rushing back inside and build a fire in the huge stone hearth and heap blankets on top of the bed. The fear, even make-believe, added something to our lovemaking. My cottage was really just one big room with a shotgun kitchen and a sleeping loft beneath a cathedral ceiling that drew the dancing, ghostly shadows away from us, leaving the rest of the room in warm brown light, like the light from a dream. We would stay that way, breathless and delightfully alone, the covers thrown aside now, the sheets sticking to our backs, until we heard Mrs. Cunningham calling Shiloh in for the night, her voice rising and falling, holding on the *Shi* a few beats, then dropping off on *loh*. She would call maybe a dozen times and we would hear her door close and the house lights would begin to go off, one by one, leaving the yard in darkness.

The night of the fire, we watched the firemen collecting their gear, rolling thick black hoses, sheathing extension ladders. When the last of the trucks had gone blinking sadly down the driveway, Charlotte said, "I think I wanna see it. Let's examine the wreckage." She was already heading for the door.

"That's not a good idea," I said.

"Why not?" she said. "Why are we whispering?"

I didn't have an answer for her right then, so I caught her by the belt and hauled her into my arms, hoping that maybe I could get her into my bed and keep her away from Mrs. Cunningham's house. She took an imaginary pen and paper in her hands and read along as she wrote, "Dear Mr. College President, One of your professors, a certain Parson Banks, has been making sexual advances toward me and I'm beginning to feel an uncomfortable pressure in class." She twisted free of my embrace and was out the door, marching across the lawn toward the house before I could stop her. There was no stopping Charlotte once she set her mind.

I jogged after her. We climbed through a section of collapsed wall and moved through the rooms downstairs, through
burned-out doorways like cave mouths. Water was puddled
on the floor. Somber smears of smoke streaked the walls. The
fire started on the second floor, according to the fireman who
woke me, and Mrs. Cunningham died in bed. We didn't go
upstairs. Portions of the house were strangely undamaged,
small surviving corners where a lamp stood untouched, as if
Mrs. Cunningham had just stepped out and might at any
minute return and require a little light for reading. Being in
the house felt wrong, like trespassing on sacred ground.

Shiloh was around there somewhere. He didn't try to prevent us from entering, wouldn't even come near us, as if he
understood that something dire had happened. Every now
and then, we would see him slip past a doorway, wraithlike.
It amazed me that something that big could move so silently.

"It's beautiful," Charlotte said. "In an awful way. It's more
beautiful now than it was before, I think. It's less perfect,
you know what I mean? It's like looking at someone's X ray."

She stopped to examine a rosewood dining table, running
her fingers along its dusty surface. Faint blue moonlight
slanted in through window frames—the heat had caused the
glass to explode outward—and through holes in the ceiling,
where the second floor had burned. The light caught in clean
streaks left on the table by Charlotte's fingers.

"Someone died here tonight, Charlotte," I said. "We
shouldn't be here."

"She lived here too, Parson, for a long time. That's what's
so amazing. Think of everything that happened here before
you came along." Charlotte pressed her palm flat against
the dining-room wall. "Put your hand here," she said. "It's
still warm."

"One of the guys from the fire department told me they
think she started the fire herself. On purpose," I said.

Charlotte jerked her hand away from the wall.

"She wanted to kill herself?"

I told her what the fireman had told me. That the bedroom

door was closed and locked but all the doors downstairs were
open to whatever sort of intruder might want to help himself.
The theory was that she wanted to bar Shiloh from the bedroom and be certain he had a way out of the fire. While I
was talking, I watched Charlotte for a reaction. She walked
over to the window, her steps crunching on the cooled embers
that had rained down from upstairs. She stood there, perfectly
still, and looked out at the night. A breeze moved past her
and I could smell her perfume mixed in with the scent of
ash. The moonlight was gauzy on her cheeks.

"You told me they had to carry Shiloh out of the fire,"
she said, turning toward me, her face now shadowed.

"Maybe he's too stupid to know that fire is a bad thing,"
I said.

"Maybe he didn't want to leave her." She faced the window
again and cocked her head as if listening intently. I tried to
hear what she was hearing. Cicadas ringing in the darkness.
A train rumbling along the tracks that divided Mrs. Cunningham's property, just barely shaking the ground. Nothing
much but those strange country sounds that only make you
more aware of the silence behind them. Charlotte said,
"That's the saddest thing I ever heard," and I didn't know
whether she meant the plaintive night sounds or what I had
just finished telling her.

I was a quiet tenant and, until Charlotte, had never brought
a woman to the farm, so most of the complaints between
Mrs. Cunningham and me tended to be mine, regarding
Shiloh. I drink too much and occasionally wander the fields
at night. I don't know if Mrs. Cunningham was ever aware
of my roving, though I have heard that old people tend to
be light sleepers. She anyways never mentioned it, and I had
lived on her farm for two years before she died. I would wander
down to the railroad tracks or to watch the bats swarming over
the pond, skimming for insects that lit on the surface. You
could throw a stone out over the water and the bats would
dive-bomb it, kamikaze runs, plunging themselves into the

pond, blind by nature, stupid from hunger, after what they thought was food. It was a mistake, the first time I fooled the bats. I was just skipping rocks. The second stone was a test case to make sure the first wasn't a fluke or a figment of my imagination. After that, I tell myself that I was drunk, that I wouldn't have gone on tricking the bats with stones if I had been sober. But I remember the buzz of power that came with killing without laying a hand, that came at the moment of impact when a bat flashed through the night haze and smacked the surface, a sound like surprise, and didn't come up.

When we first started seeing each other, Charlotte asked me to tell her the worst thing I had ever done. She wanted to know how low I could go. She wanted to prepare herself for the worst. I thought about it for a while, then took her down to the pond and told her about the bats. She didn't say anything for a long moment, just looked at me, considering. I shifted awkwardly in her gaze, worried that telling her had been a mistake, that I had let her look into my thoughts and she had seen something too awful to stay. The bats slapped the air above us with their wings. Charlotte turned away from me to watch them. Her hands were in the pockets of her jeans and the wind was blowing, making her cheeks red, whipping her hair around her face, causing strands of it to stick to her lips. Softly, she said, "They're just bats." Then, turning back to me, smiling a little, gathering momentum, "They're bloodsuckers. Wait till deer season and look around for the blaze orange caps. Those are the nut jobs. Don't turn your back on those fuckers." I didn't know if she meant what she said, but I had never been more grateful.

There had been other women in my life during my time at Mrs. Cunningham's farm but only short-term, a weekend or two, and none of them had been invited to visit. The cottage was mine alone before Charlotte came along. She told me that she had been by herself a while too, hadn't really felt at home with a man until she stayed at my house. I can't speak for Charlotte, but I should say that I have always had

trouble getting involved. In anything. I tried newspaper re-
porting after graduate school but couldn't get over the feeling
that my work, even when writing the most innocent of stories,
birth or wedding announcements, was an invasion of privacy.
I wasn't long with the newspaper. I returned to history, for
which I was originally trained. The stories of history had
already been written.

The first night Charlotte spent with me was an accident of
sorts. I had asked my students out to the farm for a get-
acquainted picnic. Both of us were drunk, inspired, I think,
by the rest of the students, most of whom were underage.
Charlotte stayed late to help me clean. Just before we went
to bed, she said to me, "You think too much. You're educated
to within an inch of your life, aren't you?"

Maybe so. Charlotte believed I was laughably careful about
hiding our relationship from the administration. I passed her
in the hall without speaking, called her by her last name in
class. Probably, she was right, nothing would have happened
if we were discovered. But I hated the *probably*, hated its
lack of guarantee. So she smiled indulgently to ease my appre-
hensions and promised again that she had told no one, that
she would not ever tell.

We had the farm to ourselves for almost a month after the
fire. Charlotte came out on the nights when she didn't draw
the late shift at the Italian restaurant where she worked. Shiloh
still frightened Charlotte, but she had softened towards him
since hearing of his loyalty to Mrs. Cunningham. We took
to leaving bowls of food for him—raw eggs cracked over white
bread, leftover grits—on what used to be the patio of the
main house. Charlotte believed we could win him over. I told
her that I had tried bribing him before without success, but
she thought that maybe Mrs. Cunningham's death had
changed the dynamic between us.

Shiloh's enthusiasm for harassing me was beginning to flag,
and we felt sorry for him. At Charlotte's request, I made
myself an easy target. She thought it might cheer him up. I
would walk slowly around the main house, wear a groove

back and forth to my car, but he didn't take advantage of my vulnerability. My path took me down to the pond, where a family of geese would scatter at my approach, and the stillness of the water was broken occasionally by a jumping bass. I even stood too close to the edge with my back to Shiloh, which I thought would be irresistible. He would keep me in sight but never come close, breeze through the high grass on my flank or stretch out on the hilltop above the pond, looking down on me, scrunch-eyed and serious like I was an algebra problem to be solved. I have to admit that there was something lovely about the way he moved, something elemental, long and low to the ground. Once, when I had lost hope of an attack, he hit me hard from behind. I sprawled on the grass trying to catch my breath, and he curled up a few yards away. I had the feeling that he knocked me down for old-time's sake.

When the sun was almost all the way gone, Charlotte and I would drag my rocking chairs with the cane bottoms out onto the grass beneath the maples. It was warm for that early in the spring, but it was cooler on the lawn than it was in my cottage. We played at being rich on Mrs. Cunningham's farm. It was easy with the main house so close, even a charred shell of it, easier now that Mrs. Cunningham was gone. We could be her secret heirs. We debated putting in a swimming pool.

"It'll be a godsend in summer," Charlotte said. "We could put it right here under the trees and the branches would catch the pool lights at night."

"But, Charlotte, this isn't Las Vegas," I said. "A pool just wouldn't sit right."

We sat quietly a moment, considering the options. Charlotte said, "We'll never come to an agreement, my love. Ask Montague to break the tie." Montague was our imaginary butler. We laughed at our silliness. We called each other "my love" and felt very English and, when Charlotte asked for another glass of Dom Perignon, I knew that she was referring to our bottle of grocery-store wine. It seemed those nights, my thoughts pretty with wine, that everything, the house, the pond, the grand evening shadows that lingered on the lawn, all of this belonged to me.

Mornings, before my afternoons courting Shiloh and evenings with Charlotte, belonged, however, to the college. Each spring, the college cooked up some historical anniversary and served it to the students in a section called "Topical History," taught by the low man on the tenure ladder and monitored closely by the promotion committee. The class that fell to me was the fiftieth anniversary of both VE and VJ days. I told my students about the USS *Indianapolis*, the cruiser that delivered the atomic bombs to Okinawa so that they could be dropped more conveniently elsewhere in Japan. On its return voyage, the *Indianapolis* was torpedoed and its crew set adrift on life rafts.

The class was interested that day, a detail I hoped wasn't lost on the committee observer. They are always interested when the subject is sex or death. I told them that the crew watched eighty percent of their shipmates be devoured by sharks, that many of them committed suicide, shot themselves or gave themselves up to drowning, slipping their life jackets over their heads and letting the weight of their clothes drag them under. It was in their power to kill themselves. The sharks were beyond their control. One of the young men in class, a punk kid who always wore a black leather jacket embroidered with delicate chains and had *f-u-c-k* tattooed on the knuckles of his left hand and *t-h-i-s* on his right, and who was not at all impressed with me, asked, "What are we supposed to understand from that story?" This kid didn't like the grades I'd been giving him and had a knack for flustering me.

That night, Charlotte and I walked down to the pond and she said, "Every action has a consequence, my love."

The bats darted above us, their motion spastic and somehow too quick. I wouldn't have tricked them, but I looked for stones anyway. I liked the cold feel of them in my palm.

"That's what you should have told that student today,"

she said. "That's what he should have understood from the story of the *Indianapolis*."

"That's a rather occult revisionist take," I said. "I'm not qualified to teach karmic retribution. You might try Eastern Religions."

I played the moment over in my head, the question, my embarrassed stuttering and note shuffling, like I had the answer written down right there if I could only find it, the committee observer watching all of this. What I came up with in class, after considerable flailing, was, "There's nothing to understand *per se*. It's just a story. Something interesting and terrible that happened once. Something that bears remembering."

We had several visitors to the farm after the fire. An insurance agent taking Polaroids, then an artist who wanted to paint the ruined house. Shiloh greeted each visitor ferociously, chasing them back to their cars and pressing his muzzle to the window, foaming on the glass. I would leave whatever I was doing and cross the lawn from my cottage, a toothless dog, to inspect the stranger, to bestow or withhold my approval like the lord of the manor. One evening, about a month after Mrs. Cunningham's death, we heard Shiloh barking, then a woman's voice dismissing him, "Quiet, dog. Lay one paw on me and you're history," and before I could leave my chair to reconnoiter, she rapped once on the door and let herself in without waiting for an invitation. "You're Parson Banks," she said. "I'm Brady Cunningham. Your landlady's daughter."

I hadn't even realized that Mrs. Cunningham had children. I had imagined for her a spinster's existence with maybe a lover lost at sea or leaving her at the altar. But here was this woman, small and wiry like Mrs. Cunningham, with Mrs. Cunningham's red hair, standing in my cottage, one hand still loosely on the doorknob, claiming to be her child and informing me that they were putting the property on the market. "Don't get up. I just thought you should know," she said. "As eldest daughter, I'm serving as executrix for the estate. I've got a sister who isn't altogether happy with me in charge, but the one thing we can agree on is to get rid of this old place. It's a financial sinkhole."

Two children, daughters. Charlotte was in the kitchen cracking raw eggs into a bowl for Shiloh when Brady came in, and she stayed there, silent, her hands poised over the bowl, fingers dripping yolk. This daughter was all business, telling me that the cottage was still mine, until they found a buyer. I would pay my rent to an estate account. She wasn't interested in my sympathy. When I said, "I'm sorry for your loss," she said, "Don't be. I haven't spoken to that woman in almost ten years. Mother was the meanest woman I ever knew."

She stepped backwards out of the house, closed the door behind her, opened it again and leaned inside. She said, "Oh, and if you see my sister around here trying to take anything out of the house, call the police. She looks like me only blonder and taller." Before I could tell her that I didn't want to get involved, didn't want to be in the middle of an inheritance dispute, she was gone, the door shut firmly between us. I heard Shiloh barking again, then her car heading off, tires crunching on the gravel driveway. I hadn't left my chair. Wind rustled in the chimney. I turned to face Charlotte and raised my eyebrows in a question. She said, "Don't ask me what that was all about. Who does she think she is barging in here? You tell me that. Her mother's dead a month before she decides to show her face. And then only to sell the house. Her mother's house, Parson." We looked at each other a moment longer before Charlotte went back to cracking eggs.

Brady Cunningham didn't bother to do anything about Shiloh. A FOR SALE sign appeared at the end of the driveway a few days after she left, but I pulled it out of the ground and tossed it into the rain gully beside the road so it would look like it had been knocked over accidentally. A realtor began stopping by to show the house. Because of the fire, it was a bargain-basement deal. Most of the potential buyers were nice enough, assuring me that if they decided to purchase the place I would be able to stay on as a tenant. They were wealthy people from out of state, looking for a lifestyle change. I hate that word, *lifestyle*. There was an oilman from Texas, a computer genius, close to my age but worth about a million times as much, even a movie actress whose stardom was beginning to fade. Each of them asked me how I liked living on Mrs. Cunningham's farm. I didn't tell them that I would buy it in an instant, if that were within my means. When the realtor wasn't listening, I would invent reasons for them not to buy and offer them grudgingly as if I were just giving a little friendly advice. A fictitious article I had read about how expensive and ultimately impossible it was to restore fire-damaged houses to their original condition. The biblical swarms of biting insects that descended on the house at dusk or the plague of rats that infested the basement in winter. I found that the most effective technique was simply to rehash the details of Mrs. Cunningham's suicide. Often the realtor hadn't apprised them and I found that telling the story that way, adding my own specifics—Mrs. Cunningham soaking the bed and carpet in gasoline before crawling under the covers with a match—her suicide began to seem like just another invention to prevent the house from being sold.

Brady Cunningham began coming out to the farm more often once the house was on the market. We'd see her from my porch in her bib overalls and work gloves, her hair tied back with a bandana, Aunt Jemima style. She would emerge from the house sooty and disheveled, carrying a cardboard box of salvageable goods. Every now and then, she gave us a smile or a wave, which we vehemently ignored. Charlotte had an idea that Brady was somehow connected to her mother's death or, at least, that she knew something that she wasn't telling, and that in the boxes that she took away was the evidence. When she was gone, we would slip into the house and try to discern what was missing, but neither of us was familiar enough with the place to recognize an absence. We found gaps in the charred bookcase but couldn't remember what, if anything, had been there before. End tables with

blank surfaces, empty drawers in which we could not find
a clue. The only thing missing, that we could tell, was
Mrs. Cunningham.

Shiloh stayed clear when Brady was around. Charlotte wondered why he didn't attack, why he didn't drive her screaming
from the grounds. She worried that Brady Cunningham's
appearance had somehow robbed him of his spirit. I said,
"He's a dog, Charlotte. What you're saying implies that he
understands what's happening around here." But I worried,
too. Sometimes when we went down to the main house to
collect the bowls that we had left for him, we discovered
the food eaten, sometimes not. I worried that Shiloh wasn't
getting any of it, that a raccoon or something was reaping
the rewards of my generosity. I decided to become a spy.

I set the food in plain sight and climbed the stairs to find
a hiding place with a good vantage of the patio. The staircase
had at one time been a wonderful thing, with a thick, smooth
banister that curved down from the second floor like a graceful
slide, but now its surface was charred rough and I was afraid
to put weight against it for fear that it might collapse. I
stepped gingerly in the darkness. Upstairs, in the hallway
beside the master bedroom, I found a narrow break in the
wall, where a section of mortar had come loose, thin like in
a gunner's turret that let through a rectangle of light. The
moon was almost full and I could see, from my hiding place,
the dark shape of the house spreading gently on the lawn,
not moving when the breeze pushed through the high, uncut grass.

I watched the plate of food for hours, but nothing came
to eat it. Most of the wall between my hiding place and the
bedroom had burned away and I could see the moonlight
playing in there too, casting strange shadows. Something
caught my attention, a rustle, motion glimpsed out of the
corner of my eye. I wasn't alone in the house. I held my breath
and listened. Nothing. No sound but the night humming. I
felt a presence though, like knowing someone is behind a
tinted window even though they can't be seen.

I whispered, "Shiloh, that you? You don't scare me, you punk dog. I wipe my ass on punks like you." Of course, there was no answer. I was spooking myself. I had to resist the temptation to look in Mrs. Cunningham's bedroom to make certain her body was gone. I had seen her bedroom once before the fire. She had asked me to carry a box of linens upstairs for her and I sat it down on the very bed in which she died. Arched windows paneled one wall and they were full of sunlight, which drifted inside and electrified motes of dust. Mrs. Cunningham came into the room behind me, carrying a smaller, lighter box and I took it from her and held it while she caught her breath. She rested one hand softly on my arm, the other on her chest, and smiled apologetically. The meanest woman I ever knew, her daughter had said but I couldn't see it. Mrs. Cunningham was already an old woman when I met her, so it was difficult, there in the cindery darkness of her house, to imagine her with enough passion in her to do something that would drive her daughters away, enough despair to choose this particular way of dying. I imagined I could smell gas very faintly when the breeze moved through the walls.

Charlotte insisted we start riding home from the college together. She said it was high time we stopped pretending. Time to take charge. "We'll do it on a Friday," she said. "Kick start the weekend." My heart pounded until we were well past the front gate, as if I were carrying drugs or the body of a murdered colleague in the trunk. Friday night, we grilled steaks under the waning moon and when we heard dogs barking in the distance, we joined them. We crouched on the ground and howled until our throats were sore. We made love in the high grass. The grass hadn't been cut since the fire and was full of spring wildflowers.

Later, Charlotte and I lay in bed naked while I read over my lesson plan and Charlotte did her homework. The sheet was pulled up to our waists, so her chest was uncovered, and I was having a little trouble concentrating. Charlotte looked up from her book and said, "If I die tomorrow—say I'm hit by a bus—how would you commit suicide?"

"Don't be morbid," I said.

"I would probably slit my wrists in the bathtub," she said. "Not over you, understand. I wouldn't be as devastated by your death as you would by mine." Here she smiled and gave my hand a squeeze. "But if I had to commit suicide, razor blades and warm water would be the way to go."

"I'd eat a bullet," I said. "Quick and painless."

"Doesn't make for a handsome corpse though, does it?" Charlotte made a gun with her hand, put the index-finger barrel between her lips, pulled the trigger and collapsed dead with her head on my chest, her hair tickling my neck. She put her hand on my stomach and circled my belly button with her damp fingertip.

"What about hanging?" I pointed at the rafters. "Throw a rope up there and jump from the loft."

"Very romantic," she said. "But far more agonizing than a garden hose from the exhaust pipe."

"I've got it," I said. "Sleeping pills and booze."

She didn't answer. She drew in a breath and held it. Everything was quiet. The startled silence that follows a gunshot. I could feel her going still, softening against me, letting all the energy slip out of her muscles. I put my hand on her back. The only sign of life I could feel in her was her heartbeat, quickening each second she refused to breathe. I counted a hundred beats before she threw the covers back, exhaling, and put her feet on the floor, her back to me, the way a drunk steadies himself when the room spins. She lifted her hair away from the back of her neck. The underside of her hair was damp with sweat.

"What could have possibly made her want to die like that?" she said.

I scooted over on the bed and blew softly on her shoulders to cool her.

"She must have done something unspeakable," she said.

"I try not to think about it," I said.

"You must have thought about it."

• • •

Charlotte and I had been carpooling from campus for about
a week, leaving the old brick buildings together and crossing
the busy quadrangle to the parking lot, my worry easing
gradually from me with each uneventful trip, when I received
an anonymous message on my answering machine. "I know
about your little secret," the voice said. "I know all about
the teacher's pet." My skin inched along my bones. The voice
was disguised, baritone, as if the speaker were young and
imitating a grown man, but I would have sworn it was the
kid with the leather jacket and tattoos. I played the message
over for Charlotte a few times to confirm my suspicions about
the identity of the speaker. She said, "Screw that little shit.
You let me worry about him."

I discovered her by accident, a few days later, standing over
him in the men's bathroom near my office. She must have
tracked him to the spot, waited until she knew he would be
alone. He was cowering in a corner and she had the collar of
his jacket in one hand and a can of Mace in the other. The
kid was wearing some sort of kilt that day and black long-
underwear bottoms with his jacket and Doc Martens. He had
his hands in front of his face, begging her not to spray him,
and looked absolutely terrified. Neither of them heard me
come in, and I slipped back into the hall and let the door
swing quietly shut. I didn't want her to know that it frightened
me to see her like that, full of violence and potent with ire.
It excited me some as well. I didn't want to have to tell her
that, despite my anger, I didn't think that I could do what
she had done. From the kid, we never heard another word
on the subject. I eased up a little after that, when I was
grading his papers.

The computer genius bought Mrs. Cunningham's house
in April. He came down to close the deal and told me that
it would be eight months or so before the restoration was
complete. He was a nice enough guy, with wire-rimmed

glasses that kept slipping down the bridge of his nose. We had a few drinks—for a computer guy he could put it away—and he offered me a renewed lease and I accepted, pretending that I was grateful and that I was happy for him.

"You should buy," he said. "I don't want to sacrifice my tenant, but renting's a losing proposition. Land's the only real investment. Land and computers. This place is gold." I wanted to hit him right then, to warn him off somehow, as Charlotte had my student. He raised his drink in a toast to land and computers and brought it to his lips and knocked the edge against his glasses, spilling a little, bumping the glasses crooked. He blinked and straightened his glasses on his nose. Probably he had been one of those kids I used to feel sorry for when I was a kid myself, but who was sorry for whom now? Apparently, Shiloh had done his shepherding routine on my new landlord the day he signed the papers. I apologized and told him that the dog belonged to me. I assured him that it wouldn't happen again.

When the construction crews began arriving, along with hordes of people from the historical society who took it upon themselves to make certain the rebuilding fit the original model, I began to see Shiloh less. He became nocturnal. I still don't know if he ate the food that I left out for him, and I hoped sometimes that he didn't, that he was feeding himself in the wild, not depending on anyone, gorging on rabbits and opossum that he hunted.

Charlotte and I would sit on the hill above the house, concealed by the high grass, and watch the construction crews at work, watch the men walk along the spine of the roof like tightrope walkers, one foot on either side. When they had shut down the machinery and abandoned their equipment for the day, we would steal down to the site, furtive as Apaches, to inspect their progress. Where there had been charred plaster appeared new stud wall and reinforced support beams. They leveled ruined walls, chipped away damaged moldings and brought in cement and sand and hydrated lime and laid new stucco over whatever masonry was salvageable. The stucco went on wet, glistened in the evening light. Charlotte leaned close to examine the faint, slightly discolored lines where the new walls met the old. She pressed the stucco with her thumb and it gave a little, allowed itself to be manipulated like putty, nearly hardened. She circled through the house, running her fingers along the walls, eyes narrow with apprehension, toeing piles of rubble and surveying the contents a little too closely, kneeling to examine the seams between blocks of new marble. I liked the way she looked with her hair pulled back, her eyes intent on her careful inspection.

Mounds of debris, ruined shingles and mortar, blackened pieces of the original frame and chalky hunks of drywall accumulated on the lawn and Charlotte couldn't stand the sight of them, so every once in a while, we hauled a load down to the railroad tracks to make a bonfire. A train would come rumbling by and the conductor would see our fire and blow his whistle. We stood close to the train to feel the wind in its wake, close enough that it became a passing blur, the lettering on the cars unreadable. We didn't say much. Most nights we were too tired to make love.

The fire made a genial orange circle in the clearing, sent up looping streams of sparks like fireflies. Shiloh would wander down to watch us and sit at the fringe of the light. Charlotte would whistle and call his name, trying to get him to join us in the firelight. He'd whine and pace back and forth in the shadows, as if he wanted to come closer but something was holding him back.

Brady Cunningham returned on a Saturday. Charlotte was working the day shift at the restaurant, and I was alone. I was grading papers and heard voices outside and went to the window to see who was trespassing on my property. Two women, one of them Brady, stalked circles around each other in the gravel behind the house. They were wearing similar black dresses and heels, both of them reddish blond, looking almost identical from a distance. It occurred to me that there might have been some sort of memorial service that day and

I wasn't invited, which made me a little angry. They were too far away for me to make out all of what they were saying, but I could catch snatches of name-calling, and it was easy enough to hear the anger in their voices. Their movements were jerky and tense, like marionettes, and it seemed from my vantage point as if this whole thing weren't real, were being staged for my benefit.

Brady turned suddenly and looked at my window. Her shoulders relaxed and she pushed her fingers through her hair. It was a moment before I realized she was looking at me, watching me watch them, and I threw myself prone on the floor beneath the window. When I had gathered the courage to look again, she was crossing the lawn to my cottage, wobbling a little when her heels sunk into the ground. I flopped down again and belly-crawled to the front door to lock it and then to the bathroom to hide. I was certain she was going to drag me into the middle of their argument somehow. I sat in the shower with the curtain pulled. I didn't move, even when she pounded on the door and circled the house trying windows, shouting, "I know you're in there. You aren't fooling anybody."

The longer I listened to her shouts and reproachful knocks, the more humiliated I became. I felt pathetic and weak sitting there, damp from the shower floor, my arms circling my knees. She could outwait me. She knocked long enough that it became apparent she wasn't going to leave. Eventually, I went slinking to the door, a beaten dog, and let her inside.

"I was in the bathroom," I said.

She waved my explanation away. Her eyes were red from crying and she wanted to know if I had any gin.

"I just wanted to take a last look at the place," she said.

I went inside and fixed us glasses of gin and grapefruit juice and brought them back out onto the porch. We made small talk—she was living in New Mexico; I was originally from Louisiana. I prepared a dozen statements in my mind to rebuke her for the way she had treated her mother in death. But I didn't say anything.

"Are you married?" she said.

"No. You?"

"Not me. Mother was married three times," she said, swirling her drink. She pressed her fingertips to her eyes. "Did you know that?"

"No." I did not. It occurred to me, then, not for the first time, that there were other things I didn't know. I had no idea what had happened between Brady and her mother. But something *had* happened. And, all of a sudden, I didn't want to know. I was afraid that she was going to tell me. It took me eight drinks to get through her visit. She stayed on my front porch long enough for night to settle on us and bring the fireflies out. There must have been a thousand of them, winking and twisting, leaving faint impressions of themselves on the darkness. I could see them in the most distant fields, adding depth, making the land look as big as the sky.

Brady said, "When I was a girl, I used to try and catch them in mason jars with holes punched in the lids. Right out there. I had this idea that I could light my room with their tails."

"That's a nice memory," I said.

"It's one of those things," she said. "You don't even know you've forgotten it, until it's right there in front of you."

It was dark enough that I couldn't see her face.

"Do you want me to turn a light on?" I said.

"No," she said. "Please don't."

I could tell that she was crying again.

The next day it rained and the construction crew didn't come. Charlotte arrived after work and we walked down to the driveway and sat in the cab of a hauling truck the crew had left behind. We watched the house through blooms of rain on the windshield. It felt like we were waiting for something. The keys were dangling from the ignition, so I gave them a half-turn to run the wipers and the radio. The only station we could get played country songs.

"Should we go in?" she said.

"I don't really feel like it," I said.

She didn't answer. The rain came down in fits and starts, one minute hard enough that our view was completely obscured, the next so gently that the wipers whined across the windshield. We saw Shiloh come up over a hill behind the pond and stand there looking down on everything. His fur was matted to his body with rain, showing clearly the weight he had lost; he looked wolfish and severe. He trotted to the water's edge, padded in a circle, then curled up, throwing his tail over his nose.

"What are you thinking about?" I said.

"I was wondering about a dog's memory," Charlotte said. "I've heard it's out of sight out of mind for dogs. They forget their owners, if they're separated for more than a couple of weeks."

"I think he remembers her," I said.

"What does he remember about her?"

"Her voice, her smell," I touched the keys, the rabbit's foot key chain. "He remembers the way she looked."

"What else?"

"You name it," I said. "He remembers everything."

The rain was coming down hard again and it was difficult to pick Shiloh out in the high grass. Charlotte covered my hand, the one that was jangling the keys, with hers. I thought I was bothering her, that she was going to ask me to stop, but she didn't. She just sat there, looking out, touching my fingers.

That evening—the quiet and the rain, Charlotte's hand on mine—had a dusty feeling, was colored with the hazy light of something that had already happened. I didn't know then that the end for the two of us was already beginning. A second ticked by, and another, and on and on, relegated by their passing to history, joining the long stream of time that already included Mrs. Cunningham's death and would eventually, after just a few more months of marking time, encompass the day that Charlotte would return to California

to give acting another shot. She would leave before the house
was finished, gleaming and perfect, as though it had never
caught fire. And she would leave before Shiloh disappeared.
I would begin to see him less and less as the house neared
completion, and then, one morning, I would wake and walk
outside to stand beneath the trees and he would be gone.
But I, of course, didn't know any of this then, sitting there
with Charlotte in the fading rain. As we watched, bats began
to materialize in the air above the pond as if from nowhere.
Shiloh's head snapped up at the sound of them, their chirp-
ing, their fluttering wings. I wondered if it was true that he
remembered everything about Mrs. Cunningham, even what
it was that made him love her. Shiloh got to his feet and
snapped at the bats that flew too near. He charged into the
shallow water after them and they cartwheeled above him,
frenzied by his pursuit. Shiloh rose up on his hind legs, still
snapping, reaching higher, swatting with his paws and for
an instant, with Shiloh standing precariously and the bats
whirling above him, it was as if they were performing an
ancient ritual dance, as old and as candid as time. That I
would remember. Shiloh dancing with the bats in the leathery
twilight. I would make it mine.

Andrew Hudgins

Rain

It's raining women here in Cincinnati.
Parts of women, parts of one woman—
the police aren't really sure. Last week
they found an arm, a leg, another arm,
and at eleven last night, while I sipped
the meticulously measured
good bourbon of my middle age,
reporters blandly announced the torso,
no horror in their voices—a slight
professional hush to show they're human too
and they're affected by what they tell us.
Not too much of course. TV is not
the place for outrage, those coiffed homunculi
appropriate for weather, sports—nothing
more tragic than lost football games. Let us
save outrage for our private lives.
(Though isn't this my private life?)
Let the family that has not, as yet, missed her
live outraged. For me, it's pity and terror,
then off to bed unpurged of them,
to seek catharsis in my nightmares. There,
the search continues. How can we bury her,
the human jigsaw scattered, half lost, half found?

Like the student who rushed up after class,
I thought we'd passed beyond the ancient myths.
"That stuff you said? About the olden times,
blood sacrifice and fate?
That was true then. It's not true any more,
is it?" She was almost sobbing.
                                        Listen,

my undivided sum, unsundered darling,
listen: Attis, Adonis, Christ, Osiris,
the flute player, the cropped green ear of corn,
whom butchery has transformed into gods:
and this poor slaughtered housewife, whore, hitchhiker,
whom we cannot make whole, though we must try.
Fate. Blood obligation. They're in the news.
We live them every day.

                        But I said, "No,
it's not true anymore. We aren't all Isis.
We won't all be Osiris."
She smiled. I smiled. She wiped her tears.
Let living teach her what it has to teach her.
She's young. American. Let her resist.
But let the red dismembered gods safeguard
her unsevered flesh. Let those whose work it is
die for her and be scattered on the planet:
God's Scavenger Hunt, God's Hide and Seek, God's Tag,
You're It. Amputate, then sew. Explode,
then gather. Smash, repair.
Like a small boy with a radio or frog,
we hack and reassemble our old unmurderable gods
so we won't tear each other into pieces.

Eternity's a ball, history is a stick.

Judy Longley

First Breakfast at Home
Following an Emergency Appendectomy

Had I glanced from buttering my toast
a moment before, would my heart

have been riven by the fierce thrust
of beak and claw? Great wings

shadowing the window like fate,
my parakeet trills, swinging

in its cage like bait until a thump
thunders the pane. I look up

into a drizzle of feathers, the hawk
dying on the ground below, wings

unfurled against the snow in a swoop
that seemed a sure thing.

Some call it grace, our innocent
preoccupation in the face of death.

How serene I felt my last day of work.
One hand sheltering the fox

that gnawed at my belly, I gazed
past my patient's glassy calm

for the ruffle and stir of her pain.
Next day, spread on the operating table,

arms bound to winglike extensions,
anesthesia hurled me toward the sun.

A knife sinks into butter, caged
creatures sing for their supper.

How bold we are, flying full tilt
into nothing we can see, how we persist.

Michael Burns

Joy's Grape

A naked woman rides a naked man
and vamps, and moans, and both pretend to mount
the summit of desire, although in these
small hours they seem a long distance from me,
and my own passionate wave is a pain
like a volcano that has come awake
deep underneath a right back molar.
To pass the time until my next Darvon,
I write a poem in my head about a man
whose heart maybe once was like a live
volcano—but now it's harmless—and lava
that ran from his head to the tip of his toes
has solidified into that cold, hard flake
of light people see in the back of his eyes.

Soon the ache begins to grow itself
into a shape that is almost tangible,
and I don't know if it will help, but I go
get the grapes out of the refrigerator
and wash them, carry them in to the TV
in a dark green bowl. I place the roundness
of one ripe grape right on top of the pain
and then, as if testing the tightness of
its skin and how much pressure it can stand
upon my throbbing tooth before it splits,
I bite. It bursts. The porno couple arch
and bare their teeth, and somewhere far away
I feel a tremor, as if that dormant heart
were trying to remember how to explode.

Three Poems by Leslie Richardson

Leftovers

The bread and the candle: pale leftovers
    from the last milling, the last box of singular suns.

There will be no more questions, no more serving you
    at sundown.

The earth—for all others, she continues.
    She continues for me as well.

It is of no importance how you blaze or abandon.

As if on a dare I will not be salty, nor sulk.
    I will be as vital as green vines.

And if I hear your old tinny songs, and because of them feel

your rounded, full-fleshed dancing, envision the
    amaranth shaking,
        there will be no late syllables from me.

I will not trace and retrace the artifacts of you like irritations.
    All will be eaten, or will burn down.

To D.H. Lawrence

The female should always be secret, you said.
Women, like figs—rotten
when open.

Your mother, the moment
she contorted to conceive
and to send—

the inward-growing flower
that pushed itself open
to give you your life—
Rotten!

That's how you've named it. Shameful.

Was it her doing when you passed through?
Is it *she* who puts
shame on you?

Actors

I sit at a table of actors, who show us all
how incredible the corn chowder tastes to them,
or how aghast they were backstage last night.
These actors are all famous, each with a Tony
or TV show, and I realize they are the same
as the actors with whom I went to school, those
who can't stop being themselves for you,
who must show you all their possibilities—
brimming with Hedda and capped teeth, brandishing
their cigarettes with long arched fingers. They knew;
they know—they are beautiful; we watch them.

Crammed together in their New York City apartments—
puddles standing beneath the whistling radiators,
tomato paste drying on the dishes, manic cats batting
crumpled cigarette packs—the actors
haven't been home in days. They've been

out scavenging, more than hungry for what
their mothers could not give them quite enough.
I see them, with their bitter-torn mouths, entire
bodies of white pancake makeup, wigs and hairnets
and *it's all so splendid, this business*. It seems that such
must be your condition if you are going to be a mask,
a vessel, a glass thing for words to shine through—
if you are going to let yourself be used. . . .

The student actors were good at waiting, at dancing,
at melting into one another publicly, at standing on crates
and proclaiming themselves in need. I was invited to all
their parties, for when actors are together at once, as they are

here, now, at the trendy and expensive restaurant,
who has eyes to observe? No one is the audience,
except, you know, the writer, who will go home
and melt, dance, pull up to a desk and proclaim.

Three Poems by Alexander Theroux

Imagine Black

I am what I deserve, blinkered, public,
Get-atable, indecorate, with finch-like tints,
Neither black nor white but always gray,
Much as my weak internal self must strike

Who considers me in fact. Objects are smoke.
In myopes, posture tends to be extremely bad.
Yet who's not bent with failures? Who not
formed by shaven shapes? Identity's a joke.

We choose any sort of seeing, any sort of sight.
We are stipple. I am striped. You are plaid.
But what better calculated to drive you mad,
Than never solid darkness, nor bright light?

Imagine black. A forest where you can lose
All of a thousand huntresses, coal mine hope,
Reclusion, a blind, nightmare housed by sleep,
Death, a wall, color you can't even choose.

Ped Xing

What man, tell me, ever
crossed the street like that,
an angle boxed on a sign,
no hands, no feet, no hat?

With Muppetless arms abrake,
He doesn't know where to go.

Is that raised arm idiotic
a plea for cars to go slow?

Its arms are not connected.
Nor is there a sense at all
Of motion in this patron
saint of perpetual stall.

Is he walking over a curb?
Or toward a thought or a thing?
Is he mute with frozen hope?
Or doing a buck and wing?

The bowling-ball head intense,
sexless with anticipation,
insists we find, I'm certain,
some charm in exaggeration,

but what with its detachment
from the neck is being said,
that something clearly half
alive is one half dead?

My vote it says in streets,
even if traffic increases,
Whether there's caution or not,
Man's essentially pieces.

Culver City, 1930

for Pola Negri and Lya de Putti

There was an odd community giddiness
in that orange-stand shaped like a pagoda,
but also a fabulous wittiness.
A cuckoo man with a head like a leek
served me a squash with an Ecuador odor
in a glass that was wearing a beak.

Two Poems by Lynn Doyle

In Another Comedy, English

God appeared to Dante as a cloud.
Dante had been lying on the ground

like a clod, compressed
by the weight of a love gone wrong.

And Dante, lifting his head as if to see,
saw not that he was still lost in an isolated fog,

but encompassed and embraced—able
to walk again—and in an atmosphere of grace.

And as he walked, he was delivered
from his passion for certain buttocks

and the round, if not succulent features
of lust's treacherous terrain,

for he entered the spirit of Rock
and climbed the cliffs of Cloud.

It was yet another coming
to overturn our view of the world

—the place of rock and cloud, and the seamy
human cumulation between.

Heresy of the Dodge, Polara

I was in the third seat of the station
   wagon and facing backward
when my mother veered
right to the story of creation.
And it has not left me.

What she said had nothing to do
   with the North Star
or any other star of wonder, star
of night I had sung about so certainly
in the season of virgin birth.

Maybe I was old
   enough to have known
the hows and whys of hymens
and yes men and no menses,
especially in the backseat of cars.

But still I had to hear
   about sticking,
and the ways of getting stuck, all
so perfectly natural yet never to be
spoken of again, an awful burden.

And only later did I realize
   that in turning toward my mother
I was seeing beyond her,
from a higher seat
I could only have assumed by kneeling.

Two Poems by Maureen Seaton

Jubilee for the Bomb

Blessings on the hunter and the hunted
whose iconography of rifle and bone
whined and hissed and sparked and charred,
on ghostly downtown schoolrooms where
children fractured into half-notes mornings
of Hiroshima, Nagasaki. War
makes so much sense sometimes,
asleep the blood a riotous red, awake
rust beneath the fingernails.
I said something wrong to my mother
who walked through midtown Manhattan
those days in a manless trance. I
said something about *Enola Gay's* golden
anniversary. I think I said: *Peace.*
I forgot she was there for the paranoia.
I forgot that her man (seventeen)
wrote to her daily and witnessed death up-close,
the kind I saw today on the Lincoln Avenue
Bridge multiplied by a thousand, more,
too much sticky red to register, not this
small dry patch that, touched, feels
warm and sad and pointless.
We were eating German food with my
father and my favorite aunt, Claire.
There were all kinds of enemy foods
around us and inside us: things we couldn't say
and things we could: schnitzel and dumpling,
wiener and wurst. Our waitress
lived peaceably down the street, her son
a dentist in Chicago with his own
phobias and retirement plan. Mom plunged
her spoon into liver soup and said:

Do you mean you regret we dropped it?
Who are you, we both thought then, looking
into our bowls for something familiar
from the forties we could swallow.
Here is the meaning of the word *Jubilee:*
from the Hebrew: a year every fifty
when slaves are emancipated, property
restored, and cultivation of land ceases.
The boy who died in the drive-by was seventeen,
like my father translating Morse code
in the middle of the Pacific Ocean
one year before he married my mother and
they almost conceived me—on their wedding night—
the very first time they made love.

Vows of Chasity and Indulgence

When I was born my mother said she had prayed so long I
    must be a miracle.
There was only one way to go with a reputation like that—very
    bad or very good.

I chose good and admired the quiet Mary who sat at Jesus'
    feet and drank him in,
content to be there with her hair on his arches, oil dripping
    down his toes.

Jesus was the only boyfriend I ever wanted. I could be the
    Virgin Mary one day, Mary
Magdalen the next—but most of the time I preferred to be
    his girl, not his mom.

Thus I chose bad to round myself out and relate to humans,
    radical notoriety and
fluent glossolalia at the same time so I could see who was
    right: Galileo or the Pope.

*If it were conceivable that in obeying God one should bring
    about one's own damnation
while in disobeying him one could be saved, I should still
    choose the way of obedience.*

Here I am clumped in a circle of roses red, white, and
    bittersweet. All the girls
melting and cohesive, our flames tonguing the walls, banked
    on universal principles.

Come all ye faith-filled, goals preempted and useless as
    menstrual blood.
Some think this is the better way, some say we better stop
    now and get saved.

Forty-four maidens in a boat and one big mother. Pop!—a
    leak of seawater sprouting
beneath five acres, across the tops of trees. Some women
    welcome the same

diversions as men yet need to stay put, we can't help it, we
    require faithfulness.
Now I'm surrounded by Christian memorabilia, some of it
    pink, some purple—

Lenten grief and circumstance. A man puts on his special
    clothes, swallows the bones
of Christ, the eighty-proof claret, lifts the wafer up and brings
    down blood and fruit.

There is turbulence in the room, hypervigilance. Never mind
    the show-off in the corner,
the wracking cough—proceed to any holy place, the sweet
    marrow of your own amen.

There is nothing here to mourn, you pretty, the ocean flows
    over your right lobe,
everything you expected flows in: succulence, salt, the dark
    raw deep.

— Telegram.

Gjenerali mbushi gotat.

— Dërgojnë telegrame, kujtojnë se mund të zgjidhet ndonjë gjë me anë të telegrameve.

Gjenerallejtënanti i nguli sytë e lodhur dhe u bë gati të pyeste, por pastaj ndezi një cigare.

— A e dini ç'më ka thënë një plakë shqiptare në një dasmë? — tha gjenerali. — Ti ke ardhur këtu që të shikosh se si ne i martojmë bijtë tanë, që pastaj të vish për të na i vrarë.

— Fjalë të tmerrshme.

— Fjalë të tmerrshme? Ju thoni fjalë të tmerrshme? Po ç'do të thoshit, sikur të dinit atë që ndodhi pastaj?

— Nuk e di, — tha tjetri.

— Dhe më mirë të mos e dini.

— Pini, koleg, — tha gjenerallejtënanti. — Për shëndetin tuaj! Të mbërrini shëndoshë e mirë në atdhe! Sa jua kam

— Falemnderit, koleg!

Gjenerali e ndiente se po dehej.

— Na u infektua një punëtor, — tha ai.

— Ma thatë një herë.

— Vdiq.

— E di, — tha gjenerallejtënanti.

Tani salloni dalngadalë po zbrazej nga njerëzit dhe shkallët e tavernës atje në fund kërcisnin më rrallë, por muzika dëgjohej vazhdimisht.

— Ku është ati juaj i shenjtë? — pyeti papritur gjenerallejtënanti.

— Nuk e di, — tha gjenerali. — Se ku vërtitet këndej dhe me siguri vazhdon t'u përgjigjet telegrameve.

Tjetri përsëri ia nguli sytë e tij të habitur dhe deshi të pyeste, por pastaj ndërroi mendje.

— E dini ç'më ndodhi në një fshat? — tha. — Toka ishte e fortë, ranore dhe me kripë. Mezi gërmohej. Kur hapëm varret, i gjetëm trupat të paprishur. Ishte një pamje e rëndë. Na u desh të porositnim arkivole të mëdha, tamam si për të vdekurit e vërtetë.

— Interesant, — tha gjenerali. — Mua s'më ka ndodhur një rast i tillë.

16 — 89

221

An Ismail Kadaré manuscript page.

Ismail Kadaré

The Art of Fiction CLIII

*In 1970 a novel by an unknown Albanian writer took literary
Paris by storm.* The General of the Dead Army *was the story
of an Italian general who goes back to Albania after the
Second World War to find the bodies of the Italian soldiers
killed there and take them back to Italy for burial. It was
hailed as a masterpiece, and its author was invited to France,
where he was welcomed by French intellectuals as an original
and powerful voice from behind the Iron Curtain.* The General *was translated into a dozen languages and inspired two
films: one under the same title starring Michel Piccoli, the*

other Bernard Tavernier's outstanding Life and Nothing Else
(La vie et rien d'autre).

*Since then over a dozen of his novels and several collections
of his poetry and essays have been translated into French,
English and other languages. He is considered one of the
world's major writers, and has been suggested for the Nobel
Prize several times. His French publishers are currently publishing his complete works in six volumes, in both French and
the original Albanian. The first three have already appeared.*

*Ismail Kadaré was born and raised in the town of Gjinokas-
tër in Albania. He read literature at the University of Tiranë
and spent three years doing postgraduate work at the Gorky
Institute in Moscow.* The General *was his first novel, published on his return to Albania in 1962, when he was
twenty-six.*

*Kadaré has been compared to Kafka and Orwell, but his
is an original voice, at once universal and deeply rooted in
his own soil. For over forty years Albania lived under the
Communist dictatorship of Enver Hoxha, whose particularly
vicious brand of Stalinism lasted longer than in any other
Eastern European country. Kadaré used a variety of literary
genres and devices—allegory, satire, historical distancing, mythology—to escape Hoxha's ruthless censorship and deadly
reprisals against any form of dissent. His work is a chronicle
of those terrible decades though the stories are often situated
in the distant past and in different countries. Two of his most
famous novels,* The Palace of Dreams *and* The Pyramid, *take
place respectively during the Ottoman Empire and in ancient
Egypt, while* The Great Winter *and* The Concert *clearly refer
to Hoxha's break with Russia under Khrushchev and with
China after Mao's death.*

*Ismail Kadaré left Albania in 1990 and settled in Paris.
In 1996 he was elected an Associate Member of the French
Academy of Moral and Political Sciences (L'Académie des
Sciences Morales et Politiques), replacing Austrian-born Brit-
ish philosopher Karl Popper, who died that year.*

He lives with his wife and daughter in the Latin Quarter,

THE ART OF FICTION

*in a spacious and bright apartment overlooking Luxembourg
Gardens; he often travels to Albania. This interview took place
at his home in February and October, 1997, with telephone
conversations in between.*

*Kadaré has the reputation of not suffering fools gladly,
but I found him gentle and courteous, and rather patient
with someone who does not know his country and its literature, about both of which he cares passionately. He speaks
French fluently with a distinct accent in a quiet measured
voice.*

INTERVIEWER

You are the first contemporary Albanian writer to achieve
international fame. For the majority of people, Albania is a
tiny country of three and a half million inhabitants on the
edge of Europe. So my first question concerns the Albanian
language. What is it?

ISMAIL KADARÉ

Half of the Albanian population lives next door, in Yugoslavia, in the region of Kosovo. In all, ten million people in
the world speak Albanian, which is one of the basic European
languages. I'm not saying this out of national pride—it is a
fact. Linguistically speaking, there are six or seven fundamental families of languages in Europe: Latin, Germanic, Slavic,
Baltic (spoken in Latvia and Estonia) and three languages
without families, so to speak: Greek, Armenian and Albanian. Therefore, the Albanian language is more considerable
than the little country where it is spoken, since it occupies
an important place in Europe's linguistic cartography. Hungarian and Finnish are not Indo-European languages.

Albanian is also important for being the only descendant
of the ancient Ilyrians' language. In antiquity there were
three regions in southern Europe: Greece, Rome and Ilyria.
Albanian is the only survivor of the Ilyrian languages. That
is why it has always intrigued the great linguists of the past.

The first person to make a serious study of Albanian was the German philosopher Gottfried Leibnitz in 1695.

INTERVIEWER

The one Voltaire parodied in *Candide* as Dr. Pangloss, who said, "All is well in this the best possible of worlds."

KADARÉ

Exactly. Yet Albania did not exist at that time as a separate entity—it was part of the Ottoman Empire, like the rest of the Balkans, including Greece. But this German genius found the language interesting. After him, other German scholars produced long studies of Albanian, Franz Bopp for example, whose book is very detailed.

INTERVIEWER

What about Albanian literature? What is its origin? Is there an Albanian Dante, Shakespeare or Goethe?

KADARÉ

Its sources are essentially oral. The first literary book in Albanian was published in the sixteenth century, and it was a translation of the Bible. The country was then Catholic. After that there were writers. The founding father of Albanian literature is the nineteenth-century writer Naim Frasheri. Without having the greatness of Dante or Shakespeare, he is nonetheless the founder, the emblematic character. He wrote long epic poems, as well as lyrical poetry, to awaken the national consciousness of Albania. After him came Gjergj Fishta. We can say that these two are the giants of Albanian literature, the ones that children study at school. Later came other poets and writers, who produced perhaps better works than those two, but they don't occupy the same place in the nation's memory.

INTERVIEWER

The Turks took Constantinople in 1454, and then the rest of the Balkans and Greece. What was the impact of Turkish on Albanian?

KADARÉ

Hardly any. Except in the administrative vocabulary, or in cooking—words like *kebab, café, bazaar*. But it had no influence on the structure of the language, for the simple reason that they are two totally different machines, and one can't use the spare parts of one for the other. The Turkish language was not known anywhere outside Turkey. Modern Turkish has been constructed by Turkish writers of the nineteenth and twentieth centuries, while the dry, administrative Turkish was not a living language and therefore could not have any influence on the other languages of the Ottoman Empire. I have met Turkish writers who have told me that they have problems with their language.

INTERVIEWER

On the other hand, a great deal of foreign vocabulary has entered Turkish—Persian, Arabic, French, among others. Before modern times, Turkish authors wrote in Persian, or in Arabic if the subject was theology.

KADARÉ

For me as a writer, Albanian is simply an extraordinary means of expression—rich, malleable, adaptable. As I have said in my latest novel, *Spiritus*, it has modalities that exist only in classical Greek, which puts one in touch with the mentality of antiquity. For example, there are Albanian verbs that can have both a beneficent or a malevolent meaning, just as in ancient Greek, and this facilitates the translation of Greek tragedies, as well as of Shakespeare, the latter being the closest European author to the Greek tragedians. When Nietzsche says that Greek tragedy committed suicide young because it only lived one hundred years, he is right. But in a global vision it has endured up to Shakespeare, and continues to this day. On the other hand, I believe that the era of epic poetry is over. As for the novel: it is still very young. It has hardly begun.

INTERVIEWER
Yet the death of the novel has been foretold for fifty years!

KADARÉ
There are always people who talk a lot of nonsense! But in a universal perspective, if the novel is to replace the two important genres of epic poetry—which has disappeared—and of tragedy—which continues—then it has barely begun, and has still two thousand years of life left.

INTERVIEWER
It seems to me that in your oeuvre you have tried to incorporate Greek tragedy into the modern novel.

KADARÉ
That is exact. I have tried to make a sort of synthesis of the grand tragedy and the grotesque, of which the supreme example is *Don Quixote*—one of the greatest works of world literature.

INTERVIEWER
The novel has since divided into many genres . . .

KADARÉ
Not at all! For me these genre divisions do not exist. The laws of literary creation are unique; they don't change, and they are the same for everyone everywhere. I mean that you can tell a story that covers three hours of human life, or three centuries—it comes to the same thing. Each writer who creates something authentic, in a natural way, instinctively also creates the technique that suits him. So all forms, or genres, are natural.

Listen, I think that in the history of literature there has been only one decisive change: the passage from orality to writing. For a long time literature was only spoken, and then suddenly with the Babylonians and the Greeks came writing. *That* changed everything, because before, when the poet recited or sang his poem and could change it at every performance as he pleased, he was free. By the same token he was ephemeral, as his poem changed in oral transmission from one generation to the next. Once written, the text becomes fixed. The author gains something by being read, but he also loses something—freedom. That is the great change in the history of literature. Little developments such as division in chapters and paragraphs, punctuation, are relatively insignificant; they are details.

For example, they say that contemporary literature is very dynamic because it is influenced by the cinema, the television, the speed of communication. But the opposite is true! If you compare the texts of the Greek antiquity with today's literature, you'll notice that the classics operated in a far larger terrain, painted on a much broader canvas, and had an infinitely greater dimension: a character moves between sky and earth, from a god to a mortal, and back again, in no time at all! The speed of action, the cosmic vision in a page and a half of the second book of the *Iliad* is impossible to find in a modern author. The story is simple: Agamemnon has done something that has displeased Zeus, who decides to punish him. He calls a messenger and tells him to fly to earth, find the Greek general called Agamemnon and put a false dream into his head. The messenger arrives in Troy, finds Agamemnon asleep and pours a false dream into his head like a liquid, and goes back to Zeus. In the morning Agamemnon calls his officers and tells them that he has had a beautiful dream, and that they should attack the Trojans. He suffers a crushing defeat. All that in a page and a half! One passes from Zeus's brain to Agamemnon's, from the sky to earth. Which writer today could invent that? Ballistic missiles are not as fast!

INTERVIEWER

Nevertheless, there have been literary events, such as modernism—Joyce, Kafka . . .

Kafka was very classical, so was Joyce. When Joyce became really modernist, in *Finnegans Wake*, he failed. He went too far and no one likes that book. Even Nabokov, a great admirer of Joyce, said it was worthless. There are inventions and innovations that are not acceptable, for there is a vein that one cannot cut with impunity, just as one cannot slice off certain aspects of human nature. A man meets a woman, and they fall in love. In this love there are all manner of possibilities, diversities, but one can't imagine this woman with the body of another creature. If there is a total severance from reality, it is the end, one enters the realm of signs.

INTERVIEWER

Do you mean that there is a certain continuity in human creativity?

KADARÉ

Exactly. We are in a way trapped by the past of humankind; we don't need to know the psychology of, say, crocodiles or giraffes. The past may be a burden, but there is nothing we can do about that. All this noise about innovations, new genres, is idle. There is *real* literature, and then there is the rest.

INTERVIEWER

You have also spoken about *negative creation*. What do you mean by that?

KADARÉ

Negative creation for a writer is what he *doesn't* write. You need a great talent to know what you shouldn't write, and in a writer's consciousness nonwritten works are more numerous than the ones he has written. You make a choice. And this choice is important. On the other hand, one must liberate oneself from these corpses, bury them, for they prevent one from writing what one should, just as it is necessary to clear up a ruin in order to prepare the site for building.

INTERVIEWER

This reminds me of Cyril Connolly, who said, "The books I have not written are so much better than the ones my friends have produced." But let us talk about your beginnings. Your childhood first. You were very small when the war broke out, after which everything changed in Albania.

KADARÉ

My childhood was rich, for I witnessed many events. The war started when I was five. I lived in Gjinokastër, a very beautiful town, through which passed the foreign armies, which was a continuous spectacle—the Italians, the Greeks . . . the town was bombarded by the Germans, the English, passed on from one hand to another. For a child it was very exciting. We lived in a large house with many empty rooms where we played—an important part of my childhood. My paternal family was modest—my father was a court messenger, the man who delivered the tribunal's letters—but my maternal family was quite rich. Paradoxically, it was my mother's family which was Communist, while my father was conservative and puritanical. We lived modestly at home, but when I went to my maternal grandfather's house I was the child of a rich family. My father was against the Communist regime, my mother and her family were for it. They did not quarrel about it, but they teased each other with irony and sarcasm. At school I belonged neither with the children from poor backgrounds, who were pro-Communist, nor with those of rich families who were terrified of the regime. But I knew both sides. That made me independent, free from childhood complexes.

INTERVIEWER

After school you moved to Tiranë, the capital, and studied literature at the university. Then you went to the Gorky Institute in Moscow. It was at the time of Khrushchev, when there was a kind of liberation, a thaw after the long Stalinist freeze. How did you find the literary scene in Moscow?

KADARÉ

I was sent to the Gorky Institute to become an official writer
of the regime—it was a factory for fabricating dogmatic hacks
of the socialist-realism school. In fact, they took three years
to kill every creativity, every originality you possessed. Luckily
I was already immunized by what I had read. At the age of
eleven I had read *Macbeth*, which had hit me like lightning,
and the Greek classics, after which nothing had any power
over my spirit. What was happening in Elsinor, or by the
ramparts of Troy, seemed to me more real than all the
wretched banality of socialist-realist novels.

At the institute I was disgusted by the indoctrination, which
in a way saved me. I kept telling myself that on no account
must I do what they taught me but the exact opposite. Their
official writers were all slaves of the party, except for a few
exceptions like Konstantin Paustovsky, Chukovsky, Yev-
tushenko.

During my stay at the institute, I wrote a novel called *The
Town Without Publicity*. When I returned to Albania, I was
worried about showing it to anyone. I published a short extract, in a magazine, entitled "A Day at the Café," which
was immediately banned. No longer was there any question
of publishing the book. The head of the Communist Youth
Organization who had recommended its publication was later
accused of liberalism and condemned to fifteen years of imprisonment. Luckily this extract exists; otherwise no one today
would believe that I wrote the novel. It was the story of two
literary crooks who want to falsify a text in order to prove
that it can be adapted to Marxism, thereby advancing their
careers. It tapped into the fundamental problem at the core
of socialist culture—falsification. This novel will be published
in the sixth volume of my complete works, which my French
publishers are preparing. Not a word of it will be changed.

INTERVIEWER

Yet in your adolescence you were attracted by communism,
weren't you?

KADARÉ

There was an idealistic side to it; you thought that perhaps certain aspects of communism were good in theory, but you could see that the practice was terrible. Very soon I realized that the whole edifice was repressive, disastrous.

INTERVIEWER

At the institute, were you permitted to read forbidden or dissident writers, such as Pasternak, Akhmatova, Tsvetay-evna, Mandelshtam?

KADARÉ

I read Gogol and Pushkin; certain novels of Dostoyevsky's, in particular *The House of the Dead* and *Brothers Karamazov*.

INTERVIEWER

What about in Albania?

KADARÉ

In Albania all these writers were forbidden. From time to time I managed to find a volume when I traveled abroad. I read Orwell and Kafka. I think the latter is more important. I liked *1984* but didn't care for *Animal Farm* because allegories of the animal kingdom don't touch me much. What happened in totalitarian countries was worse than anything that literature has ever invented.

INTERVIEWER

Orwell was unique in England. At the time when the majority of the intellectuals were sympathizers or fellow travelers, he understood the nature of totalitarianism and exposed it.

KADARÉ

I could not understand how Sartre could defend the Soviet Union. During the Cultural Revolution in China, he was told that thousands of writers, artists and intellectuals were persecuted, tortured, killed. And he became a Maoist!

INTERVIEWER

What posthumous triumph for Camus, whose reputation has gained in recent years! He turns out to have been right on every political issue, while Sartre was always wrong. Camus stood firm despite all the pressures exerted on him, which was not easy in those days.

KADARÉ

I have great respect for Camus—he was exemplary. Most Western intellectuals who lived here, free, unthreatened by totalitarian dictatorship, expected us to show courage and risk our lives. In China it was even worse than it was in Albania. Why didn't Western intellectuals protest?

INTERVIEWER

You returned to Albania in 1960 and published the novel which was to make you famous—*The General of the Dead Army*. Was the story based on a real incident, a *fait divers*?

KADARÉ

Enver Hoxha had just broken with the Soviet Union, accusing Khrushchev of revisionism, of making advances towards the West . . . attracting the interest of the West by pretending to cultural liberalism. Opposition to my novel came from the official critics *after* its publication. They blamed me for not being optimistic, for not expressing hatred toward the Italian general, for being cosmopolitan and so on.

INTERVIEWER

Your second novel, *The Monster*, tackled the theme of political anxiety. How was that received?

KADARÉ

The Monster is the story of a town in which one fine morning the Trojan Horse appears. Inside the horse there are characters from antiquity—like Ulysses—who just wait for the day the town will fall. But I did something odd: Troy does not fall; the horse stays there forever. The people live in permanent anxiety. They say: "How are we going to live, this has been going on for three thousand years, and the horse is still there, he is eternal. What can we do?" They whisper about plots, threats, and life is not normal. Because the totalitarian regime is founded on this paranoia about threats from outside, it needs an enemy to justify repression.

INTERVIEWER

This novel was banned. So what did you live on? Because if one was not an official writer, a member of the Writers' Union, one could do nothing.

KADARÉ

Though they published me and banned me by turns, once you were published and acknowledged as an author, you became a member of the Writers' Union, and you received a monthly salary, which was the same for everybody, whether a genius or a crook. This salary was one thousandth of the royalties I would have received for the number of books I sold.

INTERVIEWER

In such a climate of repression, how did you manage to have *The General* translated and published in France?

KADARÉ

In Albania, as in all Eastern European countries, there was an organization responsible for translating a number of books into a few important foreign languages. So they translated my book into French. By chance the journalist Pierre Paraf saw it, liked it and recommended it to a French publisher.

INTERVIEWER

After its great success in the West, did you feel a little more secure, protected by your international fame?

KADARÉ
Yes, but also more watched, because I was considered dangerous.

INTERVIEWER
Let us move on to your influences. First of all, your interest
in Greek tragedians, particularly Aeschylus about whom you
have written a long essay: "Aeschylus or the Eternal Loser."
Why him?

KADARÉ
I saw parallels between Greek tragedy and what was happening in totalitarian countries, above all the atmosphere of
crime and the fight for power. Take the House of Atreus,
where every crime leads to another until everybody is killed.
There were horrible crimes in Hoxha's circle. For example,
in 1981 the prime minister, Mehmet Shehu, committed "suicide"—murdered by Hoxha. For my part, I was somewhat
protected from prison by my international fame, but not from
the dagger—they could kill me and say that it was a suicide,
or a car crash.

INTERVIEWER
I'm going to become the devil's advocate, if I may, and
suggest that in such a society survival itself becomes suspect,
as in Stalin's Russia. We can mention those who perished,
like Mandelshtam, or were garrotted, like Akhmatova, or
stopped writing, like Pasternak—reduced to translating
Shakespeare—and endless others. In 1970 you wrote a six-
hundred-page novel, *The Long Winter*, which was not based
on a myth or a historical event, but on the current political
situation in your country. Your book seemed to be an attack
on revisionism, and therefore a defence of Hoxha. What
reason did you have for writing the book? After all, you could
have just gone on writing the sort of covert, allegorical stories
you had written.

KADARÉ

From 1967 to 1970 I was under the direct surveillance of the dictator himself. Remember that, to the great misfortune of the intellectuals, Hoxha regarded himself as an author and a poet, and therefore a "friend" of writers. As I was the country's best-known writer, he was interested in me. In such a situation I had three choices: to conform to my own beliefs, which meant death; complete silence, which meant another kind of death; to pay a tribute, a bribe. I chose the third solution by writing *The Long Winter*. Albania had become an ally of China, but there were frictions between the two countries, which later led to a break. Like Don Quixote, I thought that my book could accelerate this break with our latest "ally" by encouraging Hoxha. In other words, I thought that literature could accomplish the impossible—change the dictator!

INTERVIEWER

That book is the only one, to my knowledge, in which you tackle the political situation directly. Otherwise you have used various camouflages—myth, allegory, humor. I'm thinking of *The Pyramid* and *The Palace of Dreams*, set respectively in ancient Egypt and in Ottoman times. In *The Pyramid*, Pharaoh Cheops wants to build a pyramid that would be bigger and last longer than any other—an enterprise that justifies and legitimizes every sacrifice, every oppression. In *The Palace of Dreams*, the control and classification of dreams goes wrong. Did your readers in Albania understand the allusions to the Soviet empire and to the Pharaoh Hoxha?

KADARÉ

Yes. They saw clearly that I was alluding to the Communist empire, which is why they banned *The Palace of Dreams*.

INTERVIEWER

Were you influenced by writers who used the same strata-gems, such as Bulgakov in *The Master and Margarita*, Zamya-

tin in *Z*, which inspired Orwell's *1984*, as well as Hrabal
and Kundera, or Kafka in *The Castle* and *The Trial*—the
prototypes of an oppressive and closed system?

KADARÉ
I had read them, and I was conscious of certain similarities.
At the same time, I was anxious to not use banal ruses. I had
to be convinced that it would be *real* literature, with a global
vision. In this sense *The Palace of Dreams* is a success.

INTERVIEWER
The Soviet gulags have produced a rich witness literature
in the works of Solzhenitsyn, Natalia Ginzburg, Nadezhda
Mandelshtam and others. Were there gulags in Albania?

KADARÉ
Yes, but fewer, as the country was small. Hoxha built
thousands of antinuclear bunkers, in case of an atomic war
breaking out, but they were utterly useless, as he knew: his
purpose was to create a fear-psychosis.

INTERVIEWER
Despite his suspicious attitude towards you, Hoxha made
you a member of Parliament. Why?

KADARÉ
It meant nothing at all. The list of MPs was drawn by him,
and if anyone refused, he was eliminated, killed. No one ever
refused, and it involved no work whatever. Once a year the
Parliament was convened, and Hoxha dictated what he
wanted—no discussion, no debate. The deputies were chosen
from among workers, scientists, writers, so that the Parliament
appeared representative of the population.

INTERVIEWER
After the success of your books in the West, you could
have left the country. Were you ever tempted? In your book

The Albanian Spring, published in 1992, you say that several times you nearly stayed in France.

KADARÉ

I did not leave because the reprisals on the relatives, friends, even acquaintances were terrible. In 1983 I came to France with the intention of staying. Then I realized that it was not possible. There was the risk of a complete break with my country, my language, all those I loved. My French friends advised me to go back, and I did.

INTERVIEWER

The sad novel you wrote later, *The Shadow*, explains this *déchirement*: the choice between exile and freedom on the one hand, oppression and tyranny on the other. Were you afraid of exile?

KADARÉ

No. The writer is always to some extent in exile, wherever he is, because he is somehow outside, separated from others; there is always a distance.

INTERVIEWER

So why did you leave after the fall of Communism?

KADARÉ

I left in 1990, when Albania was oscillating between democracy and dictatorship. I thought that my departure would help the cause of democracy. I said that if the country chose dictatorship, I would not return, and that threat stimulated the struggle for democracy. I had come to France for the publication of *The Palace of Dreams*, and I made a public statement. The media reported it, and that played a decisive role in favor of democracy.

INTERVIEWER

The people wanted to elect you president, like Havel in Czechoslovakia, but you refused. Why?

KADARÉ

I did not hesitate a second to refuse. My case was different
from Havel's; I wanted to remain a writer and free.

INTERVIEWER

It is quite a dilemma: should one resist dictatorship, become a dissident, as did some writers in Czechoslovakia, or
leave the country, as did German writers when Hitler came
to power—they left in droves?

KADARÉ

One shouldn't be naive! The circumstances were different
in each country. You can't compare Albania under Hoxha
with Czechoslovakia. We did not have a Dubcek, the Czech
Spring, and all that followed. If Havel had been in Albania,
he would have been shot immediately. That is why there
were no dissidents in Russia under Stalin. No one could do
anything. In Albania, as in Romania, Stalinism lasted until
the very end. When Havel was in prison, he had his typewriter,
access to world media, everyone talked about him. Those who
compare our situation with Czechoslovakia have no idea of
Stalinist repression.

INTERVIEWER

So you really survived by miracle?

KADARÉ

Not entirely. Every regime needs to save face with respect
to the international community, and if you are a famous
writer, the regime has to be careful. Hoxha wanted to be
considered a poet, a Sorbonne student, a writer, not a murderer. The only thing that a writer could do under such a
dictatorship was to try to produce *true* literature. That way
one does one's duty for eternity. To expect anything else is
cynical and criminal. The Albanians had in me a writer who
connected them with the world. I dominated our cultural
life, and I was safeguarding Albanian culture with my work,

for there was on one side what I was creating, on the other the Communist product, which was worthless. When a book of mine was published, in fifteen minutes it was sold out— every copy was immediately bought. People knew that it would probably be banned, so they rushed to buy it before it was. Sometimes the book was banned before distribution, but by then thousands of copies were in circulation, and people passed them on to one another.

INTERVIEWER

Were you not supposed to submit your manuscript to the Writers' Union for inspection, which was the case in Russia?

KADARÉ

No. In Albania there was no prepublication censorship, since there was so much terror, self-censorship was enough. This was one of Hoxha's idiosyncrasies; as I said, he took himself for an intellectual. So it was the publishers who decided whether to publish a book or not. When I handed in the manuscript of *The Palace of Dreams* I knew it was a dangerous book. The publisher read it and said that he could not risk publishing it. So I told him that I accepted the responsibility: "If they start bothering you, tell them that you were impressed by my celebrity, and that I bullied you into it." In such circumstances they always punished the author, not the publisher. That is in fact what happened. He said to the authorities that considering my prestige he had not dared to refuse my manuscript.

INTERVIEWER

So writers like you gave signals, but people in the West did not want to believe how dire the situation was in Eastern European countries.

KADARÉ

In Albania everybody knew that I was an antiregime writer. And the fact that the regime couldn't condemn me gave

courage to others. That is the fundamental function of literature: maintaining the moral torch. In 1988 France made me
an honorary member of the *Institut de France*, a very great
honor. A French journalist interviewed me on the radio, asking me frankly if I was free to write what I wanted. I answered:
"No. Because freedom in our country is different from here."
What else could I say? I could not speak more openly against
the regime. What I was trying to do was give a chained people
a certain nourishment—a cultural richness comparable to that
of the free peoples of the world.

INTERVIEWER
Can you explain what you mean by true literature?

KADARÉ
You recognize it immediately, instinctively. Every time I
wrote a book, I had the impression that I was thrusting a
dagger into the dictatorship, while at the same time giving
courage to the people.

INTERVIEWER
In view of what has happened in Yugoslavia, I would like
to ask you about religious intolerance. Half the Albanians
are Muslims, including your family. Did you receive a religious
education? Is there a danger of Islamic Fundamentalism in
Albania now that religious practice has become free?

KADARÉ
I don't think so. My family were Muslims in name, but they
did not practice. No one around me was religious. Besides, the
Bektashi sect of Islam that is practiced in Albania is very
moderate, even more so than in Bosnia. So I don't think we
need to worry on that score.

INTERVIEWER
To come back to the professional side of things, how do
you divide your time between Tiranë and Paris? And your
day, wherever you are?

KADARÉ

I am more in Paris than in Tiranë because I can work better
here. There is too much politics in Tiranë, and too many
demands. I am asked to write a preface here, an article there
. . . I don't have an answer to everything.

As for my day: I write two hours in the morning, and I
stop. I can never write more—my brain gets tired. I write in
a café around the corner, away from distractions. The rest of
my time is spent reading, seeing friends, all the rest of my life.

INTERVIEWER

Is writing easy for you or difficult? Are you happy when
writing, or anxious?

KADARÉ

Writing is neither a happy nor an unhappy occupation—it
is something in-between. It is almost a second life. I write
easily, but I'm always afraid that it may be no good. You
need a stable humor; both happiness and unhappiness are
bad for literature. When you are happy, you tend to become
light, frivolous, and if you are unhappy your vision becomes
perturbed. You have to live first, experience life, and later
write about it.

INTERVIEWER

Do you write on the typewriter or by hand?

KADARÉ

I write by hand, and my wife kindly types it.

INTERVIEWER

Do you rewrite a lot?

KADARÉ

Not much, just small adjustments, but no drastic changes.

INTERVIEWER

What comes first—the plot, characters, ideas?

KADARÉ

It depends. It is different for each book. The process is
mysterious, vague. It is not the characters, but a mixture of
everything. Take *The Palace of Dreams*. In an earlier novel,
The Corner of Shame, there is one page where the idea of
dream-control is for the first time introduced. Later, I thought
it was a pity to use it so briefly, or perfunctorily. So I wrote
a short story on the theme, without any hope of publication.
But two chapters were published in a collection of short stories.
When I saw that the authorities did not notice it, I was
emboldened and expanded it into a novel. So you see, the
genesis of a book is mysterious.

INTERVIEWER

Those who read your work in the original Albanian remark
upon the beauty of your prose. Is style a conscious preoccupation for you?

KADARÉ

I am meticulous, even demanding, about language. For
example, I always write poetry, because poetry forces you
to work on the language. There are two kinds of linguistic
richnesses: the first is similar to that of precious stones—
metaphors, similies, little discoveries—the second is in the
whole. The great felicity is a perfect mixture of the two, when
a text is beautifully written and the content is substantial too.
But there is no conscious stylistic effort on my part.

INTERVIEWER

What are the things that prevent you from working? Hemingway said the telephone was the big work-killer.

KADARÉ

In Tiranë no one dared use the telephone, except for the
most anodyne purposes, because the phones were tapped.
But as I said, I only write two hours a day, and it is not
difficult to be isolated for that length of time.

INTERVIEWER

Your last novel, *Spiritus*, had a very good reception in France, and I hope it will be translated into English soon. Have you started a new novel?

KADARÉ

No. Is there any hurry?

—**Shusha Guppy**

Como Conversazione

On Travel and Travel Writing

Grey Gowrie	*Head of the Arts Council of England; Chair of the proceedings at Lake Como*
Drue Heinz	*Publisher of* The Paris Review
Stephen Brook	*The Double Eagle; New York Days, New York Nights*
William Dalrymple	*City of Djinns; In Xanadu*
Nick Danziger	*Danziger's Travels; Danziger's Britain*
Alex Frater	*Beyond the Blue Horizon; Chasing the Monsoon*
John Hatt	*The Tropical Traveller*
Edward Hoagland	*Cat Man; Notes from the Century Before*
Howard Jacobsen	*In the Land of Oz; Roots Schmoots*
Philip Marsden	*The Bronski House; The Spirit Wrestlers: A Russian Journey*
Cees Nooteboom	*Roads to Santiago; The Following Story*
Paul Theroux	*Sir Vidia's Shadow: A Friendship Across Five Continents; The Great Railway Bazaar; The Kingdom by the Sea*
Isabella Tree	*Islands in the Clouds: Travels in the Highlands of New Guinea*

On a weekend in October, 1997, Drue Heinz and Grey Gowrie chaired several sessions of conversazione *at Casa Ecco on Italy's Lake Como on the theme of travel and travel writing. With them were twelve writers who, to a greater or lesser degree, practice these two activities. That is, they all travel and they all write. But what the connection is between the two turned out to vary from writer to writer.*

The tone of the discussions was unusually cordial for a group of fellow professionals. Only one topic succeeded in producing anything like dissent—the question of how much license is permitted when reassembling the scenes of a journey. In the inevitable course the conversation took toward definitions, the travel book, travel writing and motivations for traveling were all scrutinized.

It is perhaps a measure of the eclectic nature of travel writing that the subjects covered in the discussions ranged so widely: writing for the internet, the death of Princess Diana, the poems of W.H. Auden, the use of the camera, the sexual habits of circus tigers, were all discussed at some length. And places like China, Iran, the Caucasus, Afghanistan, Papua New Guinea and Ghana were mentioned as if they were streets in a long-familiar city.

At the core of the discussions were five main topics, concerning in different ways the nature of travel and the enigmatic form of the travel book. All agreed that the travel book can slop about quite happily between genres—between history and reportage, between memoir and exploration, between metaphysics and geology. The travel book is what you make it; the consensus of the weekend was that there is no consensus. This rather watery conclusion was reached by a meandering route, but like all the best journeys it was what happened on the way that made the conversazione *so rewarding.*

—Philip Marsden

I. Ways of Seeing

The raw material for a travel book is not so much the journey as the traveler's impressions during it. Whether based on a sustained period in one place or on a continuous trip

through a region, they provide the basis for what in book
form will necessarily carry some weight. But how can a limited
time in an alien place provide valid impressions? To what
extent are travelers deceived by their passing through? Or
are we equally deceived by the familiar? Does perhaps the
stranger's eye pick up things that residents do not?

GREY GOWRIE: I spent some time in Tehran in 1978, just
before the Shah fell, and made a complete misjudgment of
what was likely to happen and reported my misjudgment to
the foreign office. Has anyone else had that experience of
getting things wrong?

PHILIP MARSDEN: I was in Yugoslavia in the summer of 1990,
a year before the war broke out. I talked to people in Sarajevo,
in Bosnian villages, in Mostar and on the Croatian coast—the
consensus was that their wonderful union was here to stay.
As evidence people would say, "My neighbor is a Croat, I'm
a Serb and my other neighbor is my good friend, this Muslim.
Look, we all live in perfect harmony." It was true, they did.
Had that gone into print, I would have made a big mistake.
You think that by talking to people you are going to get the
truth. But the actual truth, the complexities, are much greater
than the answers to just a couple of questions. You might
get all the responses to your questions, but you don't find
out that actually over the centuries this one's grandfather
killed that one's grandfather. These things remain hidden
from travel writers who pass through.

PAUL THEROUX: That's one of the problems of being a travel
writer—passing through. You talk to people; but if you live
in a place, then you get a completely different notion of it.
When I was in China in 1979, all I knew about China was
Chairman Mao. I thought, Mao's so popular, I'll talk about
Mao. So I mentioned Mao all the time. I got very oblique
looks from people, and very oblique remarks. I didn't realize
that they hated him. I think there's a problem with passing

through, in that you get a very selective idea of a place—politically a very prismatic effect.

CEES NOOTEBOOM: When you pass through a place, sometimes something happens that in a flash illuminates the whole situation for you. I was in Tehran in the same prerevolution period as Gowrie. You probably remember that everybody, including the Shah, thought that the liberals were going to take over. When in fact it was Khomeini who did. While there, I visited a mosque with a female photographer. Suddenly, we were surrounded by mullahs. They spit in our faces, but fiercely. Paaah! I thought, It's totally different—these are the people who are going to do the thing. This was just a flash. I wrote it. But nobody reads Dutch. If only the CIA could read Dutch . . . because they got all the wrong information.

STEPHEN BROOK: Could I make a wider point about information? I speak three languages, but Hungarian and Armenian are not among them. When I was traveling in those countries and trying to make sense of them, I was very dependent on people translating for me or on people speaking English. That immediately limits your circle of contact. You can't stand in a bus queue and overhear and understand what people are saying. What you get is indirect information. So it's not surprising that we all get misled and misread things from time to time, because everything has to be immediate—not everything, but in certain parts of the world there are things mediated through language that are totally strange to us.

HOWARD JACOBSEN: Can I point out the opposite of passing through? Anybody who has been born and lived in England for the last however many years would have been astonished by this year in England. You speak the language, you know what people are saying in bus queues, you think you know the system, but all sorts of things have happened in England that you would never for a second have picked: the whole

Diana business, the state of euphoria that greeted the Labor win. Nobody expected it was going to be like that. Nobody expected other people to feel as you did. *You* knew you were tired of a particular way of being, but you didn't know other people were. Now, how is it one didn't know that? Maybe there are just some things you never know, and it doesn't matter what you hear people say in bus queues—people themselves don't know.

CEES NOOTEBOOM: I remember May, 1968, in Paris. And two years later, the disappointment. I think one has to mistrust these moods, really.

EDWARD HOAGLAND: When Martin Luther King, Jr., was shot, people expected that it would work a change in America, but it didn't.

NICK DANZIGER: I was in London the day of the election, and everybody was happy. It certainly was a remarkable day. But I agree with Cees, wait for some time to pass. What permanent effect will it have?

PAUL THEROUX: Why do we have to judge it by permanent effect? There is still the question of what was being expressed then, even if it is never expressed again or nothing comes of it.

NICK DANZIGER: I was thinking of you, Paul, when I was walking around London looking at the flowers, because I envy your book (there's going to be an element of schmoozing here, so I'll start it), your terrific English book, which took as its premise what England was like after the Falkland War. Just as you felt back then that was a way of understanding the English, so it seemed to me that something important could have been found out by somebody wandering around and seeing what the English were all up to in the days after Diana's death. It did look as though some extraordinary thing was happening then. It may be that it was nothing more than a cod-shop culture triumphant. Maybe it was only that. But even that is worth knowing—if popular culture has finally got us.

STEPHEN BROOK: I wonder if sometimes we try too hard to understand. Are we there simply to sort of mirror what we see or are we there to try to understand what we are seeing. When I was in the Caucasus, just when the place was dissolving into civil war, I felt it incumbent on me to try to understand what was going on. Is that our job? I suppose our instinct is always to try to make sense of what we are seeing around us and hearing around us. But except in certain circumstances, are we really equipped to do that?

JOHN HATT: Well, the press is now failing us. We have almost no foreign correspondents, and in a way the press often can't do that sort of thing—when they're in a country they are there in the capital to file stories, they aren't out talking to people in a relaxed way. Similarly our diplomatic service. I don't know if you ever talk to diplomats, but they *never* know what is going on in the country. In Ghana, I came in overland, by the bus from the north, and it took me three days to reach the capital—all I had to do was talk to people. There was an election coming up, and it was absolutely clear to me who was going to win, but all the grandees and journalists and diplomats in Accra were saying I was wrong. When the election took place and I was right, suddenly they were all ringing me up wanting to ask questions. It was a complete joke—I'd been there three days, and these people had lived there for years. Sometimes in very brief visits you can pick up things that other people can't. Rather like when you go and photograph a country, your first photographs are the best. Later your eyes become dim.

WILLIAM DALRYMPLE: The idea of the snapshot is interesting. I lived in India for five years. After a year or two, you kind of sneer at travelers coming through—you think that having

lived in a country you know the place much better than they
do, and that they have very little of interest to say. After
about three years, I was ceasing to notice things that were
odd and interesting, which people who passed through, although very briefly, would notice. It's one of the reasons I
finally left India. If you are in any place for a long time,
however well you come to know it and however deep your
knowledge of the literature, you do cease to have that instant
impact, that instant snapshot vision of what is interesting,
what is odd, what is strange about a place. It does become
ordinary—even somewhere as weird as India. You become
less perceptive, even as you know the place better.

JOHN HATT: When I went to China during Tiananmen, I
bought a Chinese phrase book and I learned twenty words.
When I got there, this was down to three; I'd forgotten them
because they are all absolutely impossible. So I said to the
taxi driver on the way in, "Deng Xiaoping *hao bu hao*." *Bu*
means no, *hao* means good.

WILLIAM DALRYMPLE: You said he was no good.

JOHN HATT: In an interrogative way. The taxi driver said,
"*Bu hao bu hao*" very firmly. I got to my hotel, and I said
to the man who carried in my cases, "Deng Xiaoping, *hao
bu hao*." He said, "*Bu hao bu hao*." The next morning I
went to the market and the woman tried to sell me a dog. I
said, "I don't want a dog but, Deng Xiaoping *hao bu hao*."
"*Bu hao bu hao*," she said. I thought, funnily enough, I
know what a quarter of the world's population is thinking,
I've done my own little poll.

PAUL THEROUX: It's not where you live, it's how you live
there. When you live a long time in a country, you take the
path of least resistance—you don't want to be disturbed. But
when people visit, they are making a new map of the place.
They are noticing things—intentionally disturbing, upsetting

things. You came to Ghana through the back way; you went to China and asked this unbelievably rude question of people: The prime minister, he's a bad guy, you're saying. Well, who would say that? Anyone who lived in China would never say that. You are blundering in. A person coming to a new country is a bull in a china shop.

JOHN HATT: I should slightly defend myself. That's not what I said. Good or not good, is what I said.

CEES NOOTEBOOM: In the end, I think it comes down to this: you can write a very good piece on any country if you are there only very shortly and then if you are there much longer; in between is bad. I was in Mali for ten days and wrote a piece of about forty pages. I'd done my reading about the country and the religion. The people living there asked me how long I'd been there because I seemed to be terribly well-informed, though in fact I wasn't. For my book on Spain, I spent forty years of continuous travel there, and then twenty years of writing it bit by bit, always coming back. I've found that if you stay somewhere for about two to three months, you have terrible difficulties . . . all the time coming upon things you should know more about. You don't dare to write.

EDWARD HOAGLAND: It's the complexity that interests people. If you tell them something about the Sufis that is complex, then they will be interested. If you write well.

ISABELLA TREE: The point is to try to understand a different culture. I went to Papua New Guinea, talking to people who have leapt in fifty years from a tribal existence, not knowing the outside world at all, to the present day and handling computers. You can talk to a tribesman who has been educated in Australia, but he is almost always giving you what you are asking him for. I could never master the place.

GREY GOWRIE: But there *is* the eye, isn't there? The ear is only one organ of any writer. Not knowing a word, might you not be able to judge by the look of places, the look of the agriculture, the look of such towns as they are? You could start to make assessments. But are we really about assessments? People talked about an audience: some of us, I think, rather want not to have sense made for us—we want a sense of the picture before the iconography and the essay and the lecture come in.

II. Types of Travel Book

Out of the epistemology of traveling arose the question of trying to typify the travel book itself. No one who has written travel of any sort can have avoided the baffled stare that follows the declaration: I am a travel writer. In the far-flung place that is the author's subject, travel writing elicits at best confusion, at worst suspicion. Back home the confusion is even more obvious, and tinged with an added element of jealousy. As travel becomes increasingly a luxury, so doing it and writing about it appears, to those who pay for it, more and more indulgent. But if travel writing is misunderstood by those unfamiliar with it, nor does it appear to be well-defined by its practitioners.

PAUL THEROUX: All of us at this table have written travel books, but I bet that none of our books really are comparable. The range is from the travel book as a form of fiction to the travel book being as factual and objective as possible. The point is that we are all doing something different and we can't pretend that we are writing something that is going to be the authoritative book about a country.

PHILIP MARSDEN: Which is one of the great strengths and interests of the genre. Because it is a cocktail into which you can throw whatever you are interested in.

ALEX FRATER: I don't think that's a strength necessarily. You could argue that it is one of the insufficiencies of the form. It's a strange form. It's interesting that the earlier discussion focused on the authority of the travel book, but really the travel book doesn't have a lot of authority. And its authority isn't the intrinsically interesting thing about it. Personally, I think it's diaristic, it's autobiographical, it's imaginative. It's a form of painting, and some people are cubists, some people are impressionists.

EDWARD HOAGLAND: Yes. I think that V.S. Naipaul is a great writer—one of the handful of greats. But I don't agree with him about the countries frequently. Nabokov is a great writer, but I don't agree with him politically, for example. It's not that he's inaccurate, but that he has his own vision. I see that he's a genius, but I don't agree with him.

GREY GOWRIE: Is *agreement* a word you can use about travel writing?

CEES NOOTEBOOM: I'd like to point out an Anglo-Saxon tendency in travel writing—what I would very roughly call the epic. A travel book in which someone is going from the mouth of the river to its source, or from the north to the south, with a goal preset—there is a definite story. The reader knows that in the end he will end up in the mouth of the Thames. I have written one such book, but normally I would have myself parachuted somewhere, like to Bangkok or Mali and then write from being there and go on about it. I would call that lyrical. There is no preset goal of doing a journey.

DRUE HEINZ: If the British are epic writers, does that mean necessarily they are not lyrical?

CEES NOOTEBOOM: No, there is just this thing of a set mind: I am going to have this adventure, and you all are going to follow me.

HOWARD JACOBSEN: Isn't the journey as arbitrary as the plot in a novel, in fact? That's not really what we are reading it for. If you have a favorite travel writer, you aren't reading his new book because you wonder where he's going next, you just want to be acquainted with his mind again. You want to go on a journey with him again. I'll go anywhere with him.

III. The Travel Book and the Novel

The overlap of fiction and travel writing was a theme that recurred frequently through the discussions. Novels were examined as travel books, and travel books as fiction. Howard Jacobsen claimed that "the ten best travel books are all novels," adding later that "I cannot think of a single novel that isn't a travel book. Maybe Jane Austen, but I'm thinking that they're the ultimate travel books because they are about the terrible things that happen to you if you don't move."

Of the assembled writers, five at least had turned their hand to fiction. Novels were cited in the discussions at least as often as travel books. Of these, Lolita *scored the highest:* Lolita *as road book, as a motel tour of suburban America propelled by erotic obsession (in the same way as, say, Robert Byron was propelled around Asia by architectural curiosity).*

GREY GOWRIE: What about this issue of narrative—extraordinary travel adventures, where there isn't much talk. The best-seller of my youth still seems a good book, *Kon-Tiki*. And think of the great sea voyages of literature. So movement has a place. In the mention of *Lolita*, here is this highly cultivated Eastern European mind wandering around a kind of early pop art landscape of motels. *Lolita* is one of the best travel books I've ever read.

EDWARD HOAGLAND: *Lolita* has a danger too, because Humbert Humbert could be put in jail or he could destroy himself, which happens.

PAUL THEROUX: When Nabokov was preparing *Lolita*, he traveled around Ithaca, New York, making notes sitting behind schoolgirls on buses and listening to them talk.

DRUE HEINZ: Where does the imagination come into all of this?

EDWARD HOAGLAND: It is the method of empathy: imagination makes empathy possible.

PHILIP MARSDEN: The whole point of travel writing is precisely that imaginative element. You use the facts as a springboard to reach more transcendent truths. Imagination is a quest for the essence of things.

CEES NOOTEBOOM: You pick from the realities around you what you are going to describe.

ISABELLA TREE: I think travel writing is like an impressionist painting—it is over a scene, but it is an interpretation. It encourages your readers to open their eyes.

GREY GOWRIE: Aren't we saying that of course this can be an art, and an art in any form is not a literal rendition. You are trying to remake a truth, and make it come alive.

JOHN HATT: Yes, but a travel writer shouldn't get at the truth by fudging.

WILLIAM DALRYMPLE: Would you say that if it is proved, as is generally believed now, that Bruce Chatwin invented a great deal of *In Patagonia*, it is now a worthless scrap of paper?

JOHN HATT: In my opinion, yes.

NICK DANZIGER: A lot of armchair travelers are deeply disappointed now that they've discovered Chatwin made much of it up.

PAUL THEROUX: One of my problems with Chatwin, with this sort of travel book, is that it's insufficient as travel and insufficient as fiction. It's interesting to read, but you go to the country and you really have little idea where you are going.

HOWARD JACOBSEN: Is this a person who writes good sentences? Is this a mind worth keeping company with? The only point of reading a book is to hold the author in your mind for the course of the book.

PAUL THEROUX: Say I am a brilliant writer, and I describe a trip up the Amazon. I get captured by this tribe, and the first night they say, "You must sleep with three virgins for the honor of our tribe." I see all sorts of weird and wonderful customs. I think if you are honest, that if you thought I was telling the truth, you would be far more interested in *that* than however well I wrote it.

HOWARD JACOBSEN: I wouldn't be. You create what you see. There is no truth apart from you.

JOHN HATT: I think that is a very dangerous thing to say.

CEES NOOTEBOOM: You all have heard of Kapuscinski's book *The Emperor*—very highly regarded, but I don't regard it at all. He is endlessly talking to servants of the emperor: it does not smell real, each of those people do not have individual voices. I find it rather hard to take. Some people say, "Well you know this is a work of imagination, it is fiction." But the problem is that people take it as the truth, reading it as a sourcebook. These books have effects. Would you consider it acceptable if that was fiction? If those interviews were not what they purported to be?

PHILIP MARSDEN: I agree that Kapuscinski did do that. But if you get that mix right, whether it is writing under the label of fiction or the tag of fact, it is rather a thrill.

IV. Why Travel?

GREY GOWRIE: What is this trade? What about the psychology of wandering?

WILLIAM DALRYMPLE: Why travel? Why sit home for God's sake? Who wouldn't travel if they had a chance? I don't know that I feel a compulsion. If anything it is a draw. I don't think there is any psychological reason for it.

PAUL THEROUX: It's a compulsion to get away. I think it's bound up with a kind of optimism. I think that writers in their very nature are dysfunctional, incomplete, troubled people. There is something deeply wrong with anyone who wants to write. I come from a family of seven children, all of whom were clamoring for attention. With a modicum of talent, I suppose. But the talent is secondary to the obsessive nature of wanting to mark up my own space, to distinguish myself, to have my own vision of things, not wanting to be told what to do—feeling subversive against any authority, feeling that I'm always on the point of rejection. When you wander into a new society, people don't know your history. You are a new person. The idea of going to a place and talking to someone who doesn't know you is a thrill. It is why I travel. I was at my happiest in Buenos Aires—I had grown a mustache and I was walking around looking like everyone else and I thought, No one knows me, I am completely anonymous and yet I'm different from everyone else—I am the man who fell to earth.

PHILIP MARSDEN: I find it hard to divorce traveling from writing. Whether it is taking notes or for publication, I want to write it down. You say bring order to a chaotic experience— that is part of the draw of it. Deriving the order from the chaos, I find the most gratifying thing. I travel in order to write.

I came from a middle-class English family and I wanted to get out. I didn't have room in the nest. I belonged more outside and abroad than in my home—I traveled in order to belong. It reaffirms my faith in human nature when I am in a completely alien environment and I am able to share basic affection or humor or whatever with people who are completely alien to me. You have these raw human experiences. It is one of the great pleasures of traveling for me.

JOHN HATT: I wish people did travel a bit more from compulsiveness. In my case, I would say I travel not from any dysfunctionality at home, though no doubt there is plenty of that, but inquisitiveness. I think that is tremendously important. Writing can be a help with enjoying your travels, because there are certain things that you would never do unless you had the excuse for writing. For instance, I spent two weeks talking to cormorant fishermen. If I hadn't been going to write, I would have felt a banana. But I had the excuse, and I really felt that sitting in one little bit of China where I had never been before, I learned a huge amount about China.

HOWARD JACOBSEN: I think I travel to be miserable. As a writer I feed off discomfort and impatience. I travel very badly, and given the choice I wouldn't travel. I am not naturally inquisitive, I don't like sitting spending long hours talking and listening to people. I get bored with it. I am doing things that make me at all points entirely miserable. And that works. I don't know what else to write out of. It might lead to a certain creative sameness, but we all have only got a small pool to fish from. I fish from that. The business of being a wanderer—I certainly remember as a kid living the existential romanticism of wandering. But I realize that even that has not got any grander form. It is entirely about feeding off rancor and exasperation. Nothing makes you more rancid than uncomfortable traveling. It's an addiction—one gets high on being low.

PAUL THEROUX: I had hoped we might discuss traveling and not writing. I would much rather have traveling as a pure experience than feel a compulsion to have to write it down,

which is work; it's a lot of trouble. To have money and simply
wander, grinning like a dog—that would be perfect.

STEPHEN BROOK: Martin Amis said that the difference between fiction and journalism is that journalism lets you out
of the house. I think that is a large part of the reason I do travel
writing. The other reason is visceral—a love of movement. I
go to Victoria Station, and I occasionally have to go to Bat-
tersea, which is a three-minute journey across the Thames
and I get terribly excited the moment the door slams behind
me. Press my nose against the window and watch the river.
It's sort of childish, but it's very real. Of course, the longer
the journey the more exciting it is. The actual physical movement for me is very stimulating. And yes, the inquisitiveness—the curiosity about cultures. Also, I love danger. If I
hear a gunshot, I run toward it. It's the love of being stimulated in these bizarre ways. And the act of writing—I love
writing, making sense of all these experiences.

NICK DANZIGER: The first time I was asked what I wanted
to be when I grew up, when I was five or six, I said to my
father I wanted to be a tube-train driver. When he asked me
why, I said because I wanted to travel. I've tried to explore
other people's ways of life that were completely alien to
my own.

ALEX FRATER: I'm basically rootless. I was born in the south-
west Pacific, was sent to boarding school in Australia at the
age of six, then went to Fiji with my family when I was ten
and eventually, at twenty-two, ended up in London. But
nowhere have I established a permanent home base; I have
never had the feeling of belonging anywhere. Even after
thirty-five years in Britain. It's a bit like a virus, it gets in
the blood—I can't stay put for any particular length of time.
I am impelled to move. There is also a masochistic element—I
do enjoy things going wrong. I recently brought out a book
on India. A friend of mine gave it to his daughter who

was backpacking around India. When she got back, he said, "What did you think of it?" She said, "It was all right, but Alex didn't suffer enough." That was a great indictment. I believe in rough travel—it's a sort of weird prepubescent proving of masculinity. I believe in rough travel. We are all nourished by things going wrong. As for Paul's point about the purest thing of all is not to write about it—I don't agree with that. I couldn't do that. I think probably the purest thing is to keep a journal.

PAUL THEROUX: What I was suggesting is merely that all of us are travelers, all of us write. But all of us have met much greater travelers than ourselves. They have had much greater difficulties, they have been much more ambitious, have suffered more deprivations, more loneliness and have got just the satisfaction of doing it. It is a very humbling experience meeting these people. It's not so much that it is pure, it is that their journey is greater than ours and isn't recorded.

CEES NOOTEBOOM: I am not sure how much these psychological motives count. What we do have in common is the movement thing. I remember one day, before I could think or write, I just left home with a rucksack and started hitchhiking.

GREY GOWRIE: So the fundamental thing about travel is that it isn't home.

CEES NOOTEBOOM: I suppose so. There are many reasons to leave home, but I think it has to do with movement. Still now—I am sixty-four—when I arrive in some place with my wife, I say, "Well, I have to go out and see where I am." I was frustrated last night because it was dark—normally I want to get out first. I will walk a little distance with my wife, and I will say, "Well, can we just go beyond the bend because I want to see what is there." And then the next bend. And then the hill. This has stayed with me forever. It is very childish probably. When people interview me, they say, "You know what Pascal said, 'All the unhappiness in the world comes from the human being who cannot stay for twenty hours in one room.' What is your answer to that?" I have lied in all these interviews, so many lies about why I am doing it that I have stopped knowing why I am doing it. I just know that I do it.

GREY GOWRIE: You probably know that phrase you used, *beyond the bend*, also means *nuts* to us.

CEES NOOTEBOOM: Language betrays you all the time.

ISABELLA TREE: I think I travel just because I love it. I don't think I travel because it is a form of escapism. I think it excites me, in the true sense of the word—it wakes me up. As soon as I start moving, all my senses come alive. I love that feeling. It's curiosity, as well, that drives me. I love learning about another place.

EDWARD HOAGLAND: Ulysses enjoyed travel. He did want to get home, but I don't think he was in such a hurry. In terms of my own experience, I travel for joy at least as much as from compulsion. I came from a middle-class home, whose restrictions I wished to escape. I joined the circus when I was eighteen for two or three summers. Joy is twinned with a prudent danger for me. I'd like to see as much of the world before I die as possible. I believe that heaven is on earth. I spent three years legally blind, and when I recovered my sight, that principle was reaffirmed. But there is a compulsion to it. As an adult, I've usually had two homes—I need to be able to go back and forth, when one home becomes intolerable I need the other place to jump to. Like the cat on a hot tin roof—not the play, but the image of a cat that keeps moving its paws, traveling because the ground burns if it stays still. But I don't believe that contradicts this principle of life as the purpose of joy. It is not, to me, a contradiction that life is almost intolerable and also is meant to be totally joyful. I

used to masturbate my female tigers in their cages, at their
request. Then they would go to the other end of the cage
and come back and try to kill me.

PHILIP MARSDEN: What is the point of that?

EDWARD HOAGLAND: Joy and anguish are twinned. For us
travelers.

CEES NOOTEBOOM: I wanted to quote an Arab philosopher
of the eleventh century who said something about travel.
"The origin of existence is movement. Therein there can be
no immobility because if existence would be immobile, it
would return to its origin, which is nothingness. Therefore
travel never stops. Not in the higher and not in the lower
world." There is a great satisfaction for me in the idea that
the world itself travels, within a galaxy that itself travels.

GREY GOWRIE: And traveling to extinction. Everything here
will be dusted.

V. Whither the Travel Book?
*The question of the state of the art hovered around the
discussions: the place of the travel book in an era of mass travel
and mass media. In previous sessions, the great nineteenth-
century travelers, Burton particularly, were mentioned as being the grandfathers of the genre. In the 1930s, there was a
revival, with writers like Graham Greene, Peter Fleming and
Robert Byron. Then again in the 1970s the travel book re-
emerged as a forum for serious writers, a development, suggested Paul Theroux, that stemmed from a sense of frustration
with the state of the novel. In the last session, on Sunday
morning, three or four of the writers gave their assessment
of the future of their trade.*

WILLIAM DALRYMPLE: What started off as a rather prosaic
form has recently, because of the competition of televison

and guidebooks, suddenly mushroomed into a remarkably imaginative and flexible form. Paul was really responsible for kicking the new era of travel writing off in the mid-seventies with *The Great Railway Bazaar*. In the next couple of years came *In Patagonia, The Time of Gifts* and the travel-writing issue of *Granta*. Suddenly travel writing was the fashionable thing to be doing. The result was that publishers took on an awful lot of incredibly unimaginative stuff—the kind of pogo stick to the antarctic type of travel book. In about 1991 there seemed to be a terrible crisis in confidence. Everyone was suddenly saying, This form is overrated, it has been hyped in the book pages, it's really a very ordinary form of nonfiction. Now there are far fewer travel books being written but what there are are much more interesting. Amitav Ghosh for instance wrote *In an Antique Land*, about living in a very remote, very primitive Egyptian village. He crossed his own time there with another Indian, the slave of an Arab trader in the twelfth century; the result is an extraordinarily interesting hybrid.

ISABELLA TREE: The days of terra-incognita journeys are gone, of straightforward traveling for thousands and thousands of miles. I think there is now a much more important place for layering in travel writing—traveling in time as well as distance, going back to a place again and again, not moving from one spot. I think this is interesting.

ALEX FRATER: Several years ago I was a judge for the Thomas Cook Travel Book of the Year Award and that year publishers sent us ninety-four books. Of these I suppose ten were worth publishing and of those ten, five probably were made into paperbacks. But the other eighty were worthless. I think you're right, the list is being thinned down. The notion of going somewhere and writing about it is virtually dead. I think the lateral approach is the way forward. William for instance was looking at India through Delhi in *City of Djinns*, and I did a book looking at India through the monsoon.

PETER BROOK: I don't agree that it is dead, the going somewhere and writing about it. The world changes and people
want to know about it. It comes down to the writing, the
style. I mean you really ought to be able to write a travel
piece about going to the corner shop to pick up a newspaper,
as long as you do it with panache.

Four Poems by Henri Cole

Anagram

Thy word is all, if we could spell.
—George Herbert, "The Flower"

Scrawling the letters of my name,
I found and changed what I became:

first, HERON LICE emerged,
like shame usurping dignity.

Then LION CHEER assembled,
as if proof I was palimpsest.

When the strange oracle decreed,
"OH, RECLINE," I went deep

into the core of my being,
where I found LICHEN ROE,

something called IRON LEECH—germs
to help a man plow up himself.

Then the musings got profane.
"I CLONE HER!" the voice sneered,

speaking of Mother;
and there's LICE ON HER.

But I was scribe. No!
I shouted, I NO LECHER.

I am not an ECHO LINER.
I was I. So self-love came back,

replacing alphabetical tears.
Little parts of me COHEREd:

CORN, RICE & EEL.
All I was I could feel.

Charity

Naked but for dainty shoes, garter
and a ribbon in her long red hair,
she takes him in the way history takes us in:
with an unperturbed hand across the breast.
Stroking into her, the way a boot strokes a stirrup,
he seems as banal or irrelevant
as a birthmark or a hairdo. On screen,
it's her pointy attenuated legs,
smaller than life, that strain to do their work.
What he feels, for good or bad, I cannot feel.
What she feels frees her. Tenderness,
even to a stranger, corroborates the self.
Unlike the pretty jar of libidinal grease
knocked from the bed, she will not break.

The Color of Feeling and the Feeling of Color

While others were discussing
the styles of metopes,
I lay down in the Temple of Zeus
and shut my eyes.

Behind the shut eyes,
the metopes were what I saw:
a giant tugged on the arrow in his head;
a son's corpse wasted on a funeral bed;
a centaur crashed into a pit;
a wrestler cut off his head to honor his father;
and everywhere were grieving women,
tearing at their hair.

It might almost have been a lion
grazing among the war-dead
that licked the flesh of my forehead,
though it was only a bearded dog.
It was midday, and a church bell
wagged its lead tongue furiously at us,
making one think of life-in-death and all that.
Overhead, a Hades crow split the sky.
Water buffalo roamed the desolate farmland,
holding their shoulders proudly like invaders,
yet grunting in their miserable
tamed beast fashion.

All those centuries
of vengeance and maw, recapped in an hour,
clung to the mind like marble dust.
The nerves sat crumbling
like opus reticulatum—
little tufa blocks piled in a phalanx,
lantern lit at the end of the tunnel.
But when I looked up in front of me,
into a shaft of fresh, clean light,
fourteen limestone columns
rose to their doric entablature,
as if to say austerely, "Wake up!
This is the house of Zeus.
So much anguish demeans the gods."

Then I saw a little Apollonian room,
the zone of art,
asserting itself as a cure.
"Beauty is not structure,"
it seemed to say, rebuking me,
"but structure & carnage,
hurting and consoling us at once.
Neither one subordinates the other."
This was not so long ago,
in a country, many rivers and realms away,
where rooms were *stanze*,
patterns of words tethering the mind
in endless motions.

           But it was time to move on.
Our guide beckoned us from the rubble,
where the temple stood serene as Zeus.
I wiped the bitter saliva from my brow.
Far off, a lemon grove traced
the slope of a volcano,
a dolphin cut the sea.

               (Paestum, 1995)

Apollo

> *O let me clean my spirit of all doubt, give me the*
> *signature of what I am.*
> —Ovid, *The Metamorphoses, II*

I

With a shriek gulls fled across a black sky,
all of us under the pier were silent,
my blood ached from waiting, then we resumed.

"You're just like us," some bastard said;
and it was true: my hair was close-cropped,
my frame reposed against a piling, my teeth
glistened, my prick was stiff. Little by little
they had made me like them, raptly feeding
in silhouette, with exposed abdomen,
like a spider sating itself. For a moment,
I was the eye through which the universe
beheld itself, like God. And then I gagged,
stumbling through brute shadows to take a piss,
a fly investigating my wet face.

II

Stay married, God said. One marriage.
    Don't abortion. Ugly mortal sin.
Beautiful gorgeous Mary loves you
    so much. Heaven tremendous thrill
of ecstasy forever. What you are,
    they once was, God said, the beloved ones
before you; what they are, you will be.
    All the days. Don't fornicate. Pray be good.
Serpent belly thorn and dust. Serpent belly
    sing lullaby. Beautiful gorgeous Jesus
loves you so much. Only way to Heaven
    church on Sunday. You must pray rosary.
Toil in fields. Heaven tremendous thrill
    of ecstasy forever. Don't fornicate.

III

hefting me onto him
he let me cling on
like a little bear
my ardor my enemy
my cold legs clenching
the hard hairy chest

that was his body
middle-aged floating
under me until
a wall of salt
took us down
in a good clean break
I could feel like a stump
where love had been

IV

The search for a single dominant gene—
"the 'O-God' hypothesis" (one-gene,
one disorder)—which, like an oracle,
foreknows the sexual brain, is fruitless.

The human self is undeconstructable
montage, is poverty, learning, & war,
is DNA, words, is acts in a bucket,
is agony and love on a wheel that sparkles,

is a mother and father creating
and destroying, is mutable
and one with God, is man and wife speaking,
is innocence betrayed by justice,

is not sentimental but sentimentalized,
is a body contained by something bodiless.

V

"Knowledge enormous makes a God of me,"
Apollo cried, square-shouldered, naked, hair falling
down his back. Now that I am forty, nothing
I have learned proves this. Inside my chest
there is loose straw. Inside my brain there are

syllables and sound. Living inwardly,
how can I tell what is real and what is not?

Joy and grief pulse like water from a fountain
over me, a stone, but do not end as knowledge.
All my life, doing things in moderation,
I have wooed him, whose extremes are forgotten,
whose battered faceless torso fills me
with longing and shame. I lie in the grass
like a man whose being has miscarried.

VI

On the sand there were dead things from the deep.
Faint-lipped shells appeared and disappeared,
like language assembling out of gray.

Then a seal muscled through the surf,
like a fetus, and squatted on a sewage pipe.
I knelt in the tall grass and grinned at it.

Body and self were one, vaguely
coaxed onward by the monotonous waves,
recording like compound sentences.

The seal was on its way somewhere cold, far.
Nothing about it exceeded what it was
(unlike a soul reversing itself to be

something more or a pen scratching words
on vellum after inking out what came before).

VII

Walking in woods, I found him bound to a tree,
moaning like a dove, a kerchief stopping his mouth;
a sweat-smell mixed with mulch and lotion,

a ten dollar bill at his dirty feet.
How easily in him I could see myself,
poor wannabe Sebastian, sucked and bitten
like a whore! I blushed for him, hurrying home.

Memory: the diplomats in white tie
stepping from a Mercedes at the Vatican.
The limousine door swung wide like a gate
to a realm I wanted, a way of being,
formal as Bernini's rigid colonnade.
Then purple-sashed bishops flooded the square,
smearing out the white surplices of acolytes.

VIII

Dirt so fine it is like flour.
      Dirt mixed with ice.
Huge expanses of it.
      The ground frozen.
With deep exceptional holes.
       This is what I see
spilling down a nave.
      Then Daddy kissing
a cardinal's ring.
      And the long black snake
of his belt yanked
      around him. His legs
planted apart like a clergyman's.
       My body
prostrate on the counterpane
      where man and wife lay.
The inflamed buttocks.
      The Roman letters,
TU ES PETRUS,
      though I knew I was not.
Daddy's voice moving slowly,
      like a cancer

toward the brain,

        a sky-blue globe

it cannot penetrate.

            Leather flying against flesh.

In the mouth

        dirt so fine it is like flour.

IX

All I want is to trust a man with plain

unshaken faith. Because I was not loved,

I cannot love. Sometimes I think I am not alive

but frozen like debris in molten glass.

White hairs sprout from my ears like a donkey's.

I do not feel sorry so much as weak,

like a flower with a broken stem.

A little blood or forgiveness does not

improve things. My brain is staunch as a crow,

my tongue buoyant as a dolphin. Yet, I

do not grow. You, with your unfalse nature

and silver arrows, won't you take my wrist.

Speak to me. My words are sounds

and sounds are not what I feel. Make me a man.

X

To write what is human, not escapist:

that is the problem of the hand moving

away from my body.

            Yet, subject is

only pretext for assembling the words

whose real story is process is flow.

So the hand lurches forward, gliding back

serenely, radiant with tears, a million

beings and objects hypnotizing me

as I sit and stare.

            Not stupefied. Not aching.

Today, I am one. The hand jauntily
at home with evil, with unexamined feelings,
with just the facts.
                    Mind and body, like spikes,
like love and hate, recede pleasantly.
Do not be anxious. The hand remembers them.

XI

When I was a boy our father cooked
to seek forgiveness for making our house
a theatre of hysteria and despair.
How could I not eat gluttonously?

You, my Apollo, cannot see that your hands
moving over me, the plainer one,
make me doubt you, that a son's life is punishment
for a father's. Young and penniless,

you serve me lobster. Scalding in the pot,
how it shrieked as I would with nothing left!
Please forgive my little dramas of the self.
And you do . . . in an interruption of the night,

when one body falls against another—
in the endless dragging of chains that signifies love.

XII

Morning of Puritans. Ice on the pond.
Giblets boiling. Any sort of movement
makes the bluejays fly. Father's door is opening.
Why are the titmice so unafraid of him?
Wrapped in cellophane on a granite slab,
the iced heart of our turkey stops time.

I remember my life in still pictures
that fall, inflamed, as in the seventh circle

the burning rain prevents the sodomites
from standing still. But I am in motion,
stroking toward what I cannot see, like an oar
dipped into the blood that ravishes it,

until blood-sprays rouse the dissolute mind,
the ineffable tongue arouses itself.

XIII Cyparissus

"I am here. I will always succor you,"
he used to say, a little full of himself.
What did I know, I was just a boy
loved by Apollo. There had been others.
All I wanted was to ride my deer,
who made me feel some knowledge of myself,
letting me string his big antlers with violets.

One day, in a covert, not seeing the tear
stray to drink at a cool spring, I thrust
my spear inadvertently into him.
Not even Apollo could stop the grief,
which gave me a greenish tint, twisting my
forehead upward; I became a cypress.
Poor Apollo: nothing he loves can live.

XIV

This is not a poem of resurrection.
The body secretes its juices and then is gone.
This is a poem of insurrection
against the self. In the beginning was the child,
fixating on the mother, taking himself
as the sexual object . . . You know the story.
In the mirror I see a man with a firm
masculine body. Mouth open like a fish,
I look at him, one of the lucky ones

above the surface where the real me
is bronzed in the Apollonian sun.
I stay a while, mesmerized by the glass
whose four corners frame the eyes of a man
I might have been, not liquid, not pent in.

Peggy Penn

Kinshit

It's summer: none of the toilets will flush;
just enough water for a half-swirl wets
the sides, coughs and stops. No more dependable
inrush, no more effective outrush. Toilets
sweating like mad; bowl, cold as a handshake
that marks your skirt when you wipe it off.
The toilet paper build-up on top
of the crap . . . stuffed cabbage, breaking up
in the pot. Conjuring, we get the snake,
a metal catheter, force it in
then pull it out of the backed up slab;
nothing. Next the plunger hiccups the waters—
pureeing its contents, but—no flush occurs!

Just the foul floats of summer, still floating.
For the next two days Draino reigns, and four drums
later, we resort to a *case* of lemon
air freshener till the air is filled with the scent
of lemon shit. Something is running amok
with our cistern and no fool stools are
to blame. We wake at 3:00 A.M.
to gassy tank noises; jiggle the handle
in a useless ritual, watching our mini
galaxies not go down! With each pseudo-flush
it seems more strangers appear, orbiting
what has to be yours and mine—who are they?
are they *our own*? reproducing? breaking up?

The children caught in our shit again?
Intrusive mother, accusing child:
and even you (sometimes), the stale mate!

No margin of error here for shit
to happen—Whodunit? me I guess,
the usual culprit. But, I argue, shit
is the witty insurer of familia-
rity; our circuitry that stays! We lean
over the bowl, our nebula: like tea leaves
or heavenly bodies as though we were out
on the hill for our nightly count of
sanitary stars; reflecting on the
creation myths of kith and kinshit.

Three Poems by Janet Kaplan

The Child Emperor

This is how I began: a delicacy
to my mother, a scallop rocking in
her shell, one in thousands of my father's spawn.
They feasted on their housebound child, and I
would have fallen fast asleep for good beneath
their quilts, but they resolved to tear me
from the safety of their hearth. At school
I learned to build, and to defeat in rest-
lessness, any random discourse on the world.
And though I know my place above the ranks,
in darkness still I try to mend my first
displacement from the realm of human love:
I dream of meadows simmering with seeds,
and sneak away with armfuls, back toward home.

After the Sacrifice

> *The English verb* to die *is akin to the Old Irish* diune,
> *human being.*

And afterwards, the sea befriended us,
gave away its fish. It drank its own
deep cup and did not pour the fishers down
its icy throat. It always went like this.
The architect of grasses raised our corn
to the stars, the three-headed dogs howled
at the watchmen but sent us no fevers.
A woman furious with death might lift

her eyes at night: the sky would hurl no fires
at her breast but hold its meteors clenched
within its fist. Always afterwards, and
until the peace gave way, between the human
and her shadow, a kind of truce was made.

Answer

Yesterday the ocean opened its minatory door
    and suggested that the land, from South Carolina
    to New England, had best come inside.

And one day after the hurricane
    a newsphoto appears: four swimmers
    struggling an unknown body

Ashore. One man, eyes shut in effort, grips it
    from behind. A woman in mirrored sunglasses,
    big body heedless of its dainty bikini,

Hoists the limp right arm; another man tugs the left.
    Wading behind the heroes,
    one woman grabs her own hair

As if she'd tear it to the waves.
    But all's calm now; now the ocean lets them
    wade ashore with their fish-body prize

Which soon enough someone will claim,
    there will be flowers, the fuss
    over a grave. Lord gives,

Amen, Lord takes.
    But the drowned one?
    Bent at the knees, legs submerged,

Naked if it weren't for sheer white briefs:
  what could he want? His head bows
  toward its element, water,

In unspeakable—no, untranslatable—communion,
  chest collapsed, pressed into silence
  by the thumb of God.

Two Poems by Scott Cairns

The Forest of the Stylites

for Warren Farha

The way had become unbearably slow, progress
imperceptible. Even his hunger had become
less, little more than a poorly remembered myth

of never quite grasped significance. And the field
he now glimpsed far ahead appeared as a failed
forest whose cedars—bleached and branchless—clearly
     reached

past the edge of his sight. Occasional, erratic
movement at the tops of a few distant trees spun
his bearings some, induced brief vertigo, recalled

to him his hunger, if as a wave of nausea,
which abated, then poured back as he drew near and the trees
transformed to pillars, each topped by an enormous

weathered flightless bird enshrouded in a rag.

Tesserae

for Marcia Vanderlip

In paling sixth-hour light the woman cups
one azure tile fragment as if asking
of its brokenness a sign. The bright

mosaic framed before her far
from finished, she tries positioning
the speck in mind before her hand inclines

to set the fraction as a sum. In time,
this mote of clay-returned-to-element
will serve as iris for the eye

of an impossibly tinted bird
whose gaudy elegance lies entirely
comprised of likewise shattered earthenware,

which, lifted from the heap, articulates
a second purpose, free from mundane
practicalities, clearly out of nature

sprung into a flight of some duration.

Poet and Philosopher

Kirk Nesset

The Philosopher and Poet Fail to Put Out the Fire

They stand in the dark watching the cars and carport barn burn. Far below to the left, fire trucks switch up the mountain, all red flash and horn blast and echoey siren. They'll get here too late, the poet is thinking—the eucalypti above the carport will go, then the hillside and cliff and who knows how many homes. Good God, the philosopher thinks: it happens so fast. Inside the structure, where both cars (the philosopher's Nissan, the poet's old Volvo) are swallowed in orange, paint cans and tubs of thinner explode, howling, paint jets flaring straight up. They might have saved the philosopher's car—the poet's poorly wired dash is to blame—but suckled as they were on action-adventure, the ubiquitous four-wheel war-heads, well, why get too close?

Look at it go, the philosopher says, flames doing their dance in his glasses.

I'm looking, the poet responds.

A burning board falls from the roof, hits the burning hood of the Volvo. Fire trucks wind up the grade, shrieking.

Why didn't you go for the hose? the philosopher asks—the poet had dashed in for a plant mister, five minutes ago, and squirted his air vents with that.

Panic, he answers.

Panic, his neighbor repeats.

They've shared the same house for years—each has his own entrance, own gas and aluminum hearth, and own grand view, deck jutting out at San Gabriel Valley (smog-choked by day, transcendental by night); the poet's carpet's more pretty. The philosopher lives above, his friend on ground level, as Plato deemed it should be. They're employed by the same four-year liberal-arts college, a network of ears and quick tongues, and thus keep all discussions, and actions, top secret. (The poet's erotic machinations, and confessions of such, to be honest, tend to be vivid and awful, with much more potential for ruin.) Humorously, if awkwardly, too, each can hear the other's every sound in the house, down to each sigh, love grunt and belch. The acoustics astound.

You got that girl in the house? the philosopher asks, turning—meaning the nineteen-year-old student he met (he knew her from school). And couldn't help hearing.

She's in there.

Hiding?

With a groan and great hissing a falling beam slams the Nissan. Sparks leap to the tree branches.

She's afraid they'll make her a witness.

Her father'd kill her if he knew. Right? Not to mention your job.

No answer. The Nissan's windshield explodes.

The philosopher knows. His friend's a philosophical riddle, a mixture of Schopenhauer, Epicurus and somebody else—Captain Kirk, maybe—but bone-skinny, dark-skinned, prone to teeth-gnashing and worry, with black hair on his shoulders and back. They've confided a lot, the man's a good buddy, if a little unstable—unlike the philosopher, a swimmer, robust,

blond, soon to wed his old college flame; his only weakness
is booze.

The trucks hit the summit and curve out of sight onto
Skyline, veer over to Edgeridge and, whipping dry branches
and dust on the roadside, fly down the private drive to the
house. Men in glow-in-the-dark extraterrestrial outfits trot up
with gargantuan hoses. They spray, knocking cracked glass
from windows, sending charred mirrors and grill ornaments
flying. Now that it's safe—salvation is nigh—the poet affords
himself leisure to feel what he's feeling, what he's felt for
ten minutes, to maybe use later in the form of a poem. The
philosopher begins to relax, realizing how thirsty he is; visions
of beer steins dance in his head. Across the yard, past the
rose garden and fountain, the girl peers from the house (insep-
arable, almost, from the dark).

I've got to clean up, the poet says, half to himself, facing
the collapsed blackened hull of his car. This, he says, says it all.

You refer to the girl, the philosopher ventures. Girls, I
mean.

No answer.

They gape at the mini barn skeleton, stubborn last pockets
of flame, the steaming ribs, the jigsaw melt of tin roof. The
firemen spray. A paint can does a jig by the Volvo, rolls down
the road.

Don't get all symbolic on us now, the philosopher says.

Well look at this. Look at me. I'm not even *insured*.

Mine'll cover mine.

The poet glances across toward the girl. To where the girl
must be.

This is it, he announces. I'm cleaning up.

Do it, the philosopher says. Just do your work and eat your
brown rice or whatever.

And forget her.

Forget her. The other one too.

I will, the poet declares.

Good, says his friend.

After tonight. One last night. Then that's it.

The blaze is extinguished—the mountain is saved—though the firemen maintain their positions. It looks like it's out but there's heat underneath: flare-ups occur, as both poet and philosopher know. Tonight, later, they'll quaff a whole fifth of tequila and ten bottles of beer, once the girl is gone and each realizes that the other can't sleep. In the meantime they hover, and ponder and notice, now that the steam is diminished, the glowing of stars between rafters.

The Poet Vows

Lying in bed sleepless he vows, starting now, to start rising early and not forsake work, those fertile morning hours. Then again, writing and reading are addictions like anything else; sustained sleep has its place, within reason.

He vows to make peace with his body, limit the fat, sugar and salt—to eat his brown rice, or whatever. And tell his neighbor no, when he can, to hard liquor. Everybody suffers thinning hair, finally, the slump and iguana eye-pouch. No one accepts, though some suffer more.

He vows, wrenching his damp frame in the dark, to spend cash with less stupid abandon. The new sports car he bought to replace the burned Volvo, a car he'll hate in three months— toy-tiny, you can't see the hills through the miniscule windshield—sank him in debt. (The landlady, by contrast, pocketed ten grand in insurance, opting to Band-Aid the barn: new supports merely, and a fresh tin roof. The philosopher pocketed seven, settling on an older replacement, and was surprised to see the sports car roll up. Your pecker signed that contract, he told his friend.)

To not say or do cruel things to people, or vehicles or animals.

To find a woman with whom to have things in common. Bonds built on the physical, or worse, the teacher-mentor dynamic, will fail, not to mention upset and unhinge, leave you the dry salt pile you're asking to be.

To stop misrepresenting. To say you took a walk last night

in the graveyard reciting Yeats when in fact you stayed home, waiting for Letterman to come on to have someone to eat with, is a lie, however romantic.

To believe in belief and keep living. To avoid the existential quicksand midmorning, or the office when the sun wanes in the blinds. To not dwell, mind inky with thought, on splendid wrecks that once were the future, but plod on, despite that empty bullet-shell heart.

He vows to neglect any vow, if need be—briefly—for the sake of overall good, of necessary forgivable weakness. For love, however immense and irreparable.

Poet, Philosopher, Dog

Aseat on the porch the philosopher refills the shots, tipping the bottle; the poet cracks a pistachio. The valley swells like a bright circuit board—the smog has dissolved, everything shimmers.

To the dog, the philosopher says—meaning the landlady's dog, which oddly has vanished—raising his shot glass.

To the dog, the poet chimes, raising his.

May it never return, the philosopher adds. And then grimacing, gulps.

As always it's hot, October's still summer in greater L.A. Both sit in gym shorts and sandals, no shirts. A lit candle squats on the table. The poet's out of sorts because his friend's said he's leaving. The landlady, who lives down the hill, won't hear of a girl, or wife-to-be, moving in, her apartments are Gentlemen Only, so the philosopher must make an adjustment. He's house hunting already, forsaking or about to forsake this fretwork of light, this bastion of purity in the blight that surrounds: drive-by, car-jack, kidnap and rape and cop-drama terror, not to mention traffic, the countless crisscrossing freeways. How could he *move*? the poet wonders (underpaid, high on ideals, and the view). All paths lead downhill from here. Besides, the poet is jealous. Things cooled, degree by degree, as his friend waxed matrimonial.

And now the dog, which they mutually hate, nay, conspire against—that crusty ill-mannered flea-blown hopeless non-creature—has disappeared, too.

How are your balls? the philosopher asks, referring to the poet's recent vasectomy. Not so recent, actually—he's endured the ache for five months.

Ball, he says, touching himself gingerly. The right one. It's still acting up.

You might slack off more.

I did, the poet responds. He cracks a sealed pistachio between his back teeth, then fears for his molar.

Completely?

Mostly.

Give it a chance, the philosopher says.

The world's come apart, as they say, on the poet. Sex hurts, walking hurts, it hurts to just sit. (Okay, he'd gotten the dozen ejaculations out of the way fairly quickly, bent on the sterility check, then unfettered fun: and forgot the part about ice.) His young lady isn't returning his calls, and the other's away, out of state, for a while. And now his one good male friend, his confidant, confessor, is leaving. Granted, he'll inherit the philosopher's quarters, where the view is much better. You can see the burned carport from here, the mountain in winter, miles more of the valley. But who can say how long he'll last himself? The landlady's old, and old people die—once she kicks it her thousand kids'll step in, knives and forks sharpened. And out the poor poet will go.

Three tequila shots later they hear the familiar toenail click on the lower deck, the familiar thrice-circling, slower than usual, the groan and collapse. Poet and philosopher stagger up, the latter snaps on the floodlight. The poet descends to welcome the brute. The philosopher observes from above.

Long weekend, boy? the poet says to the dog.

It's a shepherd-mix mess with a ghastly exterior, the fur missing on the lower back and sides and hind parts, not unlike a baboon. Legions of fleas speckle the gray and pink flesh; the huge charcoal balls are obscene. Worst of all, though, is the odor. You can smell it eight or ten paces off, more if there's a breeze.

The thing lifts its head, blinking, thumps its tail on the deck. Obviously the beast is unwell. It'll come skulking up as a rule, fawning, mewling, pure hangdog—vile proof of the phrase—a nightmare caricature of American Fido, loyal-dog pathos, reeking its nose-wrecking stink. This above all else is why poet and philosopher hate it. Not because it's gruesome, putrid, pathetic—it can hardly help the fact that the landlady, still in her own head a Wyoming rancher, won't do a thing to relieve it—but because it *knows* what it is, and works that to advantage, inviting threats and abuse, hangdogging up despite your injunctions, inciting the cruel you you keep under wrap, the imperial you wielding the broom (*Go! Get away! Go!*), bouncing kindling sticks off the scab-addled hide.

Another toast, the philosopher intones from above, crossing the porch for the bottle.

The dog can barely raise its head. Softening, the poet bends to stroke its snout—something the philosopher won't do—where the smell is least potent. He's both relieved and sorry it's back, he'd rather not ask himself why. He sighs, then climbs the stairs, goes in to wash his fingers in the philosopher's sink.

The next day the landlady gets news from the neighbors. They returned from Tucson to find, inside their fenced court-yard, her dog clamped to their own, their expensive dalma-tian, swollen, stuck fast—they'd called the vet, evidently, to pry them apart. Chances are, they tell the landlady, they'll have to settle on something. Liability for paternity.

By this time, however, the dog, her dog, has expired.

Death by overfucking, the philosopher says, a day or two later, in his kitchen.

The poet nods, says nothing.

The philosopher stands at the stove in baby-aspirin-orange shorts, adjusting the flame on the burner. The poet leans on the counter, hairy-backed, shirtless, sweating, in his usual dark mood. The air conditioner's broken, and they can't open the windows, thanks to the smell. The landlady had her quote-unquote Mexican bury the dog in the garden, a yard or two off, unbelievably, from her tomatoes and string beans and squash. The coyotes dug it up promptly by moonlight, disemboweled it, tore at its flanks, so she's reinterred it herself, cursing, but didn't get it quite covered. The mound outside is rank, a patch of stiff fur visible still, riffled by wind.

The philosopher drops pork strips in the wok, which hiss as they hit the hot oil. A pot of rice steams behind on the back burner. Stacks of boxes stand all around—he's half-packed, he'll be out in a week, snug at home in the house he's found by the college, a nice place, roomy, old, with no view. In a bag by the door are leftover cartons of flea-bomb, bequeathed to the poet (the old tenants left the door open often, the dog had crept in, and though the philosopher'd set off two dozen bombs, eggs were still hatching).

The poet guzzles his beer. He can still smell the carcass— sweet, horrific, huge—through the closed windows, the walls, the tar-shingle roof. The philosopher dumps the remaining pork in the pan. The poet sees himself again at his HMO doctor's, supine on the table, straining up on elbows, in pain, eyeballing tubing and tissue, strangely his and not his, pale hamburger meat.

We're glad it's dead, the philosopher says, stirring the vegetables in. That's what it comes down to.

That's it, says the poet, not altogether sure he agrees.

The problem, you see, the philosopher says—waxing philo-sophical—is that exulting in the death of things living calls into question our basic humanity. Indeed, he says, pushing his glasses back on his nose, this is the question. It's dead, it was born to be dead. And we're glad. That's hard to handle.

They take their plates and forks to the table, open fresh beers and dig in, still batting paradox around, moral and existential conundrums. The philosopher flexes his mind. The poet embellishes, taking mental note, storehousing tidbits to work up later in verse. They eat, talk with their mouths full.

The poet takes a second helping, forgets to blow, burns the roof of his mouth. The philosopher's logic escapes him at times—he doesn't traffic in such, in some ways distrusts it. But his friend's in rare form. It's good to eat, drink and spout off.

May the dog rot in peace, the philosopher says, beer upraised.

In pieces! cries the poet, one of his giggling fits coming on.

May coyotes strew him all the way to El Monte—

May his rotten limbs flap! Unburied! Unwept!

The gloom's gone for a change. The poet forgets his girl's tossed him off, stops fearing the notion that he, unlike his friend, may not be nor is fit to be married. Of course they'll keep meeting, he thinks, here and in town, new wife or not, though his guts say it's unlikely. The new tenant will be quiet and pleasant, he's certain—he can't imagine at this point the brash young man who'll move in, stereo blaring, the unending shouting (Fuck, dude, fuck you!). He even stops feeling bad for the dog. And expels that lingering thought: I could've bathed and cared for the beast, which, given health and affection, would have survived. No, like the hotel keeper told Inspector Clouseau, it wasn't his dog.

Lights twinkle on in the valley. Dusk settles. The gloom's gone completely. The poet's all overflowing spontaneous feeling, so welcome in this time of no time for tranquility. He loves this man, he decides. His good true friend and fellow fire-sufferer, the philosopher. So solid and cogent, so much more upright, forthright and free of deception, than he. He'd like to say as much but can't, afraid he might cry. He imagines them mashing the dog underground thirty years hence, by letter, whatever, wherever they are, united in death by what they hated alive. All the more poignant, it seems, for on some level, with dinner over, the brandy bottle out on the table, he knows it's the end.

Later, downstairs, asleep and in bed, clad in jockstrap to protect the raw plumbing, the poet dreams of the ultimate girl, a mishmash of girls he's known and many he hasn't, the exactly right girl, who must, who does, who simply has to exist.

Asleep also, the philosopher—too philosophical to be the Christian he was as a child—dreams of heaven's tribunal. He sees the dog on high at the right hand of God, flaring its ethereal nostrils. Penitent, shambling up to the throne, the philosopher kneels, the radiant father rumbling above: *Pet the dog! Pet the dog!*

Eamon Grennan

Traveler

You could feel a passion for invisibility: to be a fly on the wall,
the pitcher's ear, the child in the corner
with his eyes closed: you could grow fat on that, full of years.

Like a dog going round and round, you circle the space
you've come back to, trying to find
some comfort, something that says you're at home now.

You'd even pray for the enlarging hush of the owl's ear
or the hawk's high wide-angle lens
that reads the world like a map: there, a grassblade shaking.

Blackbird among the daisies, you'd say, *shout across water,
wind on the shore, lamb bleating from the hill,
the song the scytheblade sings being sharpened by a stone.*

Your friend has been weeding his potato drills. He stops
and sits on a rock for a cigarette. The sun
has been shining for days and days. *Its a gift*, he tells you.

A solitary thrush, with its heart in its mouth on a high branch,
performs a dozen unfinished songs at dusk
as if it were just itself and the world. No sense to it. Listen.

Such fury and repose swelling that speckled breast, warm
in the late daylight: you can see the beak
open and close, open and close, shivering into music.

Wrapped in the web's white winding-sheet, the bluebottle
makes another music, sawing the room in half:
you note it down till it stops, each repeated live driving note.

A small egg buried in the weeds: white, broken, source
   unknown.
What else are you missing under your nose?
When you open the door, the scent of fresh-cut grass swims in.

There's a huge yellow-edged summer moon
hanging all alone in a powder-blue sky:
a body dense with its own weight, dependent on nothing.

You must stand back from nothing. No more pussyfooting
from the crux of the matter. You could travel
at the speed of light, not looking back.

Two Poems by Carin Besser

Leopold von Sacher-Masoch

Morning came, in buckles and lace,
asking to be held. The birds began
with sultry murmurs, their notes soon rising like sirens.
The bars of sunlight on the uncarpeted floor

have reminded you of something.
Somewhere it is still midnight;
a prison courtyard glows beneath a quarter moon.
But your mistress was at her cruellest by day,

her complexion blanching in the sun,
her frosted skin never warming.
Beauty must live as a fugitive
but will always leave a mark about your throat.

The clinicians have misunderstood:
to translate an abstraction into pain
was to make history felt, to ask that love
reveal its scars. Pleasure resides in its own

suspension, and your windows have kept
their watered silk, your walls, thin as parchment,
their delicate, dark-spined volumes.
An oil painting's hung above the fireplace:

your Venus, in the bolder colors
of the Flemish school, her dark hair
in a Grecian knot, shivers beneath
her heavy furs, frozen in an arctic climate.

A Tapestry

And so it happened that the two sat down
to a contest: with the blank sky sprawling
above them, the pale sun filtering through cracks
in the forest, they worked for three solid hours,

or until Athena had made from raw wool
a picture of mortal transgressions:
the barren hills that once were men,
the sad Pygmy queen become a crane,

and Cinyras on the temple steps, weeping
at the stony knees of his lost daughters.
In the foreground, a smoldering blue mountain
and a dozen heavenly powers rehearsing

their opulence. All of this in colors
that had never been imagined: rose-lavenders,
violets laced with golden thread.
Meanwhile, upon Arachne's loom,

Leda appeared, flat on her back,
awaiting the swan's feathery climax;
then the bull between Europa's thighs,
so lifelike and bleary-eyed, the onlookers wept

to see him. Of course, Arachne lost
and took her transformation badly.
From then on, she sought out darker haunts,
her hair falling out in her hands, her every mood

black and shriveled. The work suffered,
became a mere skeleton of its former self,

more raw idea than craft, but it put food on the table.
Which is not to say she didn't long

for things to be different,
for the whole fabric of her intention
to reflect the world, while the world, hopeless
and virulent, crawled to its own dusty corner.

Scott Minar

Toward the Skin

for J.S.

My friend stops his father
in the doorway, asks him
to show me the numbers burned
into his wrist like small white

promises. He asks this so easily
it surprises

me, as his father lifts
a hairy forearm to the hall
light and holds stiff
as sculpture

while we watch
and wait for history

to move past us. This is the same friend
I lie with in a tent
near the highway,
something desperate in our awkward

moves toward the skin,
some inevitable ride

we must take
away from each other. He tastes like salt,
as if he were made of it,
more like salt

than anything
I've ever known. And if after that

my landscape turned strange
and I ran from the burnt field
of my desires
as if I could get around it

and my world seemed
to collapse

from within, I ask what dark passage
was I called to, what rage
was I used, like so many others,
to answer?

Edwin Gallaher

Dreams of Ferdinand

I. New World

With a great scuffle,
the meeting adjourned.
Calm turned to storm.

Waves swung the gavels
of a spinning ship's wheel,
a rash jurisprudence.

Winds from council wars
blew dusk to midnight.
Sex, labor, crow's nest, hull—

all was out of order.
Oyster-hooded, usurped
like the dead. Father,

in the rounded Bermudas
of the soul, a storm-surge
through breaking waves

grinds music for savages.
Such howls are one urge, Father.
For neither love nor war.

II. Mirrors

Appealing to the shut-in lover
is to foresee betrayals everywhere.
Or to pen, as new kings must—
novels, letters, aphorisms—
all to imperialist air, conquering
air itself. Breathe inward,

outward, sunk in castaway rags
pervasive as armor. True solitude
forges no concerti, no messages
tucked in bottles, but hawks instead
news for Caliban: *you're puny—*
nothing—a conspiracy of shadows,

blank eyes lighting up the dark,
mirrors turned to a wall.
The loaded dice of storms roll over
the cleft sides of the island.
In the breast the heart throws itself
at an unseen and boltless door.

III. Prayer

Sea, take me with open arms,
deft sleeves, frothy collar.
Let thinned weeds flag shell-
cowled mysteries. Bilge-crested
hulls of sea are luring me.
Dawn breeds dusk, horizon's
the same. Next tide's reprise
is when I leave. To sing's to pray,·
Island. Sing of me no more.

Florence Cassen Mayers

96 and B'Way

One A.M.
two cops
three teens nabbed
four gunshots
five patrol cars
six suspects

six innocent bystanders
one ambulance
five wounded
two fatalities
four stretchers
three TV cameras

three butcher knives
six razors
four switchblades
one pipe
two machetes
five brass knuckles

five interviews:
three broken homes
two pregnant girlfriends
six high school dropouts
one ringleader
four abused childhoods

four truants
five first offenders
one parole violator:
(three armed robberies)
six drug users
two juveniles:

two names withheld
four drug dealers
six drifters
five arrests
three detained
one perpetrator flees on foot.

Two slain, five indictments,
four plea bargains, three sentences
six months/one year.

Three Poems by Michael Berryhill

Bad News

Through the blown clouds and the plate glass,
sunlight slides across the chrome fountains.
The Muzak drones like some huge machine
the last gross century switched on and then forgot.

I can put on my black suit with the faint stripes
and watch the ballet. A spider the size of a pearl
explores the blue vacancy of my tie. Meanwhile
the weevils have crawled out of the rice,
leaving their greasy dead among the spice jars.
The sunset has gone vulgar as neon.
I can choose between whiskey and tea, or have both.
There is more than one cigar and I can still write my mother.
The shoppers stroll past while you weep
into the telephone black as commas.

The Problem

The problem was, it was never quite
Expected. Days passed like water through
A sieve. To analyze: thoughts crushed like ice.
Lips creaked arguments, the sky burned blue.
One night a red glow filtered through some trees,
Filtered through some roses, pale in a pale
Light: simple hell of oil refineries.
This glow, this boil, was not a simple smell.
Beyond the city's stench, nebulae drifted,
Expanding like balloons; a gray gull

280

Bent on food careened over houses, lifted
A constant wail. Sensation's always cruel.
Still it was not expected that in that air,
She could make love seem natural, and fair.

Quitting Football

This decision has not been easy.
Daily when I pull my shorts
over my scarred knees, I think,
"Football has been good to me."
When I recall the yards of Dixie cups,
the highways of Ace bandage,
the sweet perfume of liniment,
and the trainer's gnarled hands,
I know I owe football a lot.

The sportswriters abused me with neglect,
but that's not their fault.
It's not in their nature to understand
the subtleties of the game.
It's more than Xs and Os,
more than the slotback right, the wishbone T
or splitting the zone.
It's the way a player walks as if on eggshells
off the field, it's the slow grace
of bones knitting back,
it's the nightmare huddle where
you can't remember the plays.

I know that but for artificial turf,
each fall the fresh grass would call to me.
I might have a few years left,
but would they be good years?

I want to find my wife Shirley,
whom I've never met.
This is a good town to raise kids in.
I'm hanging up my jock and getting into real estate.
I've been a free agent long enough.

Escapes

Nicole Cooley

On Christmas day, Travis calls from the rig. Miranda hears
the phone ring and runs in the house to answer it, glad for
an excuse to leave the party in the yard. All afternoon, she
has been leaning back against the wire fence that separates
Travis's mother's house from theirs, a paper plate balanced
on her knees, writing a letter to Lee Vickery in her head.
*Dear Lee, I have these dreams. Do you think about me? The
warden steals your letters—I never get them.*

For three years, as long as she and Travis have been married,
he has spent the winter working offshore, and she has gone
alone to his mother's Christmas crawfish boil. She knows
Travis's mother feels sorry for her. Once, she overheard his
mother telling him, "Not a single person loves that girl but
us." Everyone thinks Miranda is an orphan. In Travis's family,
there are one hundred and two people, not including Miranda. They crowd the backyard, grandmothers sitting in lawn
chairs, teenagers with radios on beach towels, children playing

kick the can. Travis's mother fills trash cans with crushed ice to keep the food cold.

Every year, Miranda tells Travis that she doesn't want to go to this party. Last year she offered to drive down to the coast and spend Christmas with him. "You can't do that," Travis said. "Women never come on the rig. Nobody brings their wives here." Miranda knew that was a lie. The truth is, she thinks, Travis likes to be away from her, likes to eat his dinner in the crew's television room with the other men and then go back to working on the drill pipe. After all, she knows, he could come home to New Orleans. It's not as if he's been drafted into the army. It's not as if he's in prison.

"Miranda, honey." Travis's voice crackles over the wire. "I miss you."

Miranda stands in his parents' bedroom, leaning against the wall. The room is cool and dark. The air conditioner hums. She tries to breathe slowly. Through the window, she watches Travis's mother brush shells off her lap onto the grass as her husband reaches for her, rests his arm on her shoulder.

"Are you there? They only let me make one phone call. Talk to me, honey. I've got two shifts of guys waiting behind me to call their wives."

"Merry Christmas." Her voice sounds flat. "Do you want to talk to your mother?"

"Miranda, don't be mad at me, come on. It's not my fault that I can't be with you."

Miranda lets the phone slide from her fingers; the receiver bangs against the wall. Travis hasn't left Morgan City since the beginning of the summer. Lee Vickery would come home if he could. She read in the newspaper that he has escaped three times. The police always capture him. Someday soon, she tells herself, Lee will break out and come for her. One morning, she'll open her screen door and he'll be standing on the steps, waiting there.

Every day, for the last month, Miranda's mother has called her, from a different place each time. She calls collect. The

first question Miranda always asks is, Where are you? Her
mother answers, Jackson, Corpus Christi, Little Rock, always
a city nearby Miranda but not too close. Miranda imagines
her mother circling overhead, like a plane or a dangerous
storm, before she picks a place where she will land. Her
mother talks about traveling, what it feels like to drive from
one town to another. "I'm completely free," she says. "Do
you realize that? I don't have to report to a single soul."
What Miranda doesn't mention is that her mother has been
free her whole life, at least since she had Miranda. Her mother
has never been married. When Miranda was born, her mother
left her in New Orleans with her own mother and drove away.

The year Miranda turned nineteen, her grandmother died
and her mother appeared. At the funeral home, during the
wake, a woman with short, bleached hair sat down next to
Miranda, took her hands in her lap and said, "I'm your
mother, but call me Faith." When she pressed her fingers
into Miranda's palm, her skin felt cool and dry. Miranda
stared at the woman, afraid to believe that what she said
could be true. "We're going to be together now, just the two
of us. Everything is all right."

For three days, Miranda and her mother lived in a motel
on Airline Highway, near the New Orleans airport. Miranda
only left the room to refill the ice bucket and to get more
Cokes from the soda machine to mix with her mother's gin.
She brought back peanut-butter crackers from another machine for dinner. The vending machines were at the edge of
the parking lot. All day, the lot was full of pickup trucks and
motorcycles, but it was empty every night. Miranda's mother
did not leave the room. She hooked the DO NOT DISTURB sign
over the doorknob and looked out the window at the parking
lot. "There are awful men out there," she said. "But don't
worry, we're safe and sound in here." Her mother hugged
her then, and Miranda could feel her bones, the flutter of
her heart. Her mother felt light and delicate, like a bird.

They stayed up late and slept in the same bed, curled
against each other, till past noon. Her mother pulled the

drapes—"Do you want those men to see in?"—and covered
the bedside lamp with a red scarf because she said light hurt
her eyes. The room glowed a soft pink. As they watched
TV, her mother drank gin from a water glass and brushed
Miranda's hair, smoothing the waves against her back. Her
grandmother stopped brushing Miranda's hair when she
turned twelve, telling Miranda she was too old. Her mother
was gentle, not like her grandmother, who used to pull too
hard. Miranda often fell asleep as her mother brushed.

Sometimes, her mother washed Miranda's hair. As Miranda
leaned her head back into the bathroom sink, her mother
poured warm water from the ice bucket over her head. The
water sent a tingle up and down Miranda's spine. The sham-
poo came in a glass bottle and smelled like tangerines. Afterwards, while Miranda waited for her hair to dry, a towel
twisted around her head, her mother dabbed Shalimar behind
Miranda's ears and along the back of her neck. Miranda loved
the touch of her mother's hands in her hair, on her skin.

She tried not to ask her mother questions, but she let one
slip out and ruined everything. It was the evening of the
third day. Miranda and her mother lay in bed, watching a
black and white movie. Her mother's eyes were closed. She
looked calm and peaceful, and Miranda asked the question
she'd been thinking about since her grandmother died.
"What happened to my father?" she said. "Do you know
where he is?"

Her mother's eyes snapped open. She looked mad. "Why
did you ask that?"

"I want to know." Miranda took a deep breath and went on.
"Maybe we could go see him sometime. I want to meet him."

Her mother began to laugh. She threw her head to the
side, pressed her face to the pillow and laughed and laughed.
It was a terrible, high-pitched noise. It sounded more like
crying than laughing, but when her mother sat up, Miranda
knew she wasn't crying. "You want to know about your father?" her mother said. "You don't have a father. There was
a boy at school who wanted me and I let him and I got

you. I don't know where he is. I can't even remember his last name."

There was a long silence. Miranda turned away from her mother. She stared at the carpet. She tried as hard as she could not to cry.

"Fix me another drink, will you? I'm going to take a bath." Her mother carried her glass into the bathroom.

Miranda poured the gin. She sat on the edge of the bed. She heard the tap running. Forty-five minutes went by. Miranda knocked, but there was no response. "Mama, open the door, you're scaring me," she yelled, but when she leaned on the door, it swung open easily. The bathroom was filled with steam. Water poured over the side of the tub and onto the tiled floor. The tub was filled to the top but empty. There was no one there. For a minute, Miranda thought her mother had disappeared by magic, dissolved, evaporated in a cloud of steam. Then she saw the window, cracked open to reveal a space, a wedge of moonlight, empty air.

Miranda never told anyone about those three days. Six months later, she married Travis. She told him that her mother had died at the moment she was born.

Now Miranda is careful not to ask her mother questions because she might frighten her. If she says something wrong, her mother might stop calling. She tries to tell herself that she doesn't care, that if she quit hearing from her mother, it wouldn't matter, but even as she thinks it, she knows it isn't true.

There are things Miranda hasn't told her mother, but one bothers her more than the rest: her mother doesn't know she married Travis. Miranda knows it would never occur to her mother to ask if Miranda were married or even if she has a boyfriend. Her mother never asks about anyone. She has never mentioned Miranda's grandmother, her own mother. If her mother knew about her life with Travis, maybe, Miranda thinks, her mother could listen to her story about Lee. Miranda has not talked about Lee Vickery with anyone.

Tonight, when she comes home from the crawfish boil, she fills up one of her grandmother's jelly jars with ice and vodka and waits for her mother to call. She thinks how she cannot stand to spend another Christmas alone. But she can't think of how she can make Travis come home.

Miranda walks through the house with her glass. She has not decorated any of the rooms. She doesn't see the point in fixing up a house to live in alone. She didn't want to live here in the first place. Travis's mother owns the house; she leased it to them as a wedding present. Every month, she takes the rent money out of the paycheck Travis sends to her. When they got married, Miranda wanted to leave New Orleans, to move to someplace she'd never been, someplace completely different, Texas maybe. "How could I leave my family?" Travis said, shaking his head, when she told him this. "You don't have a family, so you can't understand."

After three years, Miranda still has not unpacked her boxes with *Miranda Rivers* written on their sides, the name that isn't hers anymore. Unbleached muslin curtains left by the last tenant cover the windows. All the furniture in the house came from Travis's mother's attic. Miranda has not arranged any of the chairs or filled the bookshelves. This summer, when she was coming over everyday, Travis's mother left a pile of magazines on Miranda's porch—*Southern Living, House Beautiful*—and, for one afternoon, Miranda read them, flipped through the shiny pages, looked at the women standing proudly by their glittering floors, freshly painted cupboards and bouquets of artificial flowers. The pictures made her feel depressed. She threw them all away.

Her mother calls from Oklahoma City. "Mama?" Miranda says, when her mother pauses to take a breath in the middle of a long speech about the Oklahoma dog races. "Do you know that I'm married?"

"Hmmmm." Her mother's voice sounds sleepy now, as if Miranda woke her from a dream. "Married," she repeats.

"Three years ago, I married Travis. I wanted to invite you to the wedding, but I didn't have any idea where to find you." As soon as she says that, Miranda knows she is lying. She couldn't have invited her mother because no one knows that her mother exists.

"Married," she says in the same, slow voice. "So you're married. How long have you known Trafalgar?"

"Travis, Mama, his name is Travis."

Suddenly, her mother's tone sharpens. "Why the hell did you run off and do a thing like this? How could you get married?"

"I didn't run off. I stayed right here," Miranda tells her.

"Let me talk to this man," her mother says. "Put him on the phone right now."

"I can't." Miranda bites her lip till it hurts. "He's not here."

"He's already run away from you, hasn't he?" Her mother lets out a short laugh.

Miranda can't answer. For a few minutes, neither of them speaks. Miranda stares at the swirled pattern on the glass, at the pool of moonlight on the kitchen floor. Then her mother breaks the silence. "I was telling you about the track," she says, her voice fast and bright again. "I put two dollars on a dog named Telepathy for the daily double and got back four times my money." Through the screen door, Miranda watches Travis's mother empty the garbage cans from the party, ice glittering in the dark grass.

All summer, there was a manhunt on for Lee Vickery. The newspaper said he killed two teenage girls in West Virginia. The Louisiana police wanted him on charges of auto theft and fraud. Miranda remembers the day she opened the newspaper and saw the article, June 15, three days after Travis left for Morgan City, swearing he would be back soon. Miranda was sitting on her porch with Travis's mother, who had been coming over every day since he left. She brought over fried chicken and casserole pans full of stewed okra, the vegetable Miranda hates most. Travis's mother heated up the food, ate dinner with Miranda and went home late at night. "You're all alone in the world," she told Miranda.

Miranda saw the picture and took a deep breath, set her coffee cup down on the porch railing. She recognized him right away. Lee's features were blurred, the outlines of his body darkened. He had grown a mustache, but the newspaper photo reminded her of his yearbook picture when they were seniors. Under the photo in the newspaper were the words, "Beware: Lee Vickery is considered extremely dangerous. He is heavily armed."

"What are you looking at?" Travis's mother stood behind her chair. "Who on earth's that guy?" She pointed to the newspaper.

"Some man the police are looking for," Miranda said, trying to force her voice to sound casual.

"Well, they're always looking for somebody," Travis's mother said, settling back into her seat on the porch swing. "I hope this one is nowhere around here. Half of those criminals never get caught. If they find this one, they ought to send him to the electric chair. What'd he do?"

"He might have shot some people," Miranda said. "They're not sure." She carried the newspaper into the kitchen and cut out the story and the picture.

That night, Miranda had the first Lee Vickery dream. She is standing at the edge of Airline Highway, in front of the row of old motels. Cars and trucks whiz past in a blur of traffic, but the highway is completely silent. She can't hear any sounds. Miranda has no suitcase or shopping bag or purse. Her hands are empty. She is leaving New Orleans, but she doesn't have any idea of a place to go. Lee's blue truck pulls up. He leans out the window on the driver's side. "Hey," he calls. "Miranda, I've been looking for you. Let's go for a ride." Lee smiles. His teeth are clean and white. "Come on," he says, reaching over to unlock the door. "What are you afraid of?" Miranda climbs in. When she looks at him, she relaxes, feels happy. His hair is still sandy blond, cut short. His blue shirt is pressed and tucked into his jeans. He rests his arm on her shoulder as he begins to drive.

Now Miranda cuts the articles out and tapes them in the

empty family album she hides in her underwear drawer. She keeps her letters to Lee there too, the letters the prison sends back to her, unopened. Since the police caught Lee, on the Fourth of July, and since his trial, he has escaped three times. He has killed three more girls, the papers say.

For a long time, when she was little, Miranda believed that her grandmother was her mother. Every girl she knew lived with a woman who was her mother, so she believed it was the same for her. The other girls lived with their fathers too, but Miranda told herself she liked not having one. Fathers, she thought, got in the way. At the end of the day, they slouched in their favorite chairs, chairs no one else was allowed to sit in, drank beer from a can and yelled at whoever came near. From what Miranda observed in the houses of her friends, it was better not to have a father. Whenever she did think about her own father, she figured he must have died when she was too young to remember him.

In third grade, during a recess kickball game, Michael Belson tripped Miranda on the asphalt, saying, "You don't have a mother. Everybody knows you have to live with your grandmother because you don't have a mother." Miranda didn't cry in front of Michael, but when she got home, as she told her grandmother what happened, she began to cry.

Her grandmother listened. Then she fixed a glass of milk flavored with vanilla, and when Miranda finished drinking it, her grandmother tucked her into bed. As she was leaving Miranda's room, she said, "You've got your own mother. You might as well know. She's somewhere else."

"Where?" Miranda sat up in bed. "I could write to her and tell her to come home."

"She doesn't care about you," her grandmother said. She snapped the window shade down hard. "You have to understand that. She gave you away."

"Tell me a story about my mother," Miranda said.

"There aren't any stories about your mother." Her grandmother flicked off the ceiling light. "Now go to sleep."

The ringing of the phone wakes Miranda in the night, in the middle of one of the dreams about Lee. They sit side by side in the truck. She leans her head against his shoulder, and he drives with one hand on the wheel. She smells his skin, his sweat, the scent of cigarette smoke that clings to him. She breathes him in. He kisses her hair. Miranda does not want to wake up from this dream. As soon as she opens her eyes, everything fades.

She looks at the clock on the dresser. It's 3:15. She covers her head with her pillow to drown out the sound, but the ringing won't quit. Finally, she stumbles down the hall and into the kitchen to answer the phone. She hears Travis's voice. "Miranda, honey, I'm sorry I couldn't be with you today. Please, honey, talk to me. Why did you hang up on me this afternoon at Mama's house?" He is whispering.

Miranda imagines him standing in a dark room, the television a square of blue light, covering the receiver with his fingers to muffle the sound of his voice. She fills a glass with tap water and vodka and sits at the table without turning on a light. She wonders if Travis could be imagining her at this moment, wearing one of his undershirts, sitting in the dark kitchen. "Miranda, don't you see that things could be a lot worse? Listen, this one guy, Pike Johnson, he got assigned to a North Sea rig, and he was stuck in Norway for Christmas. Christ, he doesn't even know the language. Honey, are you there? Say something."

Miranda sips her drink; it's clean and bitter, slides easily down her throat. "Are you telling me to feel sorry for his wife?" Her voice sounds meaner than she intended.

"If you're so lonely there, call somebody," Travis says. "Call up some of the girls you hung around with in high school."

"They're married. They stay home at night with their husbands."

"Well, get a job to keep yourself busy. I don't make that much money down here."

"I wouldn't know how much money you make," Miranda says. She wants to test him, to see how far she can go before he gets mad. "I never see your money."

"That's not fair, Miranda. You know our arrangement. I sign my checks over to Mama, and she gives you as much as you need." He is speaking louder now.

Miranda looks down at her bare feet, pale against the floor, like fish glowing underwater. All of a sudden, her head aches and her eyes are filling up with tears. "Travis, come home now," she whispers. "Please. If you don't, something awful is going to happen."

"Miranda, calm down. You're just fine." Travis sounds nervous.

"You have to come home." She tries not to let him hear her crying. "This is your home, isn't it? Don't you want to see me?"

"Maybe at the end of February I can get a few days off," he says. "Look, Miranda, there's someone else waiting to use this phone. I have to hang up."

Miranda finishes her drink. She knows that Travis was lying. As she rinses her glass in the sink, the phone rings again. She grabs the receiver after the second ring. "Travis?"

The operator's voice, bored and smooth, asks her to accept the charges for a call from Faith Rivers. "Mama? Where are you? What's wrong?" Her mother only calls this late at night when she is drunk.

"I want to know something," her mother says. "Tell me the truth."

"Mama, tell me where you are." Miranda's stomach tightens.

"In Arkansas, somewhere near a tollbooth. I was driving on the highway and I pulled over to ask you this question. The truth, you swear?" Miranda hears her mother draw in a breath; she must be lighting a cigarette. Miranda thinks that she doesn't even know what brand of cigarettes her mother smokes. "Do you hate me?" her mother asks. "If you do, I want to know."

"Mama." Miranda sighs. Now she feels so tired, exhausted, that she can't think of anything but how much she wants to lie down in her own bed, close her eyes and shut out everything.

"Am I your friend? Or am I just your mother?" She asks. "Tell me the absolute truth."

Miranda takes a deep breath, ready to tell her mother what she wants to hear to calm her down, but when she starts to speak, she realizes she means it. "Mama," she says. " You're like a sister to me. You're my best friend."

Since Thanksgiving, when Travis did not come home, the only time Miranda leaves the house is when she goes next door. Travis did not take his key ring when he left in June. Although his mother doesn't know it, Miranda has the dead-bolt key to Travis's parents' house hidden in her underwear drawer with the sent-back letters and the clippings about Lee. Miranda always waits until Travis's mother has gone out, till her blue Plymouth pulls out of the driveway and down the street and then Miranda sneaks in.

She slips in through the chinaberry bush at the side of the house and onto the porch, the screen door creaking as she fits the key into the lock. She likes the fact that she breaks in using a key. It's a shotgun house, each room opening onto the next like a tunnel. Her heart always beats fast, but she walks all the way through the house, taking her time, touching her fingertips to the walls, steadying herself as she goes, as if she's walking through water.

On her journey through the house, Miranda always ends up in Travis's old room. His mother keeps his bedroom as if Travis were still a little boy, as if he had never married Miranda and any day now might change his mind, come back. His mother was pregnant seven times, but Travis is the only baby that survived. When Miranda was first getting to know him, he told her that he was an only child, and she was glad. It was one of the reasons she liked him. She imagined he would be lonely, like her, and that they would live alone together somewhere, never needing anyone but each other. Later, she found out about his family.

Lying in Travis's bed, she always has the best dreams about Lee. She sets the alarm clock to wake her in half an hour, and she makes herself dream. In her favorite dream, Lee pulls the truck off the road to stop for the night. Miranda doesn't know what state they're in, or even what town, but she is happy to be with Lee and doesn't care where they've been or where they're going. They sleep on a blanket in the open back of the truck. Lee holds her all night, his arms circling her waist, touching his lips to her shoulders, to the back of her neck.

Sometimes, she looks up at Travis's ceiling, painted blue and sprinkled with tiny silver stars. Travis wanted to be an astronaut when he was a little boy. His mother painted the ceiling to match the sky. Whenever Miranda stares at it for a long time, she gets dizzy, has to grip the edges of the mattress, hold herself stretched flat as the room spins.

Clippings of their high-school football games are taped to the wall above the bed, the newspaper yellowed, curling at the corners. Travis's mother saves these things. Two photos, of Miranda and of Mary Kay Kessler, are jammed into the rim of the dresser mirror. Mary Kay is a distant cousin of Travis's, a cheerleader he went to the prom with in tenth grade. Now she is married to another distant cousin and has two children. In Miranda's photograph, her face is blurred, her hair a dark cloud, blue-black her grandmother called it, against her face. The girl in that picture looks scared.

Sometimes, Miranda looks through the yearbooks, which are stacked under the bed. She has found three different photographs of Lee: his senior portrait, a shot of him dressed in a blue uniform for band and a baby picture. The yearbook editor collected a baby picture from everyone in the senior class, Miranda remembers. She can't recognize Travis's photograph or her own, but she often looks at Lee's picture. Travis was someone Miranda barely knew in high school, a boy she never paid attention to. When she studies Lee's picture, she thinks of how her grandmother used to tell her that every crook and criminal, every bad man, was a baby at one time, someone a mother loved.

The next day, the phone wakes Miranda at noon. "I'm going to Ocean Springs for New Year's Eve," her mother says. "I've heard they set off fireworks on the beach." It is as if she never called from Arkansas the night before.

"Mama, Travis and I went to Ocean Springs for our honeymoon. It's only a few hours from New Orleans." Miranda takes a deep breath to prepare herself for what she is going to say. "You could visit me."

Her mother continues talking, as if she doesn't hear. "They throw bottle rockets out over the Gulf to make it look like the water is on fire."

"I could take the bus to meet you someplace in between," Miranda says. "Please."

"Don't be ridiculous. You can't do that." Her mother sounds irritated now. "They sell fireworks everywhere in Mississippi at Christmas, did you know that?"

Miranda wishes that she had not asked. "Mama, I just heard Travis's car pull in the driveway. I have to go now."

"You want to get rid of me," her mother says. "Do you think I don't know that? Travis isn't home. Travis doesn't come home. He's left you. He's never coming back."

For the first time, Miranda hangs up on her mother, slams the receiver down hard, her hand shaking, and lifts it off the hook, drops it on the floor.

Miranda starts another letter to Lee Vickery. She sits at the table, wearing Travis's undershirt, sweating even though the air in the room is cool. She puts the phone in the refrigerator so she can't hear the operator's recorded voice, "If you would like to make a call, please hang up . . ." Miranda writes, *Dear Lee*, then stops, twirls the pencil between her fingers. She tries to concentrate on the letter, to not think of her mother. What she wants to say is, *if you love me, if you care anything about me, find me.* But she doesn't want to sound as if she is desperate. She wants a way to tell Lee that she needs him without sounding scared.

When she was Travis's girlfriend, before she became his

wife, Miranda was always careful not to show him how she felt, to shrug her shoulders and say, "I don't care" as much as she could. Sometimes, if she knew he was supposed to call, she would stand next to the phone and let it ring. She told Travis, "It doesn't matter to me if I see you every night or not." She let him know that at any moment she might break up with him, might leave him for some other man. In those days, she gave him a choice: he could stay with her or not. Every day, she expected him to leave, and she couldn't make herself believe that he would not. After four months, he took her on a picnic on the edge of the river, gave her an opal ring that once belonged to his mother and told her he wanted to get married.

She could send a letter to Travis, could erase *Dear Lee* and write in her husband's name. She traces the letters of his name on the tabletop. Travis has never mailed her a single letter from Morgan City, and Miranda knows there isn't anything she means that she could ever say.

Although it is the middle of the afternoon, Miranda goes back to bed. She takes off Travis's shirt, but the sheets are damp, sticking to her skin, so she pulls the shirt over her head again. Sunlight filters through the curtains. She climbs out of bed to draw them closed, but the room won't turn dark. Miranda squeezes her eyes shut to block out the light.

She wants to dream about Lee, to see herself with him, happy, driving away from her real life, but nothing works. Not imagining his hands on her body. Not picturing his face. Instead, when she finally falls asleep, she dreams a different kind of Lee Vickery dream.

She crouches on the ground at the edge of the road, smears the license plate of the truck with mud so no one can make out the numbers. Lee hands her a gun. It feels heavy: she puts it in the pocket of her jeans.

The girl stands at the side of the highway in Star City, West Virginia. Her hair is long, the color of butter, parted in the center and so clean. Her hair is important to her.

She pays attention to it every day—shampoos, special rinses, perfume on the back of her neck. Her hair ripples over her shoulders, down her back. In her purse, there is a tortoiseshell comb with a real pearl handle, given to her by her mother. She wears no makeup. Her eyes are wide, clear blue.

She waits at the edge of the highway because she and her mother had a fight. Later, her mother will not remember what they disagreed about, something small. Maybe the mother didn't like the girl's clothes that day. Maybe she told her daughter that her skirt was too short to wear to school. The girl slammed her bedroom door and ran out of the house, her purse slapping against her side as she crossed the lawn.

She has taken rides on the back streets that run through town, but never on Route 79. Lee slows the truck at the side of the road. "Go ahead," he tells Miranda. "You know what to do."

"You want a ride?" Miranda calls to the girl.

The girl looks at Miranda as if she is studying her to make sure everything's okay. There are weirdos out there; she knows you have to be careful.

Lee leans over Miranda to look out the window at the girl. He smiles. "Come on," he says. Miranda unlocks the door. "What are you afraid of?"

Miranda wants to wake up. She doesn't want to see the end of this dream. She knows that she and Lee are going to kill the girl together.

Someone is knocking on the front door, pressing the doorbell, yelling Miranda's name. "Go away," she whispers, but she is glad to be awake, out of the dream. She is curled under the quilt. "Please leave me alone." Sweat trickles down her neck; her hair is wet against her cheek. The knocking stops, then, a few minutes later, begins again, this time louder. Now there seem to be two people knocking, banging their fists against the door. Miranda wonders for a minute if the police have come for her, to ask for information about Lee. Now a hand raps on the window beside her bed. Travis's

father's voice: "If she won't let us in, she won't let us in."
Miranda pictures him standing in the grass by the fence at
the side of the house, shrugging his shoulders, giving up
on her.

Travis's mother says, "There is something wrong in there.
I know it. She's a strange one, but she's never done anything
like this before."

"We can come back tomorrow," his father says. Their shoes
crunch across the grass.

Miranda reaches one arm out of the quilt, reaches for the
warm vodka she poured into the bathroom glass. She tells
herself the drink will make her forget the dream. She will
force herself to drink slowly so she doesn't have to stand up,
get out of bed, walk through the house to get more.

When Miranda was little, her grandmother never allowed
her to touch the quilt that now covers her bed. Her grandmother made the quilt when her mother was a child. She
kept it folded in tissue paper in her hope chest, as if it were
like the family china kept in the cupboard behind glass, too
precious to use. Now Miranda knows that her grandmother
must have wanted to save the quilt, to preserve it, all those
little squares of cloth that once belonged to her mother's
dresses, all the pieces of the lost daughter she hid safely away.

Her hands shaking, Miranda dials the number of the rig.
She has never called Travis there before, but she feels that
she has to talk to him. She is tired and dizzy from lying in
bed all day. The dream runs through her mind, over and
over, and she needs to tell someone about Lee Vickery. The
receiver is cold against her ear. She has to repeat Travis's
name three times before the man at the other end agrees to
look for him. Miranda waits. She pushes her hair off the back
of her neck. She thinks how Travis will be mad and how she
doesn't care.

"Miranda? Why are you calling? Is Mama okay?"

"They're all fine," she says. She grips the phone till her
wrist hurts.

"Who?" Travis says. "What are you talking about?"

"Everybody is fine," she says.

"I only have a minute. If nothing's wrong, why are you calling? I've told you never to call me here." Travis sounds annoyed now.

"I have to tell you something." Her voice is hoarse. "Listen to me."

"I am listening." She hears talking in the background, a man laughing.

"There's someone else," she says, "I think you ought to know."

"I can't hear you. What did you say?" Travis asks.

"There is someone else," she repeats, and she waits. For a minute or two, Travis doesn't respond.

Then he says, in a slow, patient voice, as if he is talking to a child, "Miranda, honey, you don't know what you're saying. You are exhausted. You're worn out. Mama told me that you've been upset. She said you haven't been yourself. Why don't you go to bed, and we'll talk about this in a few—"

Miranda hangs up the phone in the middle of his sentence. She starts to cry. Travis does not believe her.

Miranda turns on the bathtub faucet and lets the hot water run. She opens the bathroom window to let in the moonlight, the night breeze. When the tub is full, she takes off Travis's shirt and climbs in. She leans her head against the cold porcelain. The ends of her hair float on the surface of the water. She closes her eyes.

If she ever told anyone about Lee Vickery, she thinks, what could she say? He is not her friend. He is not her lover, but she loves him. He loved her once, one time, in his car parked on the railroad tracks by the river.

She was sixteen. She did not know him. He asked her to a movie, but when he picked her up at nine o'clock that night, he drove her to the Moonwalk at the edge of the river. He stopped the car on the railroad tracks, which made her scared. "All the movies are over," he said and he looked at her and smiled. "I want to fuck you," he said, still smiling. She looked out the window at the dark water and she thought that she could open the car door and run. "What are you afraid of?" He leaned closer, reached under her skirt and touched her thigh. "You're so beautiful," he said. His fingers brushed her throat. "I've been watching you for a long time."

When he said that, Miranda turned to look at him, knowing that he loved her, knowing that she would let him do anything he wanted. She started to unbutton her blouse, but he said, "Don't." He lay her gently on the car seat, lifted her skirt above her legs with a quick movement of his hand. Outside, she heard the wind blow the flat water into waves.

When he dropped her off at her grandmother's house after midnight, he kissed her quickly then opened the door to let her out of the car. He smiled. After that night, Lee Vickery did not speak to Miranda again. He passed her in the halls at school and pretended not to know who she was. Later, she heard a rumor that Lee took any girl who would go with him to the river. When she met Travis, she told him she had never slept with anyone.

The phone rings; Miranda blinks open her eyes. She slides underwater, but she can still hear the faint ringing, five, ten, fifteen times. Whoever is calling must know she's home. Miranda rises from the bathtub, her body feeling heavy, weighted down, as if her legs are filled with sand. Her feet leave dark, wet prints on the hall floor. She walks slowly. The phone keeps ringing. Miranda stands by the table, naked, waiting, and then, on the thirtieth ring, she picks it up.

"Miranda," her mother says. No operator's voice this time. "Where are you? I'm in Mobile."

"Faith," Miranda says, trying to keep her voice steady. She knows that if she says this she can make herself believe it. "You'd better not call me anymore. I'm not staying here. I'm going to leave." Then Miranda looks out, beyond the kitchen window, past her own house, past Travis's mother's house.

NOTES ON CONTRIBUTORS

FICTION

Scott Anderson won the 1993 Pope Foundation Award for Investigative Journalism as well as a Nonfiction Fellowship at the University of Iowa. He has reported on wars in Sri Lanka, Bosnia, El Salvador, Northern Ireland, Israel, Uganda and Chechnya. A contributing editor at *Harper's* and a frequent contributor to *The New York Times Magazine*, he is the author of *The 4 O'Clock Murders* and coauthor, with his brother John Lee Anderson, of *Inside the League* and *War Zones*, all works of nonfiction. The excerpt in this issue comes from *Triage*, his first novel, which will appear this fall from Scribner.

Rick Bass is the author of twelve books of fiction and nonfiction, including *The Sky, the Stars, the Wilderness*; *The Book of Yaak*; *In the Loyal Mountains*; *The Lost Grizzlies* and *Winter*. He lives with his family on a remote ranch in Montana.

Nicole Cooley recently published a novel, *Judy Garland, Ginger Love*. Her collection of poetry, *Resurrection*, received the 1995 Walt Whitman Award from the Academy of American Poets. She teaches at Bucknell University.

Michael Knight is from Mobile, Alabama. His fiction has appeared in *Playboy, Story* and *The Paris Review*'s New Writing Issue (141). A collection of short stories, *Dogfight*, and a novel, *Divining Rod*, are both due out in October.

Kirk Nesset's stories and poems have appeared in *Ploughshares, Iowa Review*, *The Gettysburg Review, Tampa Review, Prairie Schooner* and elsewhere. His short story "Mr. Agreeable," published last year in *Fiction*, will appear this fall in *The Pushcart Prize XXIII* anthology. He teaches creative writing at Allegheny College and is at work on a novel.

POETRY

Michael Berryhill is a staff writer for *The Houston Press*.

Carin Besser recently received her MFA from the University of Florida. She now lives and works in Los Angeles.

Joel Brouwer was the 1994–1995 Hall Fellow in Poetry at the University of Wisconsin.

Michael Burns's most recent book of poems is *The Secret Names*, published in 1994. A collection of essays he edited on the poetry of Mona Van Duyn was published by the University of Arkansas Press in 1997, which will also publish a new book of his poems in 1998.

Scott Cairns's new collection, *Recovered Body*, will appear from George Braziller in October.

Henri Cole is the author of three collections of poetry, most recently *The Look of Things*. His new collection, *The Visible Man*, will be published this fall. He is Briggs-Copeland Lecturer in Poetry at Harvard.

Lynn Doyle is the author of *Living Gloves*, published in 1986. She currently teaches at Appalachian State University in Boone, North Carolina.

Sybil Pittman Estess is the coeditor of *Elizabeth Bishop and Her Art* and the author of a book of poems, *Seeing the Desert Green*. She lives in Houston, Texas.

Andrew Feld is the recipient of a 1998–1999 Stegner Fellowship.

Eamon Grennan teaches at Vassar College. His recent translation of the selected poems of Giacomo Leopardi received the 1998 PEN Prize for Poetry in Translation. He received a Guggenheim Fellowship in 1995.

Edwin Gallaher's art criticism, music journalism and poetry have appeared in *Living Blues*, *Artlies* and *Western Humanities Review*.

Andrew Hudgins's new book of poems, *Babylon in a Jar*, will be published this fall. He teaches at University of Cincinnati.

Janet Kaplan's first collection of poetry, *The Groundnote*, won the Alice James Books Competition for 1997 and is forthcoming this fall.

Judy Longley's first volume of poetry, *My Journey Toward You*, was the 1993 winner of the Marianne Moore Prize for Poetry.

Florence Cassen Mayers's work has appeared in *The Atlantic Monthly*, *Poetry*, *Commentary* and other journals. She writes and designs award-winning ABC art books for major museums including the Museum of Modern Art and the Metropolitan Museum of Art.

Czeslaw Milosz's new collection of poems, *Road-Side Dog*, is forthcoming this fall. He is a professor of Slavic languages and literature at the University of California at Berkeley and a recipient of the Nobel Prize for Literature. His cotranslator, **Robert Hass**, the former Poet Laureate, teaches at the University of California at Berkeley.

Scott Minar has published a chapbook, *The Nexus of Rain*. He teaches at Elmira College in upstate New York.

Peggy Penn lives in New York City and has just completed a book of poems, *Everything Closes*.

Susan Pliner received a New York Foundation for the Arts Fellowship in 1997. Her manuscript *What Happens Next, and Next* won the 1992 Capricorn Prize from the Writer's Voice at the West Side YMCA.

Leslie Richardson teaches at Southern Methodist University.

Maureen Seaton received the Iowa Prize for her collection of poems *Furious Cooking*.

Patty Seyburn's first collection, *Diasporatic*, which won the 1997 Marianne Moore Prize, is forthcoming this fall.

Phillip Sterling won a 1990 NEA Fellowship in Poetry. He teaches at Ferris State University in Michigan.

Alexander Theroux's most recent book is a collection of essays, *The Secondary Colors*, published in 1996.

Gene Thornton reviewed photography exhibits for *The New York Times* from 1970 to 1987 before leaving New York City for North Carolina.

Sidney Wade's first collection of poetry, *Empty Sleeves*, was published in 1991. Her new book, *Green*, is forthcoming from the University of South Carolina. She teaches at the University of Florida.

Anneliese Wagner's most recent book is a collection of poems, *Murderer's Magic*.

Michael White's most recent book, *The Island*, is a collection of poems.

Charles Wright's ninth collection, *Appalachia*, will appear this fall. In 1997, he received the Pulitzer Prize for Poetry for *Black Zodiac*.

FEATURE

Harry Mathews, author of several novels and collections of poetry, has spent the last four years preparing the *Oulipo Compendium*, a project that originated in a special issue of the magazine *New Observations*, coedited with Lynn Crawford, in 1991. His novels, *Tlooth* (originally a Paris Review Editions book) and *Cigarettes* will be reissued this fall by Dalkey Archive Press. He is the Paris Editor of *The Paris Review*.

INTERVIEWS

Shusha Guppy (Ismail Kadaré interview) is the London Editor of *The Paris Review*.

Robert Faggen (Russell Banks interview) is an associate professor of literature and the chairman of the department of literature at Claremont-McKenna College. He's the author of *Robert Frost and the Challenge of Darwin* and the editor of *The Selected Poems of Edwin Arlington Robinson*, *Early*

Poems of Robert Frost, both Penguin Editions, and also *Striving Toward Being, The Letters of Czeslaw Milosz and Thomas Merton*.

Barry Munger (Banks interview) is a freelance photographer based in New York City. He is the editor of *Caught in the Act: The Photographer in Contemporary Fiction*.

ART

Pier Consagra is represented by Holly Solomon Gallery in New York City.
Steve Miller's work has been exhibited, most recently, at Sagpond Vineyards in Sagaponack, New York, and the Karin Sachs Gallery in Munich, Germany.
Jeannie Thib is represented by the Leo Kamen Gallery, Toronto, Canada.

ERRATUM: The volume number should have changed from 39 to 40 with issue 146.

The Paris Review
Booksellers Advisory Board

THE PARIS REVIEW BOOKSELLERS ADVISORY BOARD is a group of owners and managers of independent bookstores from around the world who have agreed to share with us their knowledge and expertise.

Available now from the Flushing office
BACK ISSUES OF THE PARIS REVIEW

the modern writer as witness